KEYWORDS

*A Vocabulary of Culture
and Society*

Raymond Williams

New York

OXFORD UNIVERSITY PRESS

1976

FOR KIRSTI, ANNIKA AND DAVID

CONTENTS

INTRODUCTION

In 1945, after the ending of the wars with Germany and Japan, I was released from the Army to return to Cambridge. University term had already begun, and many relationships and groups had been formed. It was in any case strange to travel from an artillery regiment on the Kiel Canal to a Cambridge college. I had been away only four and a half years, but in the movements of war had lost touch with all my university friends. Then, after many strange days, I met a man I had worked with in the first year of the war, when the formations of the 1930s, though under pressure, were still active. He too had just come out of the Army. We talked eagerly, but not about the past. We were too much preoccupied with this new and strange world around us. Then we both said, in effect simultaneously: 'the fact is, they just don't speak the same language'.

It is a common phrase. It is often used between successive generations, and even between parents and children. I had used it myself, just six years earlier, when I had come to Cambridge from a working-class family in Wales. In many of the fields in which language is used it is of course not true. Within our common language, in a particular country, we can be conscious of social differences, or of differences of age, but in the main we use the same words for most everyday things and activities, though with obvious variations of rhythm and accent and tone. Some of the variable words, say *lunch* and *supper* and *dinner*, may be highlighted but the differences are not particularly important. When we come to say 'we just don't speak the same language' we mean something more general: that we have different immediate values or different kinds of valuation, or that we are aware, often intangibly, of different formations and distributions of energy and interest. In such a case, each group is speaking its native language, but its uses are significantly different, and especially when strong feelings or important ideas are in question. No single group is 'wrong' by any linguistic criterion, though a temporarily dominant group may try to enforce its own uses as 'correct'. What is really happening through these critical encounters, which may be very conscious or may be felt only as a certain strangeness and unease, is a

9

process quite central in the development of a language when, in certain words, tones and rhythms, meanings are offered, felt for, tested, confirmed, qualified, changed. In some situations this is a very slow process indeed; it needs the passage of centuries to show itself actively, by results, at anything like its full weight. In other situations the process can be rapid, especially in certain key areas. In a large and active university, and in a period of change as important as a war, the process can seem unusually rapid and conscious.

Yet it had been, we both said, only four or five years. Could it really have changed that much? Searching for examples we found that some general attitudes in politics and religion had altered, and agreed that these were important changes. But I found myself preoccupied by a single word, *culture*, which it seemed I was hearing very much more often: not only, obviously, by comparison with the talk of an artillery regiment or of my own family, but by direct comparison within the university over just those few years. I had heard it previously in two senses: one at the fringes, in teashops and places like that, where it seemed the preferred word for a kind of social superiority, not in ideas or learning, and not only in money or position, but in a more intangible area, relating to behaviour; yet also, secondly, among my own friends, where it was an active word for writing poems and novels, making films and paintings, working in theatres. What I was now hearing were two different senses, which I could not really get clear: first, in the study of literature, a use of the word to indicate, powerfully but not explicitly, some central formation of values (and *literature* itself had the same kind of emphasis); secondly, in more general discussion, but with what seemed to me very different implications, a use which made it almost equivalent to *society*: a particular *way of life* – 'American culture', 'Japanese culture'.

Today I can explain what I believe was happening. Two important traditions were finding in England their effective formations: in the study of literature a decisive dominance of an idea of criticism which, from Arnold through Leavis, had *culture* as one of its central terms; and in discussions of society the extension to general conversation of an anthropological sense which had been clear as a specialist term but which now, with increased American influence and with the parallel influence of such thinkers as Mannheim, was becoming naturalized. The two earlier senses had evidently weakened: the teashop sense, though still active, was more distant and was becoming comic; the sense of activity in the arts, though it held its national place, seemed more and more excluded both by the emphasis of criticism and by the larger and dissolving reference to a whole way of life. But I knew nothing of this at the time. It was just a difficult word, a word I could think of as an example of the change which we were trying, in various ways, to understand.

My year in Cambridge passed. I went off to a job in adult education. Within two years T. S. Eliot published his *Notes Towards the Definition of Culture* (1948) – a book I grasped but could not accept – and all the elusive strangeness of those first weeks back in Cambridge returned with force. I began exploring the word in my adult classes. The words I linked it with, because of the problems its uses raised in my mind, were *class* and *art*, and then *industry* and *democracy*. I could feel these five words as a kind of structure. The relations between them became more complex the more I considered them. I began reading widely, to try to see more clearly what each was about. Then one day in the basement of the Public Library at Seaford, where we had gone to live, I looked up *culture*, almost casually, in one of the thirteen volumes of what we now usually call the OED: the Oxford *New English Dictionary on Historical Principles*. It was like a shock of recognition. The changes of sense I had been trying to understand had begun in English, it seemed, in the early nineteenth century. The connections I had sensed with *class* and *art*, with *industry* and *democracy*, took on, in the language, not only an intellectual but an historical shape. I see these changes today in much more complex ways. *Culture* itself has now a different though related history. But this was the moment at which an inquiry which had begun in trying to understand several urgent contemporary problems – problems quite literally of understanding my immediate world – achieved a particular shape in trying to understand a tradition. This was the work which, completed in 1956, became my book *Culture and Society*.

It was not easy then, and it is not much easier now, to describe this work in terms of a particular academic subject. The book has been classified under headings as various as cultural history, historical semantics, history of ideas, social criticism, literary history and sociology. This may at times be embarrassing or even difficult, but academic subjects are not eternal categories, and the fact is that, wishing to put certain general questions in certain specific ways, I found that the connections I was making, and the area of concern which I was attempting to describe, were in practice experienced and shared by many other people, to whom the particular study spoke. One central feature of this area of interest was its vocabulary, which is significantly not the specialized vocabulary of a specialized discipline, though it often overlaps with several of these, but a general vocabulary ranging from strong, difficult and persuasive words in everyday usage to words which, beginning in particular specialized contexts, have become quite common in descriptions of wider areas of thought and experience. This, significantly, is the vocabulary we share with others, often imperfectly, when we wish to discuss many of the central processes of our common life. *Culture*, the original difficult word, is an exact example. It has specialized meanings in particular fields of study, and it might seem an appropriate task simply to sort these out. But it was the significance of its general and variable usage that had first attracted my attention: not in separated disciplines but in general discussion. The very fact that it was important in two areas that are often thought of as separate – *art* and *society* – posed new questions and suggested new kinds of connection. As I went on I found that this seemed to be true of a significant range of words – from *aesthetic* to *work* – and I began collecting them and trying to understand them. The significance, it can be said, is in the selection. I realize how arbitrary some inclusions and exclusions may seem to others. But out of some two hundred words, which I chose because I saw or heard them being used in quite general discussion in what seemed to me interesting or difficult ways, I then selected sixty and wrote notes and short essays on them, intending them as an appendix to *Culture and Society*, which in its main text was dealing with a number of specific writers and thinkers. But when that book was finished my publisher told me it had to be shortened: one of the items that could be taken out was this appendix. I had little effective choice. I agreed, reluctantly. I put in a note promising this material as a separate paper. But the file of the Appendix stayed on my shelf. Over nearly twenty years I have been adding to it: collecting more examples, finding new points of analysis, including other words. Recently I began to feel that this might make a book on its own. I went through the whole file again, rewrote all the notes and short essays, excluded some words and again added others. The present volume is the result.

I have emphasized this process of the development of *Keywords* because it seems to me to indicate its dimension and purpose. It is not a dictionary or glossary of a particular academic subject. It is not a series of footnotes to dictionary histories or definitions of a number of words. It is, rather, the record of an inquiry into a *vocabulary*: a shared body of words and meanings in our most general discussions, in English, of the practices and institutions which we group as *culture* and *society*. Every word which I have included has at some time, in the course of some argument, virtually forced itself on my attention because the problems of its meanings seemed to me inextricably bound up with the problems it was being used to discuss. I have often got up from writing a particular note and heard the same word again, with the same sense of significance and difficulty: often, of course, in discussions and arguments which were rushing by to some other destination. I began to see this experience as a problem of *vocabulary*, in two senses: the available and developing meanings of known words, which needed to be set down; and the explicit but as often implicit connections which people were making, in what seemed to me, again and again, particular formations of meaning – ways not only of discussing but of seeing many of our central experiences. What I had then to do was not only to collect examples, and look up or revise particular records of use, but to analyse, as far as I could, some of the issues and problems that were there inside the vocabulary, whether in single words or in habitual groupings. I called these words *Keywords* in two connected senses: they are significant, binding words in certain activities and their interpretation; they are significant, indicative words in certain forms of thought. Certain uses bound together certain ways of seeing culture and society, not least in these two most general words. Certain other uses seemed to me to open up issues and problems, in the same general area, of which we all needed to be very much more conscious. Notes on a list of words; analyses of certain formations: these were the elements of an active vocabulary – a way of recording, investigating and presenting problems of meaning in the area in which the meanings of *culture* and *society* have formed.

Of course the issues could not all be understood simply by

analysis of the words. On the contrary, most of the real issues remained, however complete the analysis. But most of them, I found, could not really be thought through, and some of them, I believe, cannot even be focused unless we are conscious of the words as elements of the problems. This point of view is now much more widely accepted. When I raised my first questions about the differing uses of *culture* I was given the impression, in kindly and not so kind ways, that these arose mainly from the fact of an incomplete education, and the fact that this was true (in real terms it is true of everyone) only clouded the real point at issue. The surpassing confidence of any particular use of a word, within a group or within a period, is very difficult to question. I recall an eighteenth-century letter:

> What, in your opinion, is the meaning of the word *sentimental*, so much in vogue among the polite . . . ? Everything clever and agreeable is comprehended in that word . . . I am frequently astonished to hear such a one is a *sentimental* man; we were a *sentimental* party; I have been taking a *sentimental* walk.

Well, that vogue passed. The meaning of *sentimental* changed and deteriorated. Nobody now asking the meaning of the word would be met by that familiar, slightly frozen, polite stare. When a particular history is completed, we can all be clear and relaxed about it. But *literature, aesthetic, representative, empirical, unconscious, liberal:* these and many other words which seem to me to raise problems will, in the right circles, seem mere transparencies, their correct use a matter only of education. Or *class, democracy, equality, evolution, materialism:* these we know we must argue about, but we can assign particular uses to sects, and call all sects but our own *sectarian.* Language depends, it can be said, on this kind of confidence, but in any major language, and especially in periods of change, a necessary confidence and concern for clarity can quickly become brittle, if the questions involved are not faced.

The questions are not only about meaning; in most cases, inevitably, they are about meanings. Some people, when they see a word, think the first thing to do is to define it. Dictionaries are produced and, with a show of authority no less confident because it is usually so limited in place and time, what is called a proper meaning is attached. I once began collecting, from correspondence in newspapers, and from other public arguments, variations on the phrases 'I see from my Webster' and 'I find from my Oxford Dictionary'. Usually what was at issue was a difficult term in an argument. But the effective tone of these phrases, with their interesting overtone of possession ('my Webster'), was to appropriate a meaning which fitted the argument and to exclude those meanings which were inconvenient to it but which some benighted person had been so foolish as to use. Of course if we want to be clear about *banxring* or *baobab* or *barilla*, or for that matter about *barbel* or *basilica* or *batik*, or, more obviously, about *barber* or *barley* or *barn*, this kind of definition is effective. But for words of a different kind, and especially for those which involve ideas and values, it is not only an impossible but an irrelevant procedure. The dictionaries most of us use, the defining dictionaries, will in these cases, and in proportion to their merit as dictionaries, list a range of meanings, all of them current, and it will be the range that matters. Then when we go beyond these to the historical dictionaries, and to essays in historical and contemporary semantics, we are quite beyond the range of the 'proper meaning'. We find a history and complexity of meanings; conscious changes, or consciously different uses; innovation, obsolescence, specialization, extension, overlap, transfer; or changes which are masked by a nominal continuity so that words which seem to have been there for centuries, with continuous general meanings, have come in fact to express radically different or radically variable, yet sometimes hardly noticed, meanings and implications of meaning. *Industry, family, nature* may jump at us from such sources; *class, rational, subjective* may after years of reading remain doubtful. It is in all these cases, in a given area of interest which began in the way I have described, that the problems of meaning have preoccupied me and have led to the sharpest realization of the difficulties of any kind of definition.

The work which this book records has been done in an area where several disciplines converge but in general do not meet. It has been based on several areas of specialist knowledge but its purpose is to bring these, in the examples selected, into general availability. This needs no apology but it does need explanation of some of the complexities that are involved in any such attempt. These can be grouped under two broad headings: problems of information and problems of theory.

The problems of information are severe. Yet anyone working

on the structures and developments of meaning in English words has the extraordinary advantage of the great Oxford *Dictionary*. This is not only a monument to the scholarship of its editors, Murray, Bradley and their successors, but also the record of an extraordinary collaborative enterprise, from the original work of the Philological Society to the hundreds of later correspondents. Few inquiries into particular words end with the great *Dictionary*'s account, but even fewer could start with any confidence if it were not there. I feel with William Empson, who in *The Structure of Complex Words* found many faults in the *Dictionary*, that 'such work on individual words as I have been able to do has been almost entirely dependent on using the majestic object as it stands'. But what I have found in my own work about the OED, when this necessary acknowledgment has been made, can be summed up in three ways. I have been very aware of the period in which the *Dictionary* was made: in effect from the 1880s to the 1920s (the first example of the current series of Supplements shows addition rather than revision). This has two disadvantages: that in some important words the evidence for developed twentieth-century usage is not really available; and that in a number of cases, especially in certain sensitive social and political terms, the presuppositions of orthodox opinion in that period either show through or are not far below the surface. Anyone who reads Dr Johnson's great *Dictionary* soon becomes aware of his active and partisan mind as well as his remarkable learning. I am aware in my own notes and essays that, though I try to show the range, many of my own positions and preferences come through. I believe that this is inevitable, and all I am saying is that the air of massive impersonality which the Oxford *Dictionary* communicates is not so impersonal, so purely scholarly, or so free of active social and political values as might be supposed from its occasional use. Indeed, to work closely in it is at times to get a fascinating insight into what can be called the ideology of its editors, and I think this has simply to be accepted and allowed for, without the kind of evasion which one popular notion of scholarship prepares the way for. Secondly, for all its deep interest in meanings, the *Dictionary* is primarily philological and etymological; one of the effects of this is that it is much better on range and variation than on connection and interaction. In many cases, working primarily on meanings and their contexts, I have found the historical evidence invaluable but have drawn different and at times even opposite conclusions from it. Thirdly, in certain areas I have been reminded very sharply of the change of perspective which has recently occurred in studies of language: for obvious reasons (if only from the basic orthodox training in dead languages) the written language used to be taken as the real source of authority, with the spoken language as in effect derived from it; whereas now it is much more clearly realized that the real situation is usually the other way round. The effects are complex. In a number of primarily intellectual terms the written language is much nearer the true source. If we want to trace *psychology* the written record is probably adequate, until the late nineteenth century. But if, on the other hand, we want to trace *job*, we have soon to recognize that the real developments of meaning, at each stage, must have occurred in everyday speech well before they entered the written record. This is a limitation which has to be recognized, not only in the *Dictionary*, but in any historical account. A certain foreshortening or bias in some areas is, in effect, inevitable. Period indications for origin and change have always to be read with this qualification and reservation. I can give one example from personal experience. Checking the latest Supplement for the generalizing contemporary use of *communications*, I found an example and a date which happened to be from one of my own articles. Now not only could written examples have been found from an earlier date, but I know that this sense was being used in conversation and discussion, and in American English, very much earlier. I do not make the point to carp. On the contrary, this fact about the *Dictionary* is a fact about any work of this kind, and needs especially to be remembered when reading my own accounts.

For certain words I have added a number of examples of my own, from both general and deliberate reading. But of course any account is bound to be incomplete, in a serious sense, just as it is bound to be selective. The problems of adequate information are severe and sometimes crippling, but it is not always possible to indicate them properly in the course of an analysis. They should, nevertheless, always be remembered. And of one particular limitation I have been very conscious. Many of the most important words that I have worked on either developed key meanings in languages other than English, or went through a complicated and interactive development in a number of major languages. Where I have been able in part to follow this, as in *alienation* or *culture*, its significance is so evident that we are bound to feel the lack of it when such tracing has not been possible. To do such comparative studies adequately would be an extraordinary international collaborative enterprise, and the difficulties of that may seem sufficient excuse. An inquiry into the meanings of *democracy*, sponsored by UNESCO and intended to be universal and comparative, ran into every kind of difficulty, though even the more limited account that Naess and his colleagues had to fall back on is remarkably illuminating. I have had enough experience of trying to discuss two key English Marxist terms – *base* and *superstructure* – not only in relation to their German originals, but in discussions with French, Italian, Spanish, Russian and Swedish friends, in relation to their forms in these other languages, to know not only that the results are fascinating and difficult, but that such comparative analysis is crucially important, not just as philology, but as a central matter of intellectual clarity. It is greatly to be hoped that ways will be found of encouraging and supporting these comparative inquiries, but meanwhile it should be recorded that while some key developments, now of international importance, occurred first in English, many did not and in the end can only be understood when other languages are brought consistently into comparison. This limitation, in my notes and essays, has to be noted and remembered by readers. It is particularly marked in very early developments, in the classical languages and in medieval Latin, where I have almost invariably simply relied on existing authorities, though with many questions that I could not answer very active in my mind. Indeed, at the level of origins, of every kind, this is generally true and must be entered as an important reservation.

This raises one of the theoretical problems. It is common practice to speak of the 'proper' or 'strict' meaning of a word by reference to its origins. One of the effects of one kind of classical education, especially in conjunction with one version of the defining function of dictionaries, is to produce what can best be called a sacral attitude to words, and corresponding complaints of vulgar contemporary misunderstanding and misuse. The original meanings of words are always interesting. But what is often most interesting is the subsequent variation. The complaints that get into the newspapers, about vulgar misuse, are invariably about very recent developments. Almost any random selection of actual developments of meaning will show that what is now taken as 'correct' English, often including many of the words in which such complaints are made, is the product of just such kinds of change. The examples are too numerous to quote here but the reader is invited to consider only *interest* or *determine* or *improve*, though *organic*, *evolution* and *individual* are perhaps more spectacular examples. I have often found a clue to an analysis by discovery of an origin, but there can be no question, at the level either of practice or of theory, of accepting an original meaning as decisive (or where should we be with *aesthetic*?) or of accepting a common source as directive (or where should we be as between *peasant* and *pagan*, *idiot* and *idiom*, or *employ* and *imply*?). The vitality of a language includes every kind of extension, variation and transfer, and this is as true of change in our own time (however much we may regret some particular examples) as of changes in the past which can now be given a sacral veneer. (*Sacral* itself is an example; the extension from its physical sense of the fundament to its disrespectful implication of an attitude to the *sacred* is not my joke, but it is a meaningful joke and thence a meaningful use.)

The other theoretical problems are very much more difficult. There is the basic problem of meaning itself, which underlies every procedure of definition. This book is an active exercise in semantics, but *semantics* itself is one of the variable words, referring to highly varied and distinct disciplines, which ought to be analysed. It has an important use in philosophy, to indicate the area in which the meanings of statements are tested for consistency within a logical system, with a consequent specialized analysis of what is involved in *meaning* at all. In linguistics there is an associated tendency, in which language is analysed as a system of signs, with a predominant emphasis on the qualities of the *system*; in one extreme but popular tendency the system alone generates meaning, and references outside it are irrelevant or mistaken. A particular sense of the root term (Greek *sema*, a sign) is developed towards a sense of systematic signification, which in its most general emphasis can be readily accepted but which in its assumption of an autonomous system (language or a language independent of reference to factors outside it) is at once highly productive and highly controversial. The point is especially relevant to my own notes and essays, which pick out particular words. I have explained that my starting-point was what I would call a cluster, a particular set of interrelated (though not obviously interrelated) words and meanings, from which my whole selection of words then developed. It is thus an intrinsic part of the work to emphasize such interconnections, some of which are systematic, in spite of problems of presentation which I shall discuss. But it could be said that individual words should never be isolated; they depend for their meanings not only on contexts but on deep structural rules. At one level this can be readily conceded. Many of the variable senses that I have analysed are determined, in practice, by contexts. Moreover, even in the course of an active concern with the available currency of meanings, certain systematic properties become evident; I would instance, though I have only occasionally remarked on it, the formation of active verbs (like *create*, but there are many other examples) from past participles; many similar cases can be found. Yet while I am sure that no word ever finally stands on its own, but must be returned to its general and relational uses and to the language-system of which it is a part, I am sure also that to pick out a word of a problematical kind and to consider, for the moment, its own internal structure, is one necessary way of considering the active interrelations of words in sentences and in the larger system of the language itself. The laws of the relationships are of crucial importance, but it is only in reductive kinds of analysis that these are seen as the laws of a system of units; many of the qualities of the system are within the apparent units (which are always relatively variable social signs) as well as in the more describable formal relations between them. This is especially the case if one holds, as I do, that the area of signification is not confined to the system itself, but in one dimension necessarily extends to the users of language and to the objects and relationships about which language speaks, and that none of these can be limited to the formal system but exist, indeed primarily, in material and historical ways. To study meanings, then, in different actual speakers and writers, and in and through historical time, is a deliberate choice. The limitations are obvious and are admitted. The emphasis is equally obvious and is conscious. One kind of semantics is the study of meaning as such; another kind is the study of formal systems of signification. The kind of semantics to which these notes and essays belong is one of the tendencies within *historical semantics*, where the theoretical problems are indeed acute but where even more fundamental theoretical problems must be seen as at issue. The emphasis on history, as a way of understanding contemporary problems of meaning and structures of meaning, is a basic choice from a position of historical materialism rather than from the now more powerful positions of objective idealism or non-historical (synchronic) structuralism.

In one way this theoretical position, which in this space I can do little more than assert, is too large for the actual and very limited notes and essays which follow. I know from repeated experience that it is possible to contribute certain kinds of awareness and certain more limited kinds of clarification by taking certain words at the level at which they are generally used, and this, for reasons related to and probably clear from all my other work, has been my overriding purpose. I have more than enough material on certain words (for example *class* and *culture*) and on certain formations (for example *art, aesthetic, subjective, psychological, unconscious*) to write, as an alternative, extended specialist studies, some themselves of book length. I may eventually do this, but the choice of a more general form and of a wider range was again deliberate. I do not share the optimism, or the theories which underlie it, of that popular kind of inter-war and surviving semantics which supposed that clarification of difficult words would help in the resolution of disputes conducted in their terms and often visibly confused by them. I believe that to understand the complexities of the meanings of *class* contributes virtually nothing to the resolution, for example, of actual class disputes and class struggles. It is not only that nobody can 'purify the dialect of the tribe', nor only that anyone who really knows himself to be a member of a society knows better than to want, in those terms, to try. It is also that the variations and confusions of meaning are not just faults in a system, or errors of feedback, or deficiencies of education. They are in many cases, in my terms, historical and contemporary substance. Indeed they have often, as variations, to be insisted upon, just because they embody different experiences and readings of experience, and this will continue to be true, in active relationships and conflicts, over and above the clarifying exercises of scholars or committees. What can really be contributed is not resolution but perhaps, at times, just that extra edge of consciousness. In a social history in which many crucial meanings have been shaped by a dominant class, and by particular professions operating to a large extent within its terms, the sense of edge is accurate. This is not a neutral review of meanings. It is an exploration of the vocabulary of a crucial area of social and cultural discussion, which has been inherited within precise historical and social conditions and which has to be made at once conscious and critical – subject to change as well as to continuity – if the millions of people in whom it is active are to see it as active: not a *tradition* to be learned, nor a *consensus* to be accepted, nor a set of meanings which, because it is 'our language', has a natural authority; but as a shaping and reshaping, in real circumstances and from profoundly different and important points of view: a vocabulary to use, to find our own ways in, to change as we find it necessary to change it, as we go on making our own language and history.

The work in historical semantics which I have found of most interest, apart from the basic work of Bréal, Volôsinov, Stern, Ullmann, Spitzer and others, has been of an applied kind: the German school which has concentrated on *Bedeutungsfelder* – specific fields of meaning, as in Trier, discussed by Springer and Öhman; and a tendency within mainly literary studies of English, as in Barfield, who distinguished several important clusters of meaning, Empson, who remarkably extended, for one kind of study, the notation of complex meanings, and a number of scholars – Willey, Danby, Barber among many others – who, for varying purposes, have traced particular key words. My sense of a field of meanings differs from that of the German school and from French work on the idea of key words. But I have found my interests closely echoed in some of the later work of the Frankfurt School, who combine analysis of key words or key terms with key concepts.

In writing about a field of meanings I have often wished that some form of presentation could be devised in which it would be clear that the analyses of particular words are intrinsically connected, sometimes in complex ways. The alphabetical listing on which I have finally decided may often seem to obscure this, although the use of cross-references should serve as a reminder of many necessary connections. The difficulty is that any other kind of arrangement, for example by areas or themes, would establish one set of connections while often suppressing another. If *representative*, for example, was set in a group of political words, perhaps centering on *democracy*, we might lose sight of a significant question in the overlap between *representative* government and *representative* art. Or if *realism* was set in a group of literary words, perhaps centering on *literature* or on *art*, another kind of overlap, with fundamental philosphical connotations and with descriptions of attitudes in business and politics, might again not be readily seen. Specialized vocabularies of known and separate academic subjects and areas of interest are, while obviously useful, very much easier both to write and to arrange. The word-lists can be fuller and they can avoid questions of overlap by deliberate limitation to meanings within the specialism. But since my whole inquiry has been into an area of general meanings and connections of meaning, I have been able to achieve neither the completeness nor the conscious limitation of deliberately specialized areas. In taking what seemed to me to be the significant vocabulary of an area of general discussion of culture and society, I have lost the props of conventional arrangement by subject and have then needed to retain the simplest conventional arrangement, by alphabetical order. However, since a book is only completed when it is read, I would hope that while the alphabetical order makes immediate use easier, other kinds of connection and comparison will suggest themselves to the reader, and may be followed through by a quite different selection and order of reading.

In this as in many other respects I am exceptionally conscious of how much further work and thinking needs to be done. Much of it, in fact, can only be done through discussion, for which the book in its present form is in part specifically intended. Often in the notes and essays I have had to break off just at the point where a different kind of analysis – extended theoretical argument, or detailed social and historical inquiry – would be necessary. To have gone in these other directions would have meant restricting the number and range of the words discussed, and in this book at least this range has been my priority. But it can also be said that this is a book in which the author would positively welcome amendment, correction and addition as well as the usual range of responses and comments. The whole nature of the enterprise is of this kind. Here is a critical area of vocabulary. What can be done in dictionaries is necessarily limited by their proper universality and by the long time-scale of revision which that, among other factors, imposes. The present inquiry, being more limited – not a dictionary but a vocabulary – is more flexible. My publishers have been good enough to include some blank pages, not only for the convenience of making notes, but as a sign that the inquiry remains open, and that the author will welcome all amendments, corrections and additions as developments (which will be acknowledged) towards the revised edition which it is hoped will be necessary. In the use of our common language, in so important an area, this is the only spirit in which this work can be properly done.

I have to thank more people than I can now name who, over twenty-five years, in many kinds of formal and informal discussion, have contributed to these analyses. I have also especially to thank Mr R. B. Woodings, my editor, who has not only been exceptionally helpful with the book itself, but who, as a former colleague, came to see me at just the moment when I was actively considering whether the file should become a book and whose encouragement was then decisive. My wife has helped me very closely at all stages of the work. I have also to record the practical help of Mr W. G. Heyman who, as a member of one of my adult classes twenty-five years ago, told me after a discussion of a word that as a young man he had begun buying the paper parts of the great Oxford *Dictionary*, and a few years later astonished me by arriving at a class with three cardboard boxes full of them, which he insisted on giving to me. I have a particular affection for his memory, and through it for these paper parts themselves – so different from the bound volumes and smooth paper of the library copies; yellowing and breaking with time, the rough uncut paper, the memorable titles – *Deject to Depravation*, *Heel to Hod*, *R to Reactive* and so on – which I have used over the years. This is a small book to offer in return for so much interest and kindness.

Cambridge, 1975   R.W.

ABBREVIATIONS

The following abbreviations are used in the text.

    fw: immediate forerunner of a word, in the same or another language.

    rw: ultimate traceable word, from which 'root' meanings are derived.

  q.v.: see entry under word noted.

     C: followed by numeral, century (C19: Nineteenth Century).

   eC: first period (third) of a century.

  mC: middle period (third) of a century.

  lC: last period (third) of a century.

    c.: (before a date) approximately.

 AN: Anglo-Norman.

 mE: Middle English (c. 1100–1500)

 oE: Old English (to c. 1100)

   F: French.

 mF: Medieval French

 oF: Old French.

   G: German.

 Gk: Classical Greek.

  It: Italian.

   L: Latin.

  lL: late Latin.

 mL: Medieval Latin.

 vL: Vulgar Latin.

Rom: Romanic.

 Sp: Spanish.

OED: *New Dictionary on Historical Principles* (Oxford). Quotations followed by a name and date only, or a date only, are from examples cited in OED. Other quotations are followed by specific sources.

A

AESTHETIC

Aesthetic first appeared in English in C19, and was not common before mC19. It was in effect, in spite of its Greek form, a borrowing from German, after a critical and controversial development in that language. It was first used in a Latin form as the title of two volumes, *Aesthetica* (1750–58) by Alexander Baumgarten (1714–62). Baumgarten defined beauty as phenomenal perfection, and the importance of this, in thinking about art, was that it placed a predominant stress on apprehension through the *senses*. This explains Baumgarten's essentially new word, derived from rw *aisthesis*, Gk – sense perception. In Greek the main reference was to material things, that is things perceptible by the senses, as distinct from things which were immaterial or which could only be thought. Baumgarten's new use was part of an emphasis on subjective sense activity, and on the specialized human creativity of art, which became dominant in these fields and which inherited his title-word, though his book was not translated and had limited circulation. In Kant beauty was also seen as an essentially and exclusively sensuous phenomenon, but he protested against Baumgarten's use and defined **aesthetics** in the original and broader Greek sense of the science of 'the conditions of sensuous perception'. Both uses are then found in occasional eC19 English examples, but by mC19 reference to 'the beautiful' is predominant and there is a strong regular association with art. Lewes, in 1879, used a variant derived form, **aesthesics**, in a definition of the 'abstract science of feeling'. Yet **anaesthesia**, a defect of physical sensation, had been used since eC18; and from mC19, with advances in medicine, **anaesthetic** – the negative form of the increasingly popular adjective – was widely used in the original broad sense to mean deprived of sensation or the agent of such deprivation. This use of the straight negative form led eventually to such negatives as **unaesthetic** or **nonaesthetic** in relation to the dominant use referring to beauty or to art.

In 1821 Coleridge wished that he could 'find a more familiar word than aesthetics for works of TASTE and CRITICISM' (qq.v.), and as late as 1842 **aesthetics** was referred to as 'a silly pedantical term'. In 1859 Sir William Hamilton, understanding it as 'the Philosophy of Taste, the theory of the Fine Arts, the Science of the Beautiful, etc.', and acknowledging its general acceptance 'not only in Germany but throughout the other countries of Europe', still thought **apolaustic** would have been more appropriate. But the word had taken hold and became increasingly common, though with a continuing uncertainty (implicit in the theory which had led to the coinage) between reference to art and more general reference to the beautiful. By 1880 the noun **aesthete** was being widely used, most often in a derogatory sense. The principles and practices of the 'aesthetic movement' around Walter Pater were both attacked and sneered at (the best-remembered example is in Gilbert's *Patience* (1880)). This is contemporary with similar feeling around the use of *culture* by Matthew Arnold and others. **Aesthete** has not recovered from this use, and the neutral noun relating to aesthetics as a formal study is the earlier (mC19) **aesthetician**. The adjective **aesthetic**, apart from its specialized uses in discussion of art and literature, is now in common use to refer to questions of visual appearance and effect.

It is clear from this history that **aesthetic**, with its specialized references to ART (q.v.), to visual appearance, and to a category of what is 'fine' or 'beautiful', is a key formation in a group of meanings which at once emphasized and isolated SUBJECTIVE (q.v.) sense-activity as the basis of art and beauty as distinct, for example, from *social* or *cultural* interpretations. It is an element in the divided modern consciousness of *art* and *society*: a reference beyond social use and social valuation which, like one special meaning of *culture*, is intended to express a human dimension which the dominant version of *society* appears to exclude. The emphasis is understandable but the isolation can be damaging, for there is something irresistibly displaced and marginal about the now common and limiting phrase 'aesthetic considerations', especially when contrasted with *practical* or UTILITARIAN (q.v.) considerations, which are elements of the same basic division.

See ART, CREATIVE, CULTURE, LITERATURE, SUBJECTIVE, UTILITARIAN

ALIENATION

Alienation is now one of the most difficult words in the language. Quite apart from its common usage in general contexts, it carries specific but disputed meanings in a range of disciplines from social and economic theory to philosophy and psychology. From mC20, moreover, it has passed from different areas of this range into new kinds of common usage where it is often confusing because of overlap and uncertainty in relation both to the various specific meanings and the older more general meanings.

Though it often has the air of a contemporary term, **alienation** as an English word, with a wide and still relevant range of meanings, has been in the language for several centuries. Its fw is *aliénacion*, mF, from *alienationem*, L, from rw *alienare* – to estrange or make another's; this relates to *alienus*, L, – of or belonging to another person or place, from rw *alius* – other, another. It has been used in English from C14 to describe an action of estranging or state of estrangement (i): normally in relation to a cutting-off or being cut off from God, or to a breakdown of relations between a man or a group and some received political authority. From C15 it has been used to describe the action of transferring the ownership of anything to another (ii), and especially the transfer of rights, estates or money. There are subsidiary minor early senses of (ii), where the transfer is contrived by the beneficiary (*stealth*) or where the transfer is seen as diversion from a proper owner or purpose. These negative senses of (ii) eventually became dominant; a legal sense of voluntary and intentional transfer survived, but improper, involuntary or even forcible transfer became the predominant implication. This was then extended to the result of such a transfer, a state of something having been alienated (iii). By analogy, as earlier in Latin, the word was further used from C15 to mean the loss, withdrawal or derangement of mental faculties, and thus insanity (iv).

In the range of contemporary specific meanings, and in most consequent common usage, each of these earlier senses is variously drawn upon. By eC20 the word was in common use mainly in two specific contexts: the **alienation** of formal property, and in the phrase **alienation of affection** (from mC19) with the sense of deliberate and contrived interference in a customary family relationship, usually that of husband and wife. But the word had already become important, sometimes as a key concept, in powerful and developing intellectual systems.

There are several contemporary variants of sense (i). There is the surviving theological sense, normally a state rather than an action, of being cut off, estranged from the knowledge of God, or from his mercy or his worship. This sometimes overlaps with a more general use, with a decisive origin in Rousseau, in which man is seen as cut off, estranged from his own original nature. There are several variants of this, between the two extreme defining positions of man estranged from his *original* (often historically primitive) nature and man estranged from his *essential* (inherent and permanent) nature. The reasons given vary widely. There is a persistent sense of the loss of original human nature through the development of an 'artificial' CIVILIZATION (q.v.); the overcoming of alienation is then either an actual primitivism or a cultivation of human feeling and practice against the pressures of civilization. In the case of estrangement from an essential nature the two most common variants are the religious sense of estrangement from 'the divine in man', and the sense common in Freud and Freudian-influenced psychology in which man is estranged (again by CIVILIZATION or by particular phases or processes of CIVILIZATION) from his primary energy, either libido or explicit sexuality. Here the overcoming of **alienation** is either recovery of a sense of the divine or, in the alternative tradition, whole or partial recovery of libido or sexuality, a prospect viewed from one position as difficult or impossible (**alienation** in this sense being part of the price paid for civilization) and from another position as programmatic and radical (the ending of particular forms of repression – CAPITALISM, the BOURGEOIS FAMILY (qq.v.) – which produce this substantial alienation).

There is an important variation of sense (i) by the addition of forms of sense (ii) in Hegel and, alternatively, in Marx. Here what is alienated is an essential nature, but the process of alienation is seen as historical. Man indeed makes his own nature, as opposed to concepts of an original human nature. But he makes his own nature by a process of objectification (in Hegel a spiritual process; in Marx the labour process) and the ending of alienation would be a transcendence of this formerly inevitable and necessary alienation. The argument is difficult and is made more difficult by the relations between the German and English key words. German *entäussern* corresponds primarily to English sense (ii): to part with, transfer, lose to another, while having also an additional and in this context crucial sense of 'making external to oneself'. German *entfremden* is closer to English sense (i), especially in the sense of an act or state of estrangement between persons. Though the difficulties are clearly explained in some translations, English critical discussion has been confused by uncertainty between the meanings and by some loss of distinction between senses (i) and (ii): a vital matter when in the development of the concept the interactive relation between senses (i) and (ii) is crucial, as especially in Marx. In Hegel the process is seen as world-historical spiritual development, in a dialectical relation of subject and object, in which alienation is overcome by a higher unity. In a subsequent critique of religion, Feuerbach described God as an alienation – in the sense of projection or transfer – of the highest human powers; this has been repeated in modern humanist arguments and in theological apologetics. In Marx the process is seen as the history of labour, in which man creates himself by creating his world, but in class-society is **alienated** from this essential nature by specific forms of **alienation** in the division of labour, private property and the capitalist mode of production in which the worker loses both the product of his labour and his sense of his own productive activity, following the expropriation of both by capital. The world man has made confronts him as stranger and enemy, having power over him who has transferred his power to it. This relates to the detailed legal and commercial sense of alienation (ii) or *Entäusserung*, though described in new ways by being centred in the processes of modern production. Thus **alienation** (i), in the most general sense of a state of estrangement, is produced by the cumulative and detailed historical processes of **alienation** (ii). Minor senses of **alienation** (i), corresponding to *Entfremdung*-estrangement of persons in competitive labour and production, the phenomenon of general estrangement in an industrial-capitalist factory or city – are seen as consequences of this general process.

All these specific senses, which have of course been the subject of prolonged discussion and dispute from within and from outside each particular system, have led to increasing contemporary usage, and the usual accusations of 'incorrectness' or 'misunderstanding' between what are in fact alternative uses of the word. The most widespread contemporary use is probably that derived from one form of psychology, a loss of connection with one's own deepest feelings and needs. But there is a very common combination of this with judgments that we live in an 'alienating' society, with specific references to the nature of modern work, modern education and modern kinds of community. A recent classification (Seeman, 1959) defined: (a) *powerlessness* – an inability or a feeling of inability to influence the society in which we live; (b) *meaninglessness* – a feeling of lack of guides for conduct and belief, with (c) *normlessness* – a feeling that illegitimate means are required to meet approved goals; (d) *isolation* – estrangement from given norms and goals; (e) *self-estrangement* – an inability to find genuinely satisfying activities. This abstract classification, characteristically reduced to psychological states and without reference to specific social and historical processes, is useful in showing the very wide range which common use of the term now involves. Durkheim's term, *anomie*, which has been also adopted in English, overlaps with **alienation** especially in relation to (b) and (c), the absence of or the failure to find adequate or convincing norms for social relationship and self-fulfilment.

It is clear from the present extent and intensity of the use of **alienation** that there is widespread and important experience which, in these varying ways, the word and its varying specific concepts offer to describe and interpret. There has been some impatience with its difficulties, and a tendency to reject it as merely fashionable. But it seems better to face the difficulties of the word and through them the difficulties which its extraordinary history and variation of usage indicate and record. In its evidence of extensive feeling of a division between *man* and *society*, it is a crucial element in a very general structure of meanings.

See CIVILIZATION, INDIVIDUAL, MAN, PSYCHOLOGICAL

ART

The original general meaning of **art,** to refer to any kind of skill, is still active in English. But a more specialized meaning has become common, and in **the arts** and to a large extent in **artist** has become predominant.

Art has been used in English from C13, fw *art*, oF, rw *artem*, L – skill. It was widely applied, without predominant specialization, until lC17, in matters as various as mathematics, medicine and angling. In the medieval university curriculum the **arts** ('the seven arts' and later 'the LIBERAL (q.v.) arts') were grammar, logic, rhetoric, arithmetic, geometry, music and astronomy, and **artist**, from C16, was first used in this context, though with almost contemporary developments to describe any skilled person (as which it is in effect identical with **artisan** until lC16) or a practitioner of one of the **arts** in another grouping, those presided over by the seven muses: history, poetry, comedy, tragedy, music, dancing, astronomy. Then, from lC17, there was an increasingly common specialized application to a group of skills not hitherto formally represented: painting, drawing, engraving and sculpture. The now dominant use of **art** and **artist** to refer to these skills was not fully established until lC19, but it was within this grouping that in lC18, and with special reference to the exclusion of engravers from the new Royal Academy, a now general distinction between **artist** and **artisan** – the latter being specialized to 'skilled manual worker' without 'intellectual' or 'imaginative' or 'creative' purposes – was strengthened and popularized. This development of **artisan**. and the mC19 definition of *scientist*, allowed the specialization of **artist** and the distinction not now of the *liberal* but of the **fine arts**.

The emergence of an abstract, capitalized **Art**, with its own internal but general principles, is difficult to localize. There are several plausible C18 uses, but it was in C19 that the concept became general. It is historically related, in this sense, to the development of CULTURE and AESTHETICS (qq.v.). Wordsworth wrote to the painter Haydon in 1815: 'High is our calling, friend, Creative Art.' The now normal association with *creative* and *imaginative*, as a matter of classification, dates effectively from lC18 and eC19. The significant adjective **artistic** dates effectively from mC19. **Artistic temperament** and **artistic sensibility** date from the same period. So too does **artiste**, a further distinguishing specialization to describe performers such as actors or singers, thus keeping **artist** for painter, sculptor and eventually (from mC19) writer and composer.

It is interesting to notice what words, in different periods, are ordinarily distinguished from or contrasted with **art**. **Artless** before mC17 meant 'unskilled' or 'devoid of skill', and this sense has survived. But there was an early regular contrast between **art** and *nature*: that is, between the product of human skill and the product of some inherent quality. **Artless** then acquired, from mC17 but especially from lC18, a positive sense to indicate spontaneity even in 'art'. While **art** still meant skill and INDUSTRY (q.v.) diligent skill, they were often closely associated, but when each was abstracted and specialized they were often, from eC19, contrasted as the separate areas of imagination and utility. Until C18 most sciences were **arts**; the modern distinction between *science* and **art**, as contrasted areas of human skill and effort, with fundamentally different methods and purposes, dates effectively from mC19.

This complex set of historical distinctions between various kinds of human skill and between varying basic purposes in the use of such skills is evidently related both to changes in the practical division of labour and to fundamental changes in practical definitions of the purposes of the exercise of skill. It can be primarily related to the changes inherent in capitalist commodity production, with its specialization and reduction of use values to exchange values. There was a consequent defensive specialization of certain skills and purposes to **the arts** or *the humanities* where forms of general use and intention which were not determined by immediate exchange could be at least conceptually abstracted. This is the formal basis of the distinction between **art** and *industry*, and between **fine arts** and **useful arts** (the latter eventually acquiring a new term specialized from another general word for skill, *technique*, fw *technicus*, L, rw *techne*, Gk – art or craft; *technical* developed for 'useful skills' from lC19, and *technology*, originally from C17 scientific study of the arts, developed in C20 to describe applied useful skills).

The **artist** is then distinct within this fundamental perspective not only from *scientist* and *technologist* – each of whom in earlier periods would have been called **artist** – but from *artisan* and *craftsman* and *skilled worker*, who are now *operatives* in terms of a specific definition and organization of WORK (q.v.). As these practical distinctions are pressed, within a given mode of production, **art** and **artist** acquire ever more general (and more vague) associations, offering to express a general *human* (i.e. non-utilitarian) interest, even while, ironically, most **works of art** are effectively treated as commodities and most **artists**, even when they justly claim quite other intentions, are effectively treated as a category of independent *craftsmen* or *skilled workers* producing a certain kind of marginal commodity.

See AESTHETIC, CREATIVE, CULTURE, INDUSTRY, SCIENCE

B

BEHAVIOUR

Behave is a very curious word which still presents difficulties. There was an oE *behabban* – to contain, from rw *be* – about, *habban* – to hold. But the modern word seems to have been introduced in C15 as a form of qualification of the verb *have* (cf. *sich behaben*, in G), and especially in the reflexive sense of 'to have (bear) oneself'. In C16 examples the past tense can be *behad*. The main sense that came through was one of public conduct or bearing: the nearest modern specialization would perhaps be *deportment*, or the specialized sense (from C16) of *manners* (cf. C14 *mannerly*). In the verb this is still a predominant sense, and to **behave** is still colloquially to behave well, although to **behave badly** is also immediately understood. In the course of its development from its originally rather limited and dignified sense of public conduct (which Johnson still noted with an emphasis on *external*), to a term summarizing, in a general moral sense, a whole range of activities, **behave** has acquired a certain ambivalence, and this has become especially important in the associated development of **behaviour**. Use of the noun to refer to public conduct or, in a moral sense, to a general range of activities is still common enough, and it is interesting that it has become possible, within the ambivalence, to speak of someone's **private behaviour**. But the critical development is the neutral application of the term, without any moral implications, to describe ways in which someone or something acts (reacts) in some specific situation. This began in scientific description in

C17 but is not common before C19. The crucial transfer seems to take place in descriptions of material objects, with a strong sense of observation which is probably related to the earlier main sense of observable public conduct. Thus: 'to watch ... the behaviour of the water which drains off a flat coast of mud' (Huxley, 1878). But the term was also used in relation to plants, lower organisms and animals, and by lC19 was in general use in its still current sense of 'the externally apparent activity of a whole organism'. (Cf. **animal behaviour**, and its specialized synonym *ethology*; *ethology* had previously been defined as mimicry, C17; the science of *ethics*, C18; the science of character (Mill, 1843). The range from moral to neutral definitions is as evident as in **behaviour**, and can of course be seen also in *character*).

One particular meaning followed from the extension of the methodology of the physical and biological sciences to an influential school of psychology which described itself (Watson, 1913) as **behaviourist** and (slightly later) **behaviourism**. Psychology was seen as 'a purely objective experimental branch of natural science' (Watson), and data of a 'mental' or 'experiential' kind were ruled out as unscientific. The key point in this definition was the sense of *observable*, which was initially confined to 'objectively physically measurable' but which later developments, that were still called **behaviourist** or **neo-behaviourist** (this use of *neo*, Gk – new, to indicate a new or revised version of a doctrine is recorded from C17 but is most common from lC19), modified to 'experimentally measurable', various kinds of 'mental' or 'experiential' (cf. SUBJECTIVE) data being admitted under conditions of controlled observation. More important, probably, than the methodological argument within psychology was the extension, from this school and from several associated social and intellectual tendencies, of a sense of **behaviour**, in its new wide reference to all (? observable) activity, and especially human activity, as 'interaction' between 'an organism' and 'its environment', usually itself specialized to 'stimulus' and 'response'. This had the effect, in a number of areas, of limiting not only the study but the nature of human activity to interactions DETER-MINED (q.v.) by an environment, other conceptions of 'intention' or 'purpose' being rejected or treated as at best secondary, the predominant emphasis being always on (observable) effect: **behaviour**. In the human sciences, and in many socially applied (and far from neutral) fields such as COMMUNICATIONS (q.v.) and *advertising* (which developed from its general sense of 'notification', from C15, to a system of organized influence on CONSUMER (q.v.) **behaviour**, especially from lC19), the relatively neutral physical senses of *stimulus* and *response* have been developed into a reductive system of 'controlled' **behaviour** as a summary of all significant human activity. (*Controlled* is interesting because of the overlap between conditions of observable experiment – developed from the sense of a system of checks in commercial accounting, from C15 – and conditions of the exercise of restraint or power over others, also from C15. The two modern senses are held as separate, but there has been some practical transfer between them.) The most important effect is the description of certain 'intentional' and 'purposive' human practices and systems as if they were 'natural' or 'objective' stimuli, to which *responses* can be graded as 'normal' or 'abnormal' or 'deviant'. The sense of 'autonomous' or 'independent' response (either generally, or in the sense of being outside the terms of a given system) can thus be weakened, with important effects in politics and sociology (cf. 'deviant groups', 'deviant political behaviour'), in psychology (cf. RATIONALIZATION) and in the understanding of intelligence or of language (**language behaviour**), where there is now considerable argument between an extended sense of **behaviourist** explanations and explanations based on such terms as *generative* or CREATIVE (q.v.).

Apart from these particular and central controversies, it remains significant that a term for public conduct should have developed into our most widely used and most apparently neutral term for all kinds of activity.

BOURGEOIS

Bourgeois is a very difficult word to use in English: first, because although quite widely used it is still evidently a French word, the earlier Anglicization to *burgess*, from oF *burgeis* and mE *burgeis*, *burges*, *borges* – inhabitant of a borough, having remained fixed in its original limited meaning; secondly, because it is especially associated with Marxist argument, which can attract hostility or dismissal (and it is relevant here that in this context **bourgeois** cannot properly be translated by the more familiar English adjective *middle-class*); thirdly, because it has been extended, especially in English in the last twenty years, partly from this

Marxist sense but mainly from much earlier French senses, to a general and often vague term of social contempt. To understand this range it is necessary to follow the development of the word in French, and to note a particular difficulty in the translation, into both French and English, of the German *bürgerlich*.

Under the feudal regime in France **bourgeois** was a juridical category in society, defined by such conditions as length of residence. The essential definition was that of the solid citizen whose mode of life was at once stable and solvent. The earliest adverse meanings come from a higher social order: an aristocratic contempt for the mediocrity of the **bourgeois** which extended, especially in C18, into a philosophical and intellectual contempt for the limited if stable life and ideas of this 'middle' class (there was a comparable English C17 and C18 use of *citizen* and its abbreviation *cit*). There was a steady association of the **bourgeois** with trade, but to succeed as a bourgeois, and to live *bourgeoisement*, was typically to retire and live on invested income. A **bourgeois** house was one in which no trade or profession (lawyers and doctors were later excepted) could be carried on.

The steady growth in size and importance of this **bourgeois** class in the centuries of expanding trade had major consequences in political thought, which in turn had important complicating effects on the word. A new concept of SOCIETY (q.v.) was expressed and translated in English, especially in C18, as *civil society*, but the equivalents for this adjective were and in some senses still are the French *bourgeois* and the German *bürgerlich*. In later English usage these came to be translated as **bourgeois** in the more specific C19 sense, often leading to confusion.

Before the specific Marxist sense, **bourgeois** became a term of contempt, but also of respect from below. The migrant labourer or soldier saw the established **bourgeois** as his opposite; workers saw the capitalized **bourgeois** as an employer. The social dimension of the later use was thus fully established by lC18, although the essentially different aristocratic or philosophical contempt was still an active sense.

The definition of **bourgeois** society was a central concept in Marx, yet especially in some of his early work the term is ambiguous, since in relation to Hegel for whom *civil (bürgerlich) society* was an important term to be distinguished from STATE (q.v.) Marx used, and in the end amalgamated the earlier and the later meanings. Marx's new sense of **bourgeois** society followed earlier historical usage, from established and solvent burgesses to a growing class of traders, entrepreneurs and employers. His attack on what he called **bourgeois** political theory (the theory of *civil society*) was based on what he saw as its falsely universal concepts and institutions, which were in fact the concepts and institutions of a specifically **bourgeois** society: that is, a society in which the **bourgeoisie** (the class name was now much more significant) had become or was becoming dominant. Different stages of **bourgeois** society led to different stages of the CAPITAL-IST (q.v.) mode of economic production, or, as it was later more strictly put, different stages of the capitalist mode of production led to different stages of **bourgeois** society and hence **bourgeois** thought, **bourgeois** feeling, **bourgeois** ideology, **bourgeois** art. In Marx's sense the word has passed into universal usage. But it is often difficult to separate it, in some respects, from the residual aristocratic and philosophical contempt, and from a later form especially common among unestablished artists, writers and thinkers, who might not and often do not share Marx's central definition, but who sustain the older sense of hostility towards the (mediocre) established and respectable.

The complexity of the word is then evident. There is a problem even in the strict Marxist usage, in that the same word, **bourgeois**, is used to describe historically distinct periods and phases of social and cultural development. In some contexts, especially, this is bound to be confusing: the **bourgeois** ideology of settled independent citizens is clearly not the same as the **bourgeois** ideology of the highly mobile agents of a para-national corporation. The distinction of **petit-bourgeois** is an attempt to preserve some of the earlier historical characteristics, but is also used for a specific category within a more complex and mobile society. There are also problems in the relation between **bourgeois** and *capitalist*, which are often used indistinguishably but which in Marx are primarily distinguishable as social and economic terms. There is a specific difficulty in the description of non-urban capitalists (e.g. agrarian capitalist employers) as **bourgeois**, with its residual urban sense, though the social relations they institute are clearly **bourgeois** in the developed C19 sense. There is also difficulty in the relation between descriptions of **bourgeois** society and the **bourgeois** or **bourgeoisie** as a class. A **bourgeois** society, according to Marx, is one in which the **bourgeois** class is dominant, but there can then be difficulties of usage, associated with some of the most intense controversies of analysis, when the same word is used for a whole society in which one class is dominant (but in which, necessarily, there are other classes) and for a specific class within that whole society. The difficulty is especially noticeable in uses of **bourgeois** as an adjective describing some practice which is not itself defined by the manifest social and economic content of **bourgeois**.

It is thus not surprising that there is resistance to the use of the word in English, but it has also to be said that for its precise uses in Marxist and other historical and political argument there is no real English alternative. The translation *middle-class* serves most of the pre-C19 meanings, in pointing to the same kinds of people, and their ways of life and opinions, as were then indicated by **bourgeois**, and had been indicated by *citizen* and *cit* and *civic* and *civil*; general uses of *citizen* and *cit* were common until lC18 but less common after the emergence of *middle-class* in lC18. But *middle-class* (see CLASS), though a modern term, is based on an older threefold division of society – *upper*, *middle* and *lower* – which has most significance in feudal and immediately post-feudal society and which, in the sense of the later uses, would have little or no relevance as a description of a developed or fully formed **bourgeois** society. A *ruling* class, which is the socialist sense of **bourgeois** in the context of historical description of a developed capitalist society, is not easily or clearly represented by the essentially different *middle* class. For this reason, especially in this context and in spite of the difficulties, **bourgeois** will continue to have to be used.

See CAPITALISM, CIVILIZATION, CLASS, SOCIETY

BUREAUCRACY

Bureaucracy appears in English from mC19. Carlyle in *Latter-day Pamphlets* (1850) wrote of 'the Continental nuisance called "Bureaucracy"', and Mill in 1848 wrote of the inexpediency of concentrating all the power of organized action 'in a dominant bureaucracy'. In 1818, using an earlier form, Lady Morgan had written of the 'Bureaucratie or office tyranny, by which Ireland had been so long governed'. The word was taken from fw *bureaucratie*, F, rw *bureau* – writing-desk and then office. The original meaning of *bureau* was the baize used to cover desks.

The English use of **bureau** as office dates from eC18; it became more common in American use, especially with reference to foreign branches, the French influence being predominant. The increasing scale of commercial organization, with a corresponding increase in government intervention and legal controls, and with the increasing importance of organized and professional central government, produced the political facts to which the new term pointed. The older struggle between *aristocracy* and *democracy* was modified by this new phenomenon of a rule from offices. Max Weber feared that the struggle between capitalism and socialism would be overtaken by the victory of **bureaucracy** as a system.

The word thus pointed originally to a political system, and still often does so, though in this use it can mask more precise reference to the very different political systems which bureaucracies can serve. More generally it is used to refer to the complicated formalities of official procedures, what the *Daily News* in 1871 described as 'the Ministry . . . with all its routine of tape, wax, seals, and bureauism'. There is an area of uncertainty between the two kinds of reference, as can be seen by the coinage of more neutral phrases such as 'business methods' and 'office organization' for commercial use, **bureaucracy** being often reserved for similar or identical procedures in government. The relations between an elected or popular government and its administrative agencies are, nevertheless, sufficiently problematic to make the question of **bureaucracy** a real and indeed growing political issue.

See DEMOCRACY, MANAGEMENT

C

CAPITALISM

Capitalism as a word describing a particular economic system began to appear in English from eC19, and almost simultaneously in French and German. **Capitalist** as a noun is a little older; Arthur Young used it, in his journal of *Travels in France* (1792), but relatively loosely: 'moneyed men, or capitalists'. Coleridge used it in the developed sense – 'capitalists . . . having labour at demand' – in *Tabletalk* (1823). Thomas Hodgskin, in *Labour Defended against the Claims of Capital* (1825) wrote: 'all the capitalists of Europe, with all their circulating capital, cannot of themselves supply a single week's food and clothing', and again: 'betwixt him who produces food and him who produces clothing, betwixt him who makes instruments and him who uses them, in steps the capitalist, who neither makes nor uses them and appropriates to himself the produce of both'. This is clearly the description of an economic *system*.

The economic sense of **capital** had been present in English from C17 and in a fully developed form from C18. Chambers *Cyclopaedia* (1727–51) has 'power given by Parliament to the South-Sea company to increase their capital' and definition of 'circulating capital' is in Adam Smith, 1776. The word had acquired this specialized meaning from its general sense of 'head' or 'chief'; fw *capital*, F, *capitalis*, L, rw *caput*, L – head. There were many derived specialist meanings; the economic meaning developed from a shortening of the phrase 'capital stock' – a material holding or monetary fund. In classical economics the functions of **capital**, and of various kinds of **capital**, were described and defined.

Capitalism represents a development of meaning in that it has been increasingly used to indicate a particular and historical economic system rather than any economic system as such. **Capital** and at first **capitalist** were technical terms in any economic system. The later (eC19) uses of **capitalist** moved towards specific functions in a particular stage of historical development;

it is this use that crystallized in **capitalism**. There was a sense of the **capitalist** as the useless but controlling intermediary between producers, or as the employer of labour, or, finally, as the owner of the means of production. This involved, eventually, and especially in Marx, a distinction of **capital** as a formal economic category from **capitalism** as a particular form of centralized ownership of the means of production, carrying with it the system of wage-labour. **Capitalism** in this sense is a product of a developing bourgeois society; there are early kinds of **capitalist** production but **capitalism** as a system – what Marx calls 'the capitalist era' – dates only from C16 and did not reach the stage of **industrial capitalism** until lC18 and eC19.

There has been immense controversy about the details of this description, and of course about the merits and workings of the system itself, but from lC19, in most languages, **capitalism** has had this sense of a distinct economic system, which can be contrasted with other systems. There have been interesting consequent uses of language, in the course of this controversy. Thus, since lC19 but especially in mC20, the words **capitalism** and **capitalist** have often been deliberately replaced by defenders of the system by such phrases as 'private enterprise' and 'free enterprise'. These terms, recalling some of the conditions of early capitalism, are applied without apparent hesitation to very large or para-national 'public' corporations, or to an economic system controlled by them. At other times, however, **capitalism** is defended under its own now common name. There has also developed a use of **post-capitalist** and **post-capitalism**, to describe modifications of the system such as the supposed transfer of control from shareholders to professional management, or the coexistence of certain NATIONALIZED (q.v.) or 'state-owned' industries. The plausibility of these descriptions depends on the definition of capitalism which they are selected to modify. Though they evidently modify certain kinds of capitalism, in relation to its central sense they are marginal. A new phrase, **state-capitalism**, has been widely used in mC20, with precedents from eC20, to describe forms of state ownership in which the original conditions of the definition – centralized ownership of the means of production, leading to a system of wage-labour – have not really changed.

It is also necessary to note an extension of the adjective **capitalist** to describe the whole society, or features of the society, in which a **capitalist** economic system predominates. There is considerable overlap and occasional confusion here between **capitalist** and BOURGEOIS (q.v.). In strict Marxist usage **capitalist** is a description of a mode of production and *bourgeois* a description of a type of society. It is in controversy about the relations between a mode of production and a type of society that the conditions for overlap of meaning occur.

See BOURGEOIS, INDUSTRY, SOCIETY

CAREER

Career is now so regularly used to describe a person's progress in life, or, by derivation from this, his profession or vocation that it is difficult to remember, in the same context, its original meanings of a racecourse and a gallop – though in some contexts, as in the phrase 'careering about', these survive.

Career appeared in English from eC16, from fw *carrière*, F – racecourse, rw *carraria*, L – carriage road, from *carrus*, L – wagon. It was used from C16 for racecourse, gallop, and by extension any rapid or uninterrupted activity. Though sometimes applied neutrally, as of the course of the sun, it had a predominant C17 and C18 sense not only of rapid but of unrestrained activity. It is not easy to be certain of the change of implication between, for example, a use in 1767 – 'a ... beauty ... in the career of her conquests' – and Macaulay's use in 1848 – 'in the full career of success'. But it is probable that it was from eC19 that the use without derogatory implication began, especially with reference to diplomats and statesmen. By mC19 the word was becoming common to indicate progress in a vocation and then the vocation itself.

At this point, and especially in the course of C20, **career** becomes inseparable from a difficult group of words of which WORK, LABOUR (qq.v.) and especially *job* are prominent examples. **Career** is still used in the abstract spectacular sense of politicians and entertainers, but more generally it is applied, with some conscious and unconscious class distinction, to *work* or a *job* which contains some implicit promise of progress. It has been most widely used for jobs with explicit internal development – 'a career in the Civil Service' – but it has since been extended to any favourable or desired or flattered occupation – 'a career in coalmining'. **Career** now implies continuity if not necessarily promotion or advancement, yet the distinction between a **career** and a *job* only partly depends on this and is associated also with class distinctions between different kinds of work.

It is interesting that something like the original metaphor, with its derogatory C17 or C18 sense, has reappeared in descriptions of some areas of work and promotion as the *rat-race*.

See LABOUR, WORK

CHARITY

Charity came into English, in C12, from fw *charité*, oF, *caritas*, L, rw *carus* – dear. Forms of the Latin word had taken on the sense of dearness of price as well as affection (an association repeated and continued in *dear* itself, from oE onward). But the predominant use of **charity** was in the context of the Bible (Greek *agape* had been distinguished into *dilectio* and *caritas* in the Vulgate, and Wyclif translated these as *love* and *charity*. Tyndale rendered *caritas* as love, and in the fierce doctrinal disputes of C16 this translation was criticized, the ecclesiastical **charity** being preferred in the Bishop's Bible and then in the Authorized Version. *Love* was one of the key terms of the C19 Revised Version.) **Charity** was then Christian love, between man and God, and between men and their neighbours. The sense of benevolence to neighbours, and specifically of gifts to the needy, is equally early, but was at first directly related to the sense of Christian love, as in the Pauline use: 'though I bestow all my goods to feed the poor . . . and have not charity, it profiteth me nothing' (1 *Corinthians* 13) where the act without the feeling is seen as null. Nevertheless, **charity** in the predominant sense of help to the needy came through steadily; it is probably already dominant in C16 and is used with a new sense of abstraction from lC17 and eC18. A **charity** as an institution was established by lC17. These senses have of course persisted.

But there is another movement in the word. **Charity begins at home** was already a popular saying in eC17 and has precedents from C14. More significant is **cold as charity**, which is an interesting reversal of what is probably the original use in *Matthew*

24: 12, where the prophecy of 'wars and rumours of wars' and of the rise of 'many false prophets' is capped by this: 'because iniquity shall abound, the love of many shall wax cold'. This is the most general Christian sense. Earlier translations (e.g. Rhemish, 1582) had used: 'charity of many shall wax cold'. Browne (1642) wrote of 'the general complaint of these times . . . that Charity grows cold'. By lC18 the sense had been reversed. It was not the sense of a drying-up or freezing of love or bene- volence; it was the more interesting sense of what the **charitable** act feels like to the recipient from prolonged experience of the habits and manners of most charitable institutions. This sense has remained very important, and some people still say that they will not 'take charity', even from public funds to which they have themselves contributed. It is true that this includes an independent feeling against being helped by others, but the odium which has gathered around **charity** in this context comes from feelings of wounded self-respect and dignity which belong, historically, to the interaction of charity and of class-feelings, on both sides of the act. Critical marks of this interaction are the specialization of **charity** to the *deserving poor* (not neighbourly love, but reward for approved social conduct) and the calcula- tion in bourgeois political economy summed up by Jevons (1878): 'all that the political economist insists upon is that charity shall be really charity, and shall not injure those whom it is intended to aid' (not the relief of need, but its selective use to preserve the incentive to wage-labour). It is not surprising that the word which was once the most general expression of love and care for others has become (except in special contexts, following the surviving legal definition of benevolent institutions) so compromised that modern governments have to advertise welfare benefits (and with a wealth of social history in the distinction) as 'not a charity but a right'.

CITY

City has existed in English since C13, but its distinctive modern use to indicate a large or very large town, and its consequent use to distinguish urban areas from rural areas or *country*, date from C16. The later indication and distinction are obviously related to the increasing importance of urban life from C16 onward, but until C19 this was often specialized to the capital city, London. The more general use corresponds to the rapid development of urban living during the Industrial Revolution, which made England by mC19 the first society in the history of the world in which a majority of the population lived in towns.

City is derived from fw *cité*, oF, rw *civitas*, L. But *civitas* was not **city** in the modern sense; that was *urbs*, L. *Civitas* was the general noun derived from *civis*, L – citizen, which is nearer our modern sense of a 'national'. *Civitas* was then the body of citizens rather than a particular settlement or type of settlement. It was so applied by Roman writers to the tribes of Gaul. In a long and complicated development *civitas* and the words derived from it became specialized to the chief town of such a state, and in ecclesiastical use to the cathedral town. The earlier English words had been *borough*, fw *burh*, oE and *town*, fw *tun*, oE. *Town* developed from its original sense of an enclosure or yard to a group of buildings in such an enclosure (as which it survives in some modern village and village-division names) to the beginnings of its modern sense in C13. *Borough* and **city** became often interchangeable, and there are various legal distinctions between them in different periods and types of medieval and post-medieval government. One such distinction of **city**, from C16, was the presence of a cathedral, and this is still residually though now wrongly asserted. When **city** began to be distinguished from *town* in terms of size, mainly from C19 but with precedents in relation to the predominance of London from C16, each was still administratively a *borough*, and this word became specialized to a form of local government or administration. From C13 **city** became in any case a more dignifying word than *town*; it was often thus used of Biblical villages, or to indicate an ideal or significant settlement. More generally, by C16 **city** was in regular use for London, and in C17 **city** and *country* contrasts were very common. **City** in the specialized sense of a financial and commercial centre, derived from actual location in the City of London, was widely used from eC18, when this financial and commercial activity notably expanded.

The **city** as a really distinctive order of settlement, implying a whole different way of life, is not fully established, with its modern implications, until eC19. It became a dominant and pre-occupying idea from mC19. The emphasis can be traced in the word, in the increasing abstraction of **city** as an adjective from particular places or particular administrative forms, and in the

47

increasing generalization of descriptions of large-scale modern urban living. The modern **city** of millions of inhabitants is thus generally if indefinitely distinguished from several kinds of **city** – cf. *cathedral city, university city, provincial city* – characteristic of earlier periods and types of settlement.

See COUNTRY, CIVILIZATION

CIVILIZATION

Civilization is now generally used to describe an achieved state or condition of organized social life. Like CULTURE (q.v.) with which it has had a long and still difficult interaction, it referred originally to a process, and in some contexts this sense still survives.

Civilization was preceded in English by **civilize**, which appeared in eC17, from C16 *civilizer*, F, fw *civilizare*, mL – to make a criminal matter into a civil matter, and thence, by extension, to bring within a form of social organization. The rw is *civil* from *civilis*, L – of or belonging to citizens, from *civis*, L – citizen. **Civil** was thus used in English from C14, and by C16 had acquired the extended senses of orderly and educated. Hooker in 1594 wrote of 'Civil Society' – a phrase that was to become central in C17 and especially C18 – but the main development towards description of an ordered society was **civility**, fw *civilitas*, mL – community. **Civility** was often used in C17 and C18 where we would now expect **civilization**, and as late as 1772 Boswell, visiting Johnson, 'found him busy, preparing a fourth edition of his folio Dictionary . . . He would not admit *civilization*, but only *civility*. With great deference to him, I thought *civilization*, from *to civilize*, better in the sense opposed to *barbarity*, than *civility*.' Boswell had correctly identified the main use that was coming through, which emphasized not so much a process as a state of social order and refinement, especially in conscious historical or cultural contrast with *barbarism*. **Civilization** appeared in Ash's dictionary of 1775, to indicate both the state and the process. By lC18 and then very markedly in C19 it became common.

In one way the new sense of **civilization**, from lC18, is a specific combination of the ideas of a process and an achieved condition. It has behind it the general spirit of the Enlightenment, with its emphasis on secular and progressive human self-development. **Civilization** expressed this sense of historical process, but also celebrated the associated sense of modernity: an achieved condition of refinement and order. In the Romantic reaction against these claims for **civilization**, alternative words were developed to express other kinds of human development and other criteria for human well-being, notably CULTURE (q.v.). In 1C18 the association of **civilization** with refinement of manners was normal in both English and French. Burke wrote in *Reflections on the French Revolution*: 'our manners, our civilization, and all the good things which are connected with manners, and with civilization'. Here the terms seem almost synonymous, though we must note that *manners* has a wider reference than in ordinary modern usage. From eC19 the development of **civilization** towards its modern meaning, in which as much emphasis is put on social order and on ordered knowledge (later, SCIENCE q.v.) as on refinement of manners and behaviour, is on the whole earlier in French than in English. But there was a decisive moment in English in the 1830s, when Mill, in his essay on Coleridge, wrote:

Take for instance the question how far mankind has gained by civilization. One observer is forcibly struck by the multiplication of physical comforts; the advancement and diffusion of knowledge; the decay of superstition; the facilities of mutual intercourse; the softening of manners; the decline of war and personal conflict; the progressive limitation of the tyranny of the strong over the weak; the great works accomplished throughout the globe by the co-operation of multitudes . . .

This is Mill's range of positive examples of **civilization**, and it is a fully modern range. He went on to describe negative effects: loss of independence, the creation of artificial wants, monotony, narrow mechanical understanding, inequality and hopeless poverty. The contrast made by Coleridge and others was between **civilization** and *culture* or *cultivation*:

The permanent distinction and the occasional contrast between cultivation and civilization . . . The permanency of the nation . . . and its progressiveness and personal freedom . . . depend on a continuing and progressive civilization. But civilization is itself but a mixed good, if not far more a corrupting influence, the hectic of disease, not the bloom of health, and a nation so distinguished more fitly to be called a varnished than a polished people, where this civilization is not grounded in cultivation, in the harmonious development of those qualities and faculties that characterize our humanity. (*On the Constitution of Church and State*, V)

Coleridge was evidently aware in this passage of the association of civilization with the *polishing* of manners; that is the point of the remark about varnish, and the distinction recalls the curious overlap, in C18 English and French, between *polished* and *polite*, which have the same root. But the description of **civilization** as a 'mixed good', like Mill's more elaborated description of its positive and negative effects, marks the point at which the word has come to stand for a whole modern social process. From this time on this sense was dominant, whether the effects were reckoned as good, bad or mixed.

Yet it was still primarily seen as a general and indeed universal process. There was a critical moment when **civilization** was used in the plural. This is later with **civilizations** than with *cultures*; its first clear use is in French (Ballanche) in 1819. It is preceded in English by implicit uses to refer to an earlier civilization, but it is not common anywhere until the 1860s.

In modern English **civilization** still refers to a general condition or state, and is still contrasted with *savagery* or *barbarism*. But the relativism inherent in comparative studies, and reflected in the use of **civilizations**, has affected this main sense, and the word now regularly attracts some defining adjective: **Western civilization, modern civilization, industrial civilization, scientific and technological civilization**. As such it has come to be a relatively neutral term for any achieved social order or way of life, and in this sense has a complicated and much disputed relation with the modern social sense of *culture*. Yet its sense of an achieved state is still sufficiently strong for it to retain some normative quality; in this sense **civilization, a civilized way of life, the conditions of civilized society** may be seen as capable of being lost as well as gained.

See CITY, CULTURE, MODERN, SOCIETY

CLASS

Class is an obviously difficult word, both in its range of meanings and in its complexity in that particular meaning where it describes a social division. The Latin word *classis*, a division according to property of the people of Rome, came into English in lC16 in its Latin form, with a plural *classes* or *classies*. There is a lC16 use (King, 1594) which sounds almost modern: 'all the classies and ranks of vanitie'. But **classis** was primarily used in explicit reference to Roman history, and was then extended, first as a term in church organization ('assemblies are either classes or synods', 1593) and later as a general term for a division or group ('the classis of Plants', 1664). It is worth noting that the derived Latin word *classicus*, coming into English in eC17 as **classic** from fw *classique*, F, had social implications before it took on its general meaning of a standard authority and then its particular meaning of belonging to Greek and Roman antiquity (now usually distinguished in the form **classical**, which at first alternated with *classic*). Gellius wrote: '*classicus . . . scriptor, non proletarius*'. But the form **class**, coming into English in C17, acquired a special association with education. Blount, glossing *classe* in 1656, included the still primarily Roman sense of 'an order or distribution of people according to their several Degrees' but added: 'in Schools (wherein this word is most used) a Form or Lecture restrained to a certain company of Scholars' – a use which has remained common in education. The development of **classic** and **classical** was strongly affected by this association with authoritative works for study.

From lC17 the use of **class** as a general word for a group or division became more and more common. What is then most difficult is that **class** came to be used in this way about people as well as about plants and animals, but without social implications of the modern kind. (Cf. Steele 1709: 'this Class of modern Wits'.) Development of **class** in its modern social sense, with relatively fixed names for particular classes (**lower class**, **middle class**, **upper class**, **working class** and so on) belongs essentially to the period between 1770 and 1840, which is also the period of the industrial Revolution and its decisive reorganization of society. At the extremes it is not difficult to distinguish between

(i) **class** as a general term for any grouping and (ii) **class** as a would-be specific description of a social formation. There is no difficulty in distinguishing between Steele's 'Class of modern Wits' and, say, the *Declaration* of the Birmingham Political Union (1830) 'that the rights and interests of the middle and lower classes of the people are not efficiently represented in the Commons House of Parliament'. But in the crucial period of transition, and indeed for some time before it, there is real difficulty in being sure whether a particular use is sense (i) or sense (ii). The earliest use that I know, which might be read in a modern sense, is Defoe's ' 'tis plain the dearness of wages forms our people into more classes than other nations can show' (*Review*, 14 April, 1705). But this, even in an economic context, is far from certain. There must also be some doubt about Hanway's title of 1772: 'Observations on the Causes of the Dissoluteness which reigns among the lower classes of the people'. We can read this, as indeed we would read Defoe, in a strictly social sense, but there is enough overlap between sense (i) and sense (ii) to make us pause. The crucial context of this develop-ment is the alternative vocabulary for social divisions, and it is a fact that until lC18, and residually well into C19 and even C20, the most common words were *rank* and *order*, while *estate* and *degree* were still more common than **class**, *Estate, degree* and *order* had been widely used to describe social position from medieval times. *Rank* had been common from lC16. In virtually all contexts where we would now say **class** these other words were standard, and *lower order* and *lower orders* became especially common in C18.

The essential history of the introduction of **class**, as a word which would supersede older names for social divisions, relates to the increasing consciousness that social position is made rather than merely inherited. All the older words, with their essential metaphors of standing, stepping and arranging in rows, belong to a society in which position was determined by birth. Individual mobility could be seen as movement from one *estate, degree, order* or *rank* to another. What was changing conscious-ness was not only increased individual mobility, which could be largely contained within the older terms, but the new sense of a SOCIETY (q.v.) or a particular *social system* which actually created social divisions, including new kinds of division. This is quite explicit in one of the first clear uses, that of Madison in *The Federalist* (USA, c. 1787): moneyed and manufacturing interests 'grow up of necessity in civilized nations, and divide them into different classes, actuated by different sentiments and views'. Under the pressure of this awareness, greatly sharpened by the economic changes of the Industrial Revolution and the political conflicts of the American and French Revolutions, the new vocabulary of **class** began to take over. But it was a slow and uneven process, not only because of the residual familiarity of the older words, and not only because conservative thinkers continued, as a matter of principle, to avoid **class** wherever they could and to prefer the older (and later some newer) terms. It was slow and uneven, and has remained difficult, mainly because of the inevitable overlap with the use of **class** not as a specific social division but as a generally available and often *ad hoc* term of grouping.

With this said, we can trace the formation of the newly specific **class** vocabulary. **Lower classes** was used in 1772, and **lowest classes** and **lowest class** were common from the 1790s. These carry some of the marks of the transition, but do not complete it. More interesting because less dependent on an old general sense, in which the **lower classes** would be not very different from the COMMON (q.v.) *people*, is the new and increasingly self-conscious and self-used description of the **middle classes**. This has precedents in 'men of a middle condition' (1716), 'the middle Station of Life', (Defoe, 1719), 'the Middling People of England . . . generally Good-natured and Stout-hearted' (1718), 'the middling and lower classes' (1789). Gisborne in 1795 wrote an 'Enquiry into the Duties of Men in the Higher Rank and Middle Classes of Society in Great Britain'. Hannah More in 1796 wrote of the 'middling classes'. The 'burden of taxation' rested heavily 'on the middle classes' in 1809 (*Monthly Repository*, 501), and in 1812 there was reference to 'such of the Middle Class of Society who have fallen upon evil days' (*Examiner*, August). *Rank* was still used at least as often, as in James Mill (1820): 'the class which is universally described as both the most wise and the most virtuous part of the community, the middle rank' (*Essay on Government*), but here **class** has already taken on a general social sense, used on its own. The swell of self-congratulatory description reached a temporary climax in Brougham's speech of 1831: 'by the people, I mean the middle classes, the wealth and intelligence of the country, the glory of the British name'.

There is a continuing curiosity in this development. *Middle* belongs to a disposition between *lower* and *higher*, in fact as an insertion between an increasingly insupportable *high* and *low*. **Higher classes** was used by Burke (*Thoughts on French Affairs*) in 1791, and **upper classes** is recorded from the 1820s. In this model an old hierarchical division is still obvious; the **middle class** is a self-conscious interposition between persons of *rank* and the *common people*. This was always, by definition, indeterminate: this is one of the reasons why the grouping word **class** rather than the specific word *rank* eventually came through. But clearly in Brougham, and very often since, the *upper* or *higher* part of the model virtually disappears, or, rather, awareness of a *higher* class is assigned to a different dimension, that of a residual and respected but essentially displaced aristocracy.

This is the ground for the next complication. In the fierce argument about political, social and economic rights, between the 1790s and the 1830s, **class** was used in another model, with a simple distinction of the **productive** or **useful classes** (a potent term against the aristocracy). In the widely-read translation of Volney's *The Ruins, or A Survey of the Revolutions of Empires* (2 parts, 1795) there was a dialogue between those who by 'useful labours contribute to the support and maintenance of society' (the majority of the people, 'labourers, artisans, tradesmen and every profession useful to society', hence called *People*) and a **Privileged class** ('priests, courtiers, public accountants, commanders of troops, in short, the civil, military or religious agents of government'). This is a description in French terms of *the people* against an aristocratic government, but it was widely adopted in English terms, with one particular result which corresponds to the actual political situation of the reform movement between the 1790s and the 1830s: both the self-conscious **middle classes** and the quite different people who by the end of this period would describe themselves as the **working classes** adopted the descriptions **useful** or **productive classes**, in distinction from and in opposition to the *privileged* or the *idle*. This use, which of course sorts oddly with the other model of *lower*, *middle* and *higher*, has remained both important and confusing.

For it was by transfer from the sense of *useful* or *productive* that the **working classes** were first named. There is considerable overlap in this: cf. 'middle and industrious classes' (*Monthly Magazine*, 1797) and 'poor and working classes' (Owen, 1813) – the latter probably the first English use of **working classes** but still very general. In 1818 Owen published *Two Memorials on*

Behalf of the Working Classes, and in the same year *The Gorgon* (28 November 1818) used **working classes** in the specific and unmistakable context of relations between 'workmen' and 'their employers'. The use then developed rapidly, and by 1831 the *National Union of the Working Classes* identified not so much privilege as the 'laws . . . made to protect . . . property or capital' as their enemy. (They distinguished such laws from those that had not been made to protect INDUSTRY (q.v.), still in its old sense of applied labour.) In the *Poor Man's Guardian* (19 October 1833), O'Brien wrote of establishing for 'the productive classes a complete dominion over the fruits of their own industry' and went on to describe such a change as 'contemplated by the working classes'; the two terms, in this context, are inter-changeable. There are complications in phrases like the **labouring classes** and the **operative classes**, which seem designed to separate one group of the **useful classes** from another, to correspond with the distinction between *workmen* and *employers*, or *men* and *masters*: a distinction that was economically inevitable and that was politically active from the 1830s at latest. The term **working classes**, originally assigned by others, was eventually taken over and used as proudly as **middle classes** had been: 'the working classes have created all wealth' (*Rules* of Ripponden Co-operative Society; cit. J. H. Priestley, *History of RCS*; dating from 1833 or 1839).

By the 1840s, then, **middle classes** and **working classes** were common terms. The former became singular first; the latter is singular from the 1840s but still today alternates between singular and plural forms, often with ideological significance, the singular being normal in socialist uses, the plural more common in conservative descriptions. But the most significant effect of this complicated history was that there were now two common terms, increasingly used for comparison, distinction or contrast, which had been formed within quite different models. On the one hand *middle* implied hierarchy and therefore implied **lower class**: not only theoretically but in repeated practice. On the other hand *working* implied productive or useful activity, which would leave all who were not **working class** unproductive and useless (easy enough for an aristocracy, but hardly accepted by a productive **middle class**). To this day this confusion reverberates. As early as 1844 Cockburn referred to 'what are termed *the* working-classes, as if the only workers were those who wrought with their hands'. Yet *working man* or *workman* had a persistent

reference to manual labour. In an Act of 1875 this was given
legal definition: 'the expression *workman* . . . means any person
who, being a labourer, servant in husbandry, journeyman,
artificer, handicraftsman, miner, or otherwise engaged in
manual labour . . . has entered into or works under a contract
with an employer'. The association of *workman* and **working
class** was thus very strong, but it will be noted that the definition
includes contract with an employer as well as manual work. An
Act of 1890 stated: 'the provisions of section eleven of the
Housing of the Working Classes Act, 1885 . . . shall have effect
as if the expression *working classes* included all classes of persons
who earn their livelihood by wages or salaries.' This permitted a
distinction from those whose livelihood depended on fees (**professional class**), profits (**trading class**) or property (**independent**).
Yet, especially with the development of clerical and service
occupations, there was a critical ambiguity about the class
position of those who worked for a *salary* or even a *wage* and
yet did not do manual labour. (*Salary* as fixed payment dates from
C14; *wages and salaries* is still a normal C19 phrase; in 1868,
however, 'a manager of a bank or railway – even an overseer
or a clerk in a manufactory – is said to draw a salary', and the
attempted class distinction between salaries and wages is evident;
by eC20 the *salariat* was being distinguished from the *proletariat*).
Here again, at a critical point, the effect of two models of **class**
is evident. The **middle class**, with which the earners of salaries
normally aligned themselves, is an expression of relative social
position and thus of social distinction. The **working class**,
specialized from the different notion of the *useful* or *productive
classes*, is an expression of economic relationships. Thus the two
common modern class terms rest on different models, and the
position of those who are conscious of relative social position
and thus of social distinction, and yet, within an economic
relationship, sell and are dependent on their labour, is the point
of critical overlap between the models and the terms. It is absurd
to conclude that only the **working classes** WORK (q.v.), but if
those who work in other than 'manual' labour describe themselves in terms of relative social position (**middle class**) the
confusion is inevitable. One side effect of this difficulty was a
further elaboration of **classing** itself (the period from lC18 to
lC19 is rich in these derived words: **classify, classifier, classification**). From the 1860s the **middle class** began to be divided into
lower and *upper* sections, and later the **working class** was to be

divided into *skilled, semi-skilled* and *labouring.* Various other systems of classification succeeded these, notably *socio-economic group*, which must be seen as an attempt to marry the two models of **class**, and STATUS (q.v.).

It is necessary, finally, to consider the variations of **class** as an abstract idea. In one of the earliest uses of the singular social term, in Crabbe's

> To every class we have a school assign'd
> Rules for all ranks and food for every mind

class is virtually equivalent to *rank* and was so used in the definition of a *middle* class. But the influence of sense (i), **class** as a general term for grouping, was at least equally strong, and *useful* or *productive* classes follows mainly from this. The *productive* distinction, however, as a perception of an active economic system, led to a sense of **class** which is neither a synonym for *rank* nor a mode of descriptive grouping, but is a description of fundamental economic relationships. In modern usage, the sense of *rank*, though residual, is still active; in one kind of use **class** is still essentially defined by birth. But the more serious uses divide between descriptive grouping and economic relationship. It is obvious that a terminology of basic economic relationships (as between employers and employed, or propertied and propertyless) will be found too crude and general for the quite different purpose of precise descriptive grouping. Hence the persistent but confused arguments between those who, using **class** in the sense of basic relationship, propose two or three basic **classes**, and those who, trying to use it for descriptive grouping, find they have to break these divisions down into smaller and smaller categories. The history of the word carries this essential ambiguity.

When the language of **class** was being developed, in eC19, each tendency can be noted. *The Gorgon* (21 November 1818) referred quite naturally to 'a smaller class of tradesmen, termed *garret-masters*'. But Cobbett in 1825 had the newer sense: 'so that here is one class of society united to oppose another class'. Charles Hall in 1805 had argued that

> the people in a civilized state may be divided into different orders; but for the purpose of investigating the manner in which they enjoy or are deprived of the requisites to support the health of their bodies or minds, they need only be divided

into two classes, viz. the rich and the poor. (*The Effects of Civilization on the People in European States*).

Here there is a distinction between *orders* (*ranks*) and effective economic groupings (**classes**). A cotton spinner in 1818 (cit. *The Making of the English Working Class*; E. P. Thompson, p. 199) described employers and workers as 'two distinct classes of persons'. In different ways this binary grouping became conventional, though it operated alongside tripartite groupings: both the social grouping (*upper*, *middle* and *lower*) and a modernized economic grouping: John Stuart Mill's 'three classes', of 'landlords, capitalists and labourers' (*Monthly Repository*, 1834, 320) or Marx's 'three great social classes . . . wage-labourers, capitalists and landlords' (*Capital*, III). In the actual development of capitalist society, the tripartite division was more and more replaced by a new binary division: in Marxist language the *bourgeoisie* and the *proletariat*. (It is because of the complications of the tripartite division, and because of the primarily social definition of the English term **middle class**, that *bourgeoisie* and even *proletariat* are often difficult to translate.) A further difficulty then arises: a repetition, at a different level, of the variation between a descriptive grouping and an economic relationship. A **class** seen in terms of economic relationships can be a category (*wage-earners*) or a formation (**the working class**). The main tendency of Marx's description of classes was towards formations:

> The separate individuals form a class only insofar as they have to carry on a common battle against another class; otherwise they are on hostile terms with each other as competitors. On the other hand, the class in its turn achieves an independent existence over against the individuals, so that the latter find their conditions of existence predestined, and hence have their position in life and their personal development assigned to them by their class . . . (*German Ideology*)

This difficult argument again attracts confusion. A **class** is sometimes an economic category, including all who are objectively in that economic situation. But a **class** is sometimes (and in Marx more often) a formation in which, for historical reasons, consciousness of this situation and the organization to deal with it have developed. Thus:

> Insofar as millions of families live under economic conditions of existence that separate their mode of life, their interests

and their culture from those of the other classes, and put them in hostile opposition to the latter, they form a class. Insofar as there is merely a local interconnection among these small-holding peasants, and the identity of their interests begets no community, no national bond and no political organization among them, they do not form a class. (*Eighteenth Brumaire of Louis Bonaparte*)

This is the distinction between category and formation, but since **class** is used for both there has been plenty of ground for confusion. The problem is still critical in that it underlies repeated arguments about the relation of an assumed **class-consciousness** to an objectively measured **class**, and about the vagaries of self-description and self-assignation to a class scale. Many of the derived terms repeat this uncertainty. **Class consciousness** clearly can belong only to a formation. **Class struggle, class conflict, class war, class legislation, class bias** depend on the existence of formations (though this may be very uneven or partial within or between **classes**). **Class culture**, on the other hand, can swing between the two meanings: *working-class culture* can be the meanings and values and institutions of the formation, or the tastes and life-styles of the category (see also CULTURE). In a whole range of contemporary discussion and controversy, all these variable meanings of **class** can be seen in operation, usually without clear distinction. It is therefore worth repeating the basic range (outside the uncontroversial senses of general classification and education):

  (i) *group* (objective); social or economic category, at varying levels
  (ii) *rank*; relative social position; by birth or mobility
  (iii) *formation*; perceived economic relationship; social, political and cultural organization

See CULTURE, INDUSTRY, MASSES, POPULAR, SOCIETY

COLLECTIVE

Collective appeared in English as an adjective from C16 and as a noun from C17. It was mainly a specialized development from **collect**, fw *collectus*, L – gathered together; (there is also a fw *collecter*, oF – to gather taxes or other money). **Collective** as an adjective was used from its earliest appearance to describe people acting together, or in such related phrases as **collective body** (Hooker, *Ecclesiastical Polity*, VIII, iv; 1600). Early uses of the noun were in grammar or in physical description. The social and political sense of a specific unit – 'your brethren of the Collective' (Cobbett, *Rural Rides*, II, 337; 1830) – belongs to the new DEMOCRATIC (q.v.) consciousness of eC19. This use has been revived in several subsequent periods, including mC20, but is still not common. **Collectivism**, used mainly to describe socialist economic theory, and only derivatively in the political sense of **collective**, became common in lC19; it was described in the 1880s as a recent word, though its use is recorded from the 1850s.

See COMMON, DEMOCRACY, MASSES, SOCIETY

COMMERCIALISM

Commerce was a normal English word for trade from C16, from fw *commerce*, F, *commercium*, L, rw *com*, L – together, *merx*, L – ware or merchandise. **Commerce** was also extended from C16 to describe all kinds of 'dealings' – meetings, interactions – between men. **Commercial** appeared from lC17 in the more specific sense of activities connected with trade, as distinct from other activities. It was at first primarily descriptive but began to acquire critical associations from mC18. The fully critical word is **commercialism**, from mC19, to indicate a system which puts financial profit before any other consideration. Meanwhile **commerce** retained its neutral sense, and **commercial** could be used either favourably or unfavourably.

There is an interesting contemporary use of **commercial** to describe a broadcast advertisement, and in some associated popular entertainment there was, from the 1960s, a use of **commercial** to mean not only successful but also effective or powerful work, as in popular music the favourable **commercial sound**. Meanwhile, however, **commercial broadcasting** preferred to describe itself as *independent* (cf. CAPITALISM and *free* or *private enterprise*).

COMMON

Common has an extraordinary range of meaning in English, and several of its particular meanings are inseparable from a still active social history. The rw is *communis*, L, which has been derived, alternatively, from *com-*, L – together and *munis*, L – under obligation, and from *com-* and *unus*, L – one. In early uses these senses can be seen to merge: **common** to a **community** (from C14 an organized body of people), to a specific group, or to the generality of mankind. There are distinctions in these uses, but also considerable and persistent overlaps. What is then interesting is the very early use of **common** as an adjective and noun of social division: **common**, **the common** and **commons**, as contrasted with lords and nobility. The tension of these two senses has been persistent. **Common** can indicate a whole group or interest or a large specific and subordinate group. (Cf. Elyot's protest (*Governor* I, i, 1531) against **commune weale**, later **commonwealth**: 'There may appere lyke diversitie to be in Englisshe between a publike weale and a commune weale, as shulde be in Latin, betwene *Res publica* & *res plebeia*'.)

The same tension is apparent even in applications of the sense of a whole group: that is, of generality. **Common** can be used to affirm something shared or to describe something *ordinary* (itself ambivalent, related to *order* as series or sequence, hence *ordinary* – in the usual course of things, but also to *order* as rank, social and military, hence *ordinary* – of an undistinguished kind); or again, in one kind of use, to describe something *low* or *vulgar* (which has specialized in this sense from a comparable origin, *vulgus*, L – the common people). It is difficult to date the derogatory sense of **common**. In feudal society the attribution was systematic and carried few if any additional overtones. It is significant that members of the Parliamentary army in the Civil War of mC17 refused to be called **common soldiers** and insisted on *private soldiers*. This must indicate an existing and significant derogatory sense of **common**, though it is interesting that this same army were fighting for **the commons** and went on to establish a **commonwealth**. The alternative they chose is remarkable, since it asserted, in the true spirit of their revolution, that they were their own men. There is a great deal of social history in this transfer across the range of ordinary description from **common** to *private*: in a way the transposition of hitherto opposed meanings, becoming *private* soldiers in a **common** cause. In succeeding British armies, *private* has been deprived of this significance and reduced to a technical term for those of lowest rank.

It is extremely difficult, from lC16 on, to distinguish relatively neutral uses of **common**, as in *common ware*, from more conscious and yet vaguer uses to mean *vulgar, unrefined* and eventually *low-class*. Certainly the clear derogatory use seems to increase from eC19, in a period of more conscious and yet less specific class-distinction (cf. CLASS). By lC19 'her speech was very *common*' has an unmistakable ring, and this use has persisted over a wide range of behaviour. Meanwhile other senses, both neutral and positive, are also in general use. People, sometimes the same people, say 'it's *common* to eat ice-cream in the street' (and indeed it is becoming **common** in another sense); but also 'it's *common* to speak of the need for a *common* effort' (which may indeed be difficult to get if many of the people needed to make it are seen as **common**).

See CLASS, MASSES, POPULAR

COMMUNICATION

Communication in its most general modern meaning has been in the language since C15. Its fw is *communicacion*, oF, from *communicationem*, L, a noun of action from the stem of the past participle of *communicare*, L, from rw *communis*, L – common: hence *communicate* – make common to many, impart. **Communication** was first this action, and then, from lC15, the object thus made common: a **communication**. This has remained its main range of use. But from lC17 there was an important extension to the *means* of communication, specifically in such phrases as **lines of communication**. In the main period of development of roads, canals and railways, **communications** was often the abstract general term for these physical facilities. It was in C20, with the development of other means of passing information and maintaining social contact, that **communications** came also and perhaps predominantly to refer to such MEDIA (q.v.) as the press and broadcasting, though this use (which is earlier in USA than in UK) is not settled before mC20. The **communications industry**, as it is now called, is thus usually distinguished from the *transport industry*: **communications** for information and ideas, in print and broadcasting; *transport* for the physical carriage of people and goods.

In controversy about communications systems and communication theory it is often useful to recall the unresolved range of the original noun of action, represented at its extremes by *transmit*, a one-way process, and *share* (cf. **communion** and especially **communicant**), a common or mutual process. The intermediate senses – make common to many, and impart – can be read in either direction, and the choice of direction is often crucial. Hence the attempt to generalize the distinction in such contrasted phrases as **manipulative communication(s)** and **participatory communication(s)**.

See COMMON

COMMUNISM

Communism and **communist** emerged, as words, in mC19. Their best-known origins, on a European scale, are the *Communist Manifesto* of Marx and Engels in 1848 and the associated *Communist League*. But the word had been in use for some time before this. The *London Communist Propaganda Society* was founded in 1841, by Goodwyn Barmby, and there is an evident connection in this use with *communion*: 'the Communist gives (the Communion Table) a higher signification, by holding it as a type of that holy millennial communitive life'. Given the affinities and overlaps of the words deriving from COMMON (q.v.), this range is understandable, and certain connections were deliberately made by Christian utopian socialists. The overlap with secular and republican terminology, basically derived from the French Revolution, is also evident. Barmby claimed that he 'first pronounced the name of Communism which has since . . . acquired that world-wide reputation'. This had been in 1840, but significantly 'in conversation with some of the most advanced minds of the French metropolis' and in particular 'in the company of some disciples of Babeoeuf (*sic*) then called Equalitarians'. *Communiste* is recorded in a use by Cabet, also in 1840, and *communisme* and *communism* (in English also *communionism*) followed quickly in the same decade. In France and Germany, but not in England, **communist** became a harder word than SOCIALIST (q.v.). Engels later explained that he and Marx could not have called the Communist Manifesto 'a *Socialist* manifesto', because one was a working-class, the other a middle-class movement; 'socialism was, on the continent at least, respectable; Communism was the very opposite'. The modern distinction between **communist** and *socialist* is often read back to this period, but this is misleading. It is not only that *socialism* and *socialist* were more widely used, in Marxist as in other parties, but that **communist** was still quite widely understood, in English, in association with *community* and thus with experiments in common property. In English, in the 1880s, *socialism* was almost certainly the harder word, since it was unambiguously linked, for all its varying tendencies, to reorganization of the society as a whole. **Communist** was used in a modern sense after the example of the Paris Commune of 1870, but significantly was challenged by some as inaccurate; the real word for that was *communard*. William Morris in the 1890s expressed his opposition to Fabian Socialism in the explicit terms of **Communism** and **Communist**.

Yet the predominant general term was still *socialism* until the Russian Revolution. In 1918 the Russian Social-Democratic Labour Party (Bolsheviks) renamed itself the Communist Party of the Soviet Union (Bolsheviks), and nearly all modern usage follows from this. The renaming reached back to the distinction felt by Marx and Engels, and to the Paris Commune, but it was an act of historical reconstitution of the word, rather than of steady continuity. Within this tradition **communism** was now a higher stage beyond *socialism*, through which, however, it must pass. But this has had less effect on general meanings than the distinction which followed 1918 (though with many earlier substantial if not nominal precedents) between REVOLUTIONARY and DEMOCRATIC SOCIALISTS (qq.v.). Subsequent splits in the communist movement have produced further variations, though **communist** is most often used of parties linked to Soviet definitions, and variants of *revolutionary* and *Marxist-Leninist* have been common to describe alternative or dissident **communist** parties.

One particularly difficult use, in this complex and intensely controversial history, is that of *Marxist*. Virtually all the revolutionary socialist parties and groups, including the Communist Parties, claim to be *Marxist*, though in controversy they often deny this title to other competing parties of the same general kind. From outside the socialist movement, *marxist* has also been widely used: partly as a catch-all description of the varying revolutionary socialist and communist parties and groups; partly as a way of describing specifically theoretical and intellectual work and tendencies, often without political or immediately political implications. (In this latter use *marxist* is often an internal or external euphemism for **communist** or *revolutionary socialist*, though the marxist principle of the union of theory and practice gives the frequency of its contemporary use some significance.)

See SOCIALISM

COMMUNITY

Community has been in the language since C14, from fw *comuneté*, oF, *communitatem*, L – community of relations or feelings, from rw *communis*, L – COMMON (q.v.). It became established in English in a range of senses: (i) the commons or common people, as distinguished from those of rank (C14–C17); (ii) a state or organized society, in its later uses relatively small (C14–); (iii) the people of a district (C18–); (iv) the quality of holding something in common, as in **community of interests**, **community of goods** (C16–); (v) a sense of common identity and characteristics (C16–). It will be seen that senses (i) to (iii) indicate actual social groups; senses (iv) and (v) a particular quality of relationship (as in *communitas*). From C17 there are signs of the distinction which became especially important from C19, in which **community** was felt to be more immediate than SOCIETY (q.v.), although it must be remembered that *society* itself had this more immediate sense until C18, and *civil society* (see CIVILIZATION) was, like *society* and *community* in these uses, originally an attempt to distinguish the body of direct relationships from the organized establishment of *realm* or *state*. From C19 the sense of immediacy or locality was strongly developed in the context of larger and more complex industrial societies. **Community** was the word normally chosen for experiments in an alternative kind of group-living. It is still so used and has been joined, in a more limited sense, by **commune** (the French *commune* – the smallest administrative division – and the German *Gemeinde* – a civil and ecclesiastical division – had interacted with each other and with **community**, and also passed into socialist thought (especially *commune*) and into sociology (especially *Gemeinde*) to express particular kinds of social relations). The contrast, increasingly expressed in C19, between the more direct, more total and therefore more significant relationships of **community** and the more formal, more abstract and more instrumental relationships of *state*, or of *society* in its modern sense, was influentially formalized by Tönnies (1887) as a contrast between *Gemeinschaft* and *Gesellschaft*, and these terms are now sometimes used, untranslated, in other languages. A comparable distinction is evident in mC20 uses of **community**. In some uses this has been given a polemical edge, as in **community politics**, which is distinct not only from *national politics* but from formal *local politics* and normally involves various kinds of direct action and direct local organization, 'working directly with people', as which it is distinct from 'service to the **community**', which has an older sense of voluntary work supplementary to official provision or paid service.

The complexity of **community** thus relates to the difficult interaction between the tendencies originally distinguished in the historical development: on the one hand the sense of direct common concern; on the other hand the materialization of various forms of common organization, which may or may not adequately express this. **Community** can be the warmly persuasive word to describe an existing set of relationships, or the warmly persuasive word to describe an alternative set of relationships. What is most important, perhaps, is that unlike all other terms of social organization (*state, nation, society*, etc.) it seems never to be used unfavourably, and never to be given any positive opposing or distinguishing term.

See CIVILIZATION, COMMON, COMMUNISM, NATIONALIST, SOCIETY

CONSENSUS

Consensus came into English in mC19, originally in a physiological sense, which from C16 had been a specialized sense of the fw *consensus*, L – an agreement or common feeling, rw *con*, L – together, *sentire* – feel. Thus in a use in 1861: 'there is a general connexion between the different parts of a nation's civilization; call it, if you will, a consensus, provided that the notion of a set of physical organs does not slip in with that term'. **Consensual** is earlier, from mC18, in two special contexts: legal – the **consensual contract** of Roman law; physiological, of involuntary (*sympathetic*) or reflex actions of the nervous system. **Consensus** and, later, **consensual** were steadily developed, by transfer, to indicate general agreement: 'the consensus of the Protestant missionaries' (1861). There are supporting subsidiary uses, in more defined forms, such as **consensus of evidence**, from the same period.

The word has become much more common in C20 and has been an important political term in mC20. The general use, for an existing agreement of opinion, is often subtly altered in its political application. **Consensus politics** can mean, from the general sense, policies undertaken on the basis of an existing body of agreed opinions. It can also mean, and in practice has more often meant, a policy of avoiding or evading differences or divisions of opinion in an attempt to 'secure the centre' or 'occupy the middle ground'. This is significantly different, in practice, from *coalition* (originally the growing together of parts, from C17; fw *coalitionem*, L from *coalescere* – to grow together, a sense still represented in *coalesce*; but from C17 the union or combination of parties, and from C18 combination by deliberate, often formal agreement). The negative sense of **consensus politics** was intended to describe deliberate evasion of basic conflicts of principle, but also a process in which certain issues were effectively excluded from political argument – not because there was actual agreement on them, nor because a coalition had arrived at some compromise, but because in seeking for the 'middle ground' which the parties would then compete to capture there was no room for issues not already important (because they were at some physical distance from normal everyday life –

faraway or foreign, or because their effects were long-term, or because they affected only minorities). **Consensus** then, while retaining a favourable sense of general agreement, acquired the unfavourable senses of bland or shabby evasion of necessary issues or arguments. Given this actual range it is now a very difficult word to use, over a range from the positive sense of seeking general agreement, through the sense of a relatively inert or even UNCONSCIOUS (q.v.) assent (cf. *orthodox opinion* and *conventional wisdom*), to the implication of a 'manipulative' kind of politics seeking to build a 'silent majority' as the power-base from which dissenting movements or ideas can be excluded or repressed. It is remarkable that so apparently mild a word has attracted such strong feelings, but some of the processes of modern electoral and 'public opinion' politics go a long way to explain this.

It is worth noticing that the word is now often spelled **con-census**, in some surprising places, including some which complain generally about a modern inability to spell. It is probable that this is from association with *census*, which if so is interesting in that it indicates a now habitual if unconscious connection with the practice of counting opinions, as in public opinion polls. But there has been a long confusion between *c* and *s* in words of this kind (cf. British *defence* and American *defense*, which go back to mE variations). **Consent** itself was often spelled *concent* to C16.

See CONVENTIONAL

CONSUMER

In modern English **consumer** and **consumption** are the predominant descriptive nouns of all kinds of use of goods and services. The predominance is significant in that it relates to a particular version of economic activity, derived from the character of a particular economic system, as the history of the word shows.

Consume has been in English since C14, from fw *consumer*, F, and the variant *consommer*, F (these variants have a complicated but eventually distinct history in French), rw *consumere*, L – to take up completely, devour, waste, spend. In almost all its early English uses, **consume** had an unfavourable sense; it meant to destroy, to use up, to waste, to exhaust. This sense is still present in 'consumed by fire' and in the popular description of pulmonary phthisis as **consumption**. Early uses of **consumer**, from C16, had the same general sense of destruction or waste.

It was from mC18 that **consumer** began to emerge in a neutral sense in descriptions of bourgeois political economy. In the new predominance of an organized market, the acts of making and of using goods and services were newly defined in the increasingly abstract pairings of *producer* and **consumer**, *production* and **consumption**. Yet the unfavourable connotations of **consume** persisted, at least until lC19, and it was really only in mC20 that the word passed from specialized use in political economy to general and popular use. The relative decline of *customer*, used from C15 to describe a buyer or purchaser, is significant here, in that *customer* had always implied some degree of regular and continuing relationship to a supplier, whereas **consumer** indicates the more abstract figure in a more abstract market.

The modern development has been primarily American but has spread very quickly. The dominance of the term has been so great that even groups of informed and discriminating purchasers and users have formed *Consumers' Associations*. The development relates primarily to the planning and attempted control of markets which is inherent in large-scale industrial capitalist (and state-capitalist) production, where, especially after the depression of lC19, manufacture was related not only to the supply of known needs (which *customer* or *user* would adequately describe) but to the planning of given kinds and quantities of production which required large investment at an early and often predictive stage. The development of modern commercial *advertising* (persuasion, or *penetration* of a market) is related to the same stage of capitalism: the creation of needs and wants and of particular ways of satisfying them, as distinct from and in addition to the notification of available supply which had been the main earlier function of *advertising* (where that kind of persuasion could be seen as *puff* and *puffery*). **Consumer** as a predominant term was the creation of such manufacturers and their agents. It implies, ironically as in the earliest senses, the using-up of what is going to be produced, though once the term was established it was given some appearance of autonomy (as in the curious phrase **consumer choice**). It is appropriate in terms of the history of the word that criticism of a wasteful and 'throw-away' society was expressed, somewhat later, by the description **consumer society**. Yet the predominance of the capitalist model ensured its extension, or attempted extension, to such fields as politics, education and health. In any of these fields, but also in the ordinary field of goods and services, to say *user* rather than **consumer** is still to express a relevant distinction.

See WEALTH

CONVENTIONAL

A **convention** was originally a coming together or assembly, from fw *convention*, F, *conventionem*, L – assembly, rw *convenire*, L – to come together. As such it has been used in English since C16, and is still quite often used in this sense. There is a natural extension of use to mean an agreement, and this has been common in English since C15.

The more difficult uses of **convention** and especially **conventional** relate to an extension of the sense of agreement to something implicitly customary or agreed, and to a different kind of extension, especially in literature and art, to an implicit agreed method. The extension to the sense of custom is from lC18. It was important in the political controversy about *rights*, which ironically were being elsewhere (in the United States and France) formally defined by **Conventions**. But its most common use was in questions of manners and behaviour, and an unfavourable sense soon appeared, in which **conventional** meant artificial or formal, and by derivation merely old-fashioned. Complaints against **conventions** and **conventional ideas** can be readily found from mC19 onwards. Most of the early special uses in art and literature are in the same sense, as part of a normal ROMANTIC (q.v.) preference for spontaneity and innovation. But a more technical sense, in which it was seen that all forms of art contain fundamental and often only implicit **conventions** of method and purpose, is also evident from mC19 and has since been important in specialized discussion. The degree of formality originally important in **convention** is now almost wholly lost, except in this specialized use. In normal use **convention** is indeed the opposite of formal agreement, and can be used quite neutrally. **Conventional**, however, usually expresses the unfavourable sense.

On the other hand, after the invention of the atom and hydrogen bombs, **conventional weapons** were favourably contrasted (from c. 1950) with *nuclear weapons*.

See CONSENSUS

COUNTRY

Country has two different meanings in modern English: broadly, a native land and the rural or agricultural parts of it.

The word is historically very curious, since it derives from the feminine adjective *contrata*, mL, rw *contra*, L – against, in the phrase *contrata terra* meaning land 'lying opposite, over against or facing'. In its earliest separate meaning it was a tract of land spread out before an observer. (Cf. the later use of *landskip*, C16, *landscape*, C18; in oE *landscipe* was a region or tract of land; the word was later adopted from Dutch *landschap* as a term in painting). *Contrata* passed into English through oF *cuntrée* and *contrée*. It had the sense of native land from C13 and of the distinctly rural areas from eC16. Tyndale (1526) translated part of *Mark* v, 14 as 'tolde it in the cyte, and in the countre'.

The widespread specialized use of **country** as opposed to *city* began in lC16 with increasing urbanization and especially the growth of the capital, London. It was then that **country people** and the **country house** were distinguished. On the other hand **countryfied** and **country bumpkin** were C17 metropolitan slang. **Countryside**, originally a Scottish term to indicate a specific locality, became in C19 a general term to describe not only the rural areas but the whole rural life and economy.

In its general use, for native land, **country** has more positive associations than either *nation* or *state*: cf. 'doing something for the country' with 'doing something for the nation' or '. . . state'. **Country** habitually includes the people who live in it, while *nation* is more abstract and *state* carries a sense of the structure of power. Indeed **country** can substitute for *people*, in political contexts: cf. 'the country demands'. This is subject to variations of perspective: cf. the English lady who said in 1945: 'they have elected a socialist government and the country will not stand for it'. In some uses **country** is regularly distinguished from government: cf. 'going to the country' – calling an election. There is also a specialized metropolitan use, as in the postal service, in which all areas outside the capital city are 'country'.

Countryman carries both political and rural senses, but the latter is stronger and the former is usually extended to **fellow-countryman**.

See CITY, NATIVE, PEASANT

CREATIVE

Creative in modern English has a general sense of original and innovating, and an associated special sense of productive. It is also used to distinguish certain kinds of work, as in **creative writing, the creative arts**. It is interesting to see how this now commonplace but still, on reflection, surprising word came to be used, and how this relates to some of its current difficulties.

Create came into English from the stem of the past participle of rw *creare*, L – make or produce. This inherent relation to the sense of something having been made, and thus to a past event, was exact, for the word was mainly used in the precise context of the original divine creation of the world: **creation** itself, and **creature**, have the same root stem. This context remained decisive until at least C16, and the extension of the word to indicate present or future making – that is to say a kind of making by men – is part of the major transformation of thought which we now describe as the humanism of the Renaissance. 'There are two creators,' wrote Torquato Tasso (1544–95), 'God and the poet.' This sense of human creation, specifically in works of the imagination, is the decisive source of the modern meaning. In his *Apologie for Poetrie*, Philip Sidney (1554–86) saw God as having made Nature but having also made man in his own likeness, giving him the capacity 'with the force of a divine breath' to imagine and make things beyond nature.

Yet use of the word remained difficult, because of the original context. Donne referred to poetry as a 'counterfeit Creation', where *counterfeit* does not have to be taken in its strongest sense of false but where the old sense of art as *imitation* is certainly present. Several uses of **create** and **creation**, in Elizabethan writers, are pejorative:

Or art thou but
A Dagger of the Mind, a false Creation,
Proceeding from the heat-oppressed Brain. (*Macbeth*)

This is the very coinage of your Brain:
This bodiless Creation extasie
Is very cunning in. (*Hamlet*)

Are you a God? Would you create me new? (*Comedy of Errors*)

Translated thus from a poor creature to a creator; for now
must I create intolerable sort of lies. (*Every Man in his
Humour*)

Indeed the clearest extension of **create**, without unfavourable
implications, was to social rank, given by the authority of the
monarch: 'the King's Grace created him Duke' (1495); 'I create
you Companions to our person' (*Cymbeline*). This is still not
quite human making.

By lC17, however, both **create** and **creation** can be found
commonly in a modern sense, and during C18 each word
acquired a conscious association with ART (q.v.), a word which
was itself changing in a complementary direction. It was in
relation to this, in C18, that **creative** was coined. Since the word
evidently denotes a faculty, it had to wait on general acceptance
of **create** and **creation** as human actions, without necessary
reference to a past divine event. By 1815 Wordsworth could
write confidently to the painter Haydon: 'High is our calling,
friend, Creative Art.' This runs back to the earliest specific
reference I have come across: 'companion of the Muse, Creative
Power, Imagination' (Mallet, 1728). (There is an earlier use of
creative in Cudworth, 1678, but in a sentence still partly carrying
the older sense: 'this Divine, miraculous, creative power'.)
The decisive development was the conscious and then conventional association of **creative** with *art* and thought. By eC19 it
was conscious and powerful; by mC19 conventional. **Creativity**, a
general name for the faculty, followed in C20.

This is clearly an important and significant history, and in its
emphasis on human capacity the term has become steadily
more important. But there is one obvious difficulty. The word
puts a necessary stress on originality and innovation, and when
we remember the history we can see that these are not trivial
claims. Indeed we try to clarify this by distinguishing between

innovation and *novelty*, though *novelty* has both serious and trivial senses. The difficulty arises when a word once intended, and often still intended, to embody a high and serious claim, becomes so conventional, as a description of certain general kinds of activity, that it is applied to practices for which, in the absence of the convention, nobody would think of making such claims. Thus any imitative or stereotyped literary work can be called, by convention, **creative writing**, and advertising copywriters officially describe themselves as **creative**. Given the large elements of simple IDEOLOGICAL and HEGEMONIC (qq.v.) reproduction in most of the written and visual arts, a description of everything of this kind as **creative** can be confusing and at times seriously misleading. Moreover, to the extent that **creative** becomes a cant word, it becomes difficult to think clearly about the emphasis which the word was intended to establish: on *human* making and innovation. The difficulty cannot be separated from the related difficulty of the senses of *imagination*, which can move towards *dreaming* and *fantasy*, with no necessary connection with the specific practices that are called *imaginative* or *creative arts*, or, on the other hand, towards *extension, innovation* and *foresight*, which not only have practical implications and effects but can be tangible in some **creative** activities and works. The difficulty is especially apparent when **creative** is extended, rightly in terms of the historical development, to activities in thought, language and social practice in which the specialized sense of *imagination* is not a necessary term. Yet such difficulties are inevitable when we realize the necessary magnitude and complexity of the interpretation of human activity which **creative** now so indispensably embodies.

See ART, IMAGE, FICTION

CRITICISM

Criticism has become a very difficult word, because although its predominant general sense is of fault-finding, it has an underlying sense of judgment and a very confusing specialized sense, in relation to art and literature, which depends on assumptions that may now be breaking down. The word came into English in eC17, from **critic** and **critical**, mC16, fw *criticus*, L, *kritikos*,

Gk, rw *kritos*, Gk – a judge. Its predominant early sense was of fault-finding: 'stand at the marke of criticisme . . . to bee shot at', Dekker (1607). It was also used for commentary on literature and especially from lC17 for a sense of the act of judging literature and the writing which embodied this. What is most interesting is that the general sense of fault-finding, or at least of negative judgment, has persisted as primary. This has even led to the distinction of *appreciation* as a softer word for the judgment of literature. But what is significant in the development of **criticism**, and of **critic** and **critical**, is the assumption of judgment as the predominant and even natural response. (**Critical** has another specialized but important and persistent use, not to describe judgment, but from a specialized use in medicine to refer to a turning point; hence decisive. *Crisis* itself has of course been extended to any difficulty as well as to any turning point.)

While **criticism** in its most general sense developed towards *censure* (itself acquiring from C17 an adverse rather than a neutral implication), **criticism** in its specialized sense developed towards TASTE (q.v.), *cultivation*, and later CULTURE (q.v.) and *discrimination* (itself a split word, with this positive sense for good or informed judgment, but also a strong negative sense of unreasonable exclusion or unfair treatment of some outside group). The formation which underlies this development is very difficult to understand because it has taken so strong a hold on our minds. In its earliest period the association is with learned or 'informed' ability. It still often tries to retain this sense. But its crucial development, from lC17, depended on the isolation of the reception of impressions: the reader, one might now say, as the CONSUMER (q.v.) of a range of works. Its generalization, within a particular class and profession, depended on the assumptions best represented by *taste* and *cultivation*: a form of social development of personal impressions and responses, to the point where they could be represented as the STANDARDS (q.v.) of *judgment*. The notion that response was judgment depended, of course, on the social confidence of a class and later a profession. The confidence was variously specified, originally as *learning* or scholarship, later as *cultivation* and *taste*, later still as SENSIBILITY (q.v.). At various stages, forms of this confidence have broken down, and especially in C20 attempts have been made to replace it by *objective* (cf. SUBJECTIVE) methodologies, providing another kind of basis for judgment. What has not been questioned is the assumption of 'judgment'. In its pretensions to authority it has of course been repeatedly challenged, and **critic** in the most common form of this specialized sense – as a reviewer of plays, films, books and so on – has acquired an understandable derogatory sense. But this cannot be resolved by distinctions of status between **critic** and *reviewer*. What is at issue is not only the association between **criticism** and fault-finding but the more basic association between **criticism** and judgment as apparently general and natural processes. As a term for the social or professional generalization of the processes of reception of any but especially the more formal kinds of COMMUNICATION (q.v.), **criticism** is ideological not only in the sense that it assumes the position of the *consumer* but also in the sense that it masks this position by a succession of abstractions of its real terms of response (as *judgment, taste, cultivation, discrimination, sensibility; disinterested, qualified, rigorous* and so on). This then actively prevents that understanding of response which does not assume the habit (or right or duty) of judgment. The continuing sense of **criticism** as fault-finding is the most useful linguistic influence against the confidence of this habit, but there are also signs, in the occasional rejection of **criticism** as a definition of conscious response, of a more significant rejection of the habit itself. The point would then be, not to find some other term to replace it, while continuing the same kind of activity, but to get rid of the habit, which depends, fundamentally, on the abstraction of response from its real situation and circumstances: the elevation to judgment, and to an apparently general process, when what always needs to be understood is the specificity of the response, which is not a judgment but a practice, in active and complex relations with the situation and conditions of the practice, and, necessarily, with all other practices.

See AESTHETIC, CONSUMER, SENSIBILITY, TASTE

CULTURE

Culture is one of the two or three most complicated words in the English language. This is so partly because of its intricate historical development, in several European languages, but mainly because it has now come to be used for important concepts in several distinct intellectual disciplines and in several distinct and incompatible systems of thought.

The fw is *cultura*, L, from rw *colere*, L. *Colere* had a range of meanings: inhabit, cultivate, protect, honour with worship. Some of these meanings eventually separated, though still with occasional overlapping, in the derived nouns. Thus 'inhabit' developed through *colonus*, L to *colony*. 'Honour with worship' developed through *cultus*, L to *cult*. *Cultura* took on the main meaning of cultivation or tending, though with subsidiary medieval meanings of honour and worship (cf. in English **culture** as 'worship' in Caxton (1483)). The French forms of *cultura* were *couture*, oF, which has since developed its own specialized meaning, and later *culture*, which by eC15 had passed into English. The primary meaning was then in husbandry, the tending of natural growth.

Culture in all its early uses was a noun of process: the tending *of* something, basically crops or animals. The subsidiary *coulter* – ploughshare, had travelled by a different linguistic route, from *culter*, L – ploughshare, *culter*, oE, to the variant English spellings *culter, colter, coulter* and as late as eC17 **culture** (Webster, *Duchess of Malfi*, III, ii: 'hot burning cultures'). This provided a further basis for the important next stage of meaning, by metaphor. From eC16 the tending of natural growth was extended to a process of human development, and this, alongside the original meaning in husbandry, was the main sense until lC18 and eC19. Thus More: 'to the culture and profit of their minds'; Bacon: 'the culture and manurance of minds' (1605); Hobbes: 'a culture of their minds' (1651); Johnson: 'she neglected the culture of her understanding' (1759). At various points in this development two crucial changes occurred: first, a degree of habituation to the metaphor, which made the sense of human tending direct; second, an extension of particular processes to a general process, which the word could abstractly carry. It is of course from the latter development that the independent noun **culture** began its complicated modern history, but the process of change is so intricate, and the latencies of meaning are at times so close, that it is not possible to give any definite date. **Culture** as an independent noun, an abstract process or the product of such a process, is not important before lC18 and is not common before mC19. But the early stages of this development were not sudden. There is an interesting use in Milton, in the second (revised) edition of *The Readie and Easie Way to Establish a Free Common-*

wealth (1660): 'spread much more Knowledg and Civility, yea, Religion, through all parts of the Land, by communicating the natural heat of Government and Culture more distributively to all extreme parts, which now lie num and neglected.' Here the metaphorical sense ('natural heat') still appears to be present, and *civility* (cf. CIVILIZATION) is still written where in C19 we would normally expect **culture**. Yet we can also read 'government and culture' in a quite modern sense. Milton, from the tenor of his whole argument, is writing about a general social process, and this is a definite stage of development. In C18 England this general process acquired definite class associations though **cultivation** and **cultivated** were more commonly used for this. But there is a letter of 1730 (Bishop of Killala, to Mrs Clayton; cit Plumb, *England in the Eighteenth Century*) which has this clear sense: 'it has not been customary for persons of either birth or culture to breed up their children to the Church'. Akenside (*Pleasures of Imagination*, 1744) wrote: '. . . nor purple state nor culture can bestow'. Wordsworth wrote 'where grace of culture hath been utterly unknown' (1805), and Jane Austen (*Emma*, 1816) 'every advantage of discipline and culture'.

It is thus clear that **culture** was developing in English towards some of its modern senses before the decisive effects of a new social and intellectual movement. But to follow the development through this movement, in lC18 and eC19, we have to look also at developments in other languages and especially in German.

In French, until C18, **culture** was always accompanied by a grammatical form indicating the matter being cultivated, as in the English usage already noted. Its occasional use as an independent noun dates from mC18, rather later than similar occasional uses in English. The independent noun *civilization* also.emerged in mC18; its relationship to **culture** has since been very complicated (cf. CIVILIZATION and discussion below). There was at this point an important development in German: the word was borrowed from French, spelled first (lC18) *Cultur* and from lC19 *Kultur*. Its main use was still as a synonym for *civilization*: first in the abstract sense of a general process of becoming 'civilized' or 'cultivated'; second, in the sense which had already been established for *civilization* by the historians of the Enlightenment, in the popular C18 form of the universal histories, as a description of the secular process of human development. There was then a decisive change of use in Herder.

In his unfinished *Ideas on the Philosophy of the History of Mankind* (1784–91) he wrote of *Cultur*: 'nothing is more indeterminate than this word, and nothing more deceptive than its application to all nations and periods'. He attacked the assumption of the universal histories that 'civilization' or 'culture' – the historical self-development of humanity – was what we would now call a unilinear process, leading to the high and dominant point of C18 European culture. Indeed he attacked what he called European subjugation and domination of the four quarters of the globe, and wrote:

> Men of all the quarters of the globe, who have perished over the ages, you have not lived solely to manure the earth with your ashes, so that at the end of time your posterity should be made happy by European culture. The very thought of a superior European culture is a blatant insult to the majesty of Nature.

It is then necessary, he argued, in a decisive innovation, to speak of 'cultures' in the plural: the specific and variable cultures of different nations and periods, but also the specific and variable cultures of social and economic groups within a nation. This sense, which has become common in C20 anthropology and sociology, and by extension in general use, remained comparatively isolated, however, in all European languages until at earliest mC19 and was not fully established until eC20.

What mainly happened in eC19, under the influence of Herder and many other writers of the Romantic movement, in Germany, England and France, was a social and historical application of an alternative idea of human development: alternative, that is, to the ideas now centred on 'civilization' and 'progress'. This application was exceptionally complicated. It was used to emphasize national and traditional cultures, including the new concept of **folk-culture**. It was used to attack what was seen as the 'MECHANICAL' (q.v.) character of the new civilization then emerging: both for its abstract rationalism and for the 'inhumanity' of current industrial development. It was used to distinguish between 'human' and 'material' development. Politically, as so often in this period, it veered between radicalism and reaction and very often, in the confusion of major social change, fused elements of both. (It should also be noted, though it adds to the real complication, that the same kind of distinction, especially between 'material' and 'spiritual' development, was made by von Humboldt and others, until as late as 1900, with a reversal of the terms, **culture** being material and *civilization* spiritual. In general, however, the opposite distinction was dominant.)

The complexity of the modern development of the word, and of its modern usage, can then be appreciated. We can easily distinguish the sense which depends on a literal continuity of physical process as now in 'sugar-beet culture' or, in the special-ized physical application in bacteriology since the 1880s, 'germ culture'. But once we go beyond the physical reference, we have to recognize three broad active categories of usage. The sources of two of these we have already discussed: (i) the independent and abstract noun which describes a general process of intellectual, spiritual and aesthetic development, from C18; (ii) the indepen-dent noun, whether used generally or specifically, which indicates a particular way of life, whether of a people, a period or a group, from Herder and C19. But we have also to recognize (iii) the independent and abstract noun which describes the works and practices of intellectual and especially artistic activity. This seems often now the most widespread use: **culture** is music, literature, painting and sculpture, theatre and film. A **Ministry of Culture** refers to these specific activities, sometimes with the addition of philosophy, scholarship, history. This use, (iii), is in fact relatively late. It is difficult to date precisely because it is in origin an applied form of sense (i): the idea of a general process of in-tellectual, spiritual and aesthetic development was applied and effectively transferred to the works and practices which represent and sustain it. In English (i) and (iii) are still close; at times, for internal reasons, they are indistinguishable as in Arnold, *Culture and Anarchy* (1867); while sense (ii) was decisively introduced into English by Tylor, *Primitive Culture* (1870). The decisive development of sense (iii) in English was in lC19 and eC20.

Faced by this complex and still active history of the word, it is easy to react by selecting one 'true' or 'proper' or 'scientific' sense and dismissing other senses as loose or confused. There is evidence of this reaction even in the excellent study by Kroeber and Kluckhohn, *Culture: A Critical Review of Concepts and Defini-tions*, where usage in North American anthropology is in effect taken as a norm. It is clear that, within a discipline, conceptual usage has to be clarified. But in general it is the range and overlap of meanings that is significant. The complex of senses indicates a complex argument about the relations between general human development and a particular way of life, and between both and the works and practices of art and intelligence. Within this complex argument there are fundamentally opposed as well as effectively overlapping positions; there are also, understandably, many unresolved questions and confused answers. But these arguments and questions cannot be resolved by reducing the complexity of actual usage. This point is relevant also to uses of forms of the word in languages other than English, where there is considerable variation. Even within English, 'social anthropology' is normally used in Britain where 'cultural anthropology' would be used in North America. The anthropological use is common in the German, Scandinavian and Slavonic language groups, but it is distinctly subordinate to the senses of art and learning, or of a general process of human development, in Italian and French. Between languages as within a language, the range and complexity of sense and reference indicate both difference of intellectual position and some blurring or over-lapping. These variations, of whatever kind, necessarily involve alternative views of the activities, relationships and processes which this complex word indicates. The complexity, that is to say, is not finally in the word but in the problems which its variations of use significantly indicate.

It is necessary to look also at some associated and derived words. **Cultivation** and **cultivated** went through the same meta-phorical extension from a physical to a social or educational sense in C17, and were especially significant words in C18. Coleridge, making a classical eC19 distinction between civiliza-tion and culture, wrote (1830): 'the permanent distinction, and occasional contrast, between cultivation and civilization'. The noun in this sense has effectively disappeared but the adjective is still quite common, especially in relation to manners and tastes. The important adjective **cultural** appears to date from the 1870s; it became common by the 1890s. The word is only available, in its modern sense, when the independent noun, in the artistic and intellectual or anthropological senses, has become familiar. Hostility to the word **culture** in English appears to date from the controversy around Arnold's views. It gathered force in lC19 and eC20, in association with a comparable hostility to *aesthete* and AESTHETIC (q.v.). Its association with class distinction produced the mime-word *culchah*. There was also an area of hostility associa-ted with anti-German feeling, during and after the 1914–18 War, in relation to propaganda about *Kultur*. The central area of hostility has lasted, and one element of it has been emphasized by the recent American phrase **culture-vulture**. It is significant that virtually all the hostility (with the sole exception of the temporary anti-German association) has been connected with uses involving claims to superior knowledge (cf. the noun INTELLECTUAL), refinement (*culchah*) and distinctions between 'high' art (**culture**) and popular art and entertainment. It thus records a real social history and a very difficult and confused phase of social and cultural development. It is interesting that the steadily extending social and anthropological use of **culture** and **cultural** and such formations as **sub-culture** (the culture of a distinguishable smaller group) has, except in certain areas (notably popular entertainment), either by-passed or effectively diminished the hostility and its associated unease and embarrassment.

See AESTHETIC, ART, CIVILIZATION, HUMANITY, SCIENCE

D

DEMOCRACY

Democracy is a very old word but its meanings have always been complex. It came into English in C16, from fw *démocratie*, F, *democratia*, mL – a translation of *demokratia*, Gk, from rw *demos* – people, *kratos* – rule. It was defined by Elyot, with specific reference to the Greek instance, in 1531: 'an other publique weal was amonge the Atheniensis, where equalitie was of astate among the people . . . This maner of governaunce was called in greke *Democratia*, in latine, *Popularis potentia*, in englisshe the rule of the comminaltie.' It is at once evident from Greek uses that everything depends on the senses given to *people* and to *rule*. Ascribed and doubtful early examples range from obeying 'no master but the law' (? Solon) to 'of the people, by the people, for the people' (? Cleon). More certain examples compare 'the insolence of a despot' with 'the insolence of the unbridled commonalty' (cit. Herodotus) or define a government as democracy 'because its administration is in the hands, not of the few, but of the many'; also, 'all that is opposed to despotic power, has the name of democracy' (cit. Thucydides). Aristotle (*Politics*, IV, 4) wrote: 'a democracy is a state where the freemen and the poor, being in the majority, are invested with the power of the state'. Yet much depends here on what is meant by 'invested with power': whether it is ultimate sovereignty or, at the other extreme, practical and unshared rule. Plato made Socrates say (in *Republic*, VIII, 10) that 'democracy comes into being after the poor have conquered their opponents, slaughtering some and banishing some, while to the remainder they give an equal share of freedom and power'.

This range of uses, near the roots of the term, makes any simple derivation impossible. It can, however, be said at once that several of these uses – and especially those which indicate a form of popular class rule – are at some distance from any orthodox modern 'Western' definition of **democracy**. Indeed the emergence of that orthodox definition, which has its own uncertainties, is what needs to be traced. 'Democracy' is now often traced back to medieval precedents and given a Greek authority. But the fact is that, with only occasional exceptions, **democracy**, in the records that we have, was until C19 a strongly unfavourable term, and it is only since lC19 and eC20 that a majority of political parties and tendencies have united in declaring their belief in it. This is the most striking historical fact.

Aquinas defined **democracy** as popular power, where the ordinary people, by force of numbers, governed – oppressed – the rich; the whole people acting like a tyrant. This strong class sense remained the predominant meaning until lC18 and eC19, and was still active in mC19 argument. Thus: 'Democracie, when the multitude have government', Fleming (1576) (for the class sense of *multitude* see MASSES); 'democratie, where free and poore men being the greater number, are lords of the estate' (1586); 'democracy . . . nothing else than the power of the multitude', Filmer, *Patriarcha* (1680). To this definition of the *people* as the *multitude* there was added a common sense of the consequent type of *rule*: a **democracy** was a state in which all had the right to rule and did actually rule; it was even contrasted (e.g. by Spinoza) with a state in which there was rule by representatives, including elected representatives. It was in this sense that the first political constitution to use the term **democracy** – that of Rhode Island in 1641 – understood it: 'popular government; that is to say it is in the power of the body of freemen orderly assembled, or major part of them, to make or constitute just Lawes, by which they will be regulated, and to depute from among themselves such ministers as shall see them faithfully executed between man and man'.

This final clause needs to be emphasized, since a new meaning of democracy was eventually arrived at by an alteration of the concept here embodied. In the case of Rhode Island, the people or a major part of them made laws in orderly assembly; the ministers 'faithfully executed' them. This is not the same as the **representative democracy** defined by Hamilton in 1777. He was referring to the earlier sense of **democracy** when he observed that 'when the deliberative or judicial powers are vested wholly or partly in the collective body of the people, you must expect error, confusion and instability. But a representative democracy, where the right of election is well secured and regulated, and the exercise of the legislative executive and judicial authorities is vested in select persons . . . etc.' It is from this modified American use that a dominant modern sense developed. Bentham formulated a general sense of democracy as rule by the majority of the people, and then distinguished between 'direct democracy' and 'representative democracy', recommending the latter because it provided continuity and could be extended to large societies. These important practical reasons have since been both assumed and dropped, so that in mC20 an assertion of **democracy** in the Rhode Island sense, or in Bentham's *direct* sense, could be described as 'anti-democratic', since the first principle of **democracy** is taken to be rule by elected representatives. The practical arguments are of course serious, and in many circumstances decisive, but one of the two most significant changes in the meaning of **democracy** is this exclusive association with one of its derived forms, and the attempted exclusion of one of its original forms; at one period, its only form.

The second major change has to do with interpretation of *the people*. There is some significant history in the various attempts to limit 'the people' to certain qualified groups: freemen, owners of property, the wise, white men, men, and so on. Where **democracy** is defined by a process of election, such limited constitutions can be claimed to be fully **democratic**: the mode of choosing representatives is taken as more important than the proportion of 'the people' who have any part in this. The development of democracy is traced through institutions using this mode rather than through the relations between all the people and a form of government. This interpretation is orthodox in most accounts of the development of English democracy. Indeed **democracy** is said to have been 'extended' stage by stage, where what is meant is clearly the right to vote for representatives rather than the old (and until eC19 normal English) sense of *popular power*. The distinction became critical in the period of the French Revolution. Burke was expressing an orthodox view when he wrote that 'a perfect democracy' was 'the most shameless thing in the world' (*Reflections on the Revolution in France*, 1790), for **democracy** was taken to be 'uncontrolled' popular power under which, among other things, minorities (including especially the minority which held substantial property) would be suppressed or oppressed. **Democracy** was still a revolutionary or at least a radical term to mC19, and the specialized development of **representative democracy** was at least in part a conscious reaction to this, over and above the practical reasons of extent and continuity.

It is from this point in the argument that two modern meanings of **democracy** can be seen to diverge. In the socialist tradition, **democracy** continued to mean *popular power*: a state in which the interests of the majority of the people were paramount and in which these interests were practically exercised and controlled by the majority. In the liberal tradition, **democracy** meant open election of representatives and certain conditions (**democratic rights**, such as free speech) which maintained the openness of election and political argument. These two conceptions, in their extreme forms, now confront each other as enemies. If the predominant criterion is popular power in the popular interest, other criteria are often taken as secondary (as in the **People's Democracies**) and their emphasis is specialized to 'capitalist democracy' or 'bourgeois democracy'. If the predominant criteria are elections and free speech, other criteria are seen as secondary or are rejected; an attempt to exercise popular power in the popular interest, for example by a General Strike, is described as **anti-democratic**, since **democracy** has already been assured by other means; to claim economic EQUALITY (q.v.) as the essence of democracy is seen as leading to 'chaos' or to **totalitarian democracy** or *government by trade-unions*. These positions, with their many minor variants, divide the modern meanings of **democracy** between them, but this is not usually seen as historical variation of the term; each position, normally, is described as 'the only true meaning', and the alternative use is seen as propaganda or hypocrisy.

Democratic (from eC19) is the normal adjective for one or other of these kinds of belief or institution. But two further senses should be noted. There is an observable use of **democratic** to describe the conditions of open argument, without necessary reference to elections or to power. Indeed, in one characteristic use freedom of speech and assembly are *the* 'democratic rights', sufficient in themselves, without reference to the institution or character of political power. This is a limiting sense derived from the liberal emphasis, which in its full form has to include election and popular sovereignty (though not popular rule). There is also a derived sense from the early class reference to the 'multitude': to be **democratic**, to have **democratic** manners or feelings, is to be unconscious of class distinctions, or consciously to disregard or overcome them in everyday behaviour: acting *as if* all people were equal, and deserved equal respect, whether this is really so or not. Thus a man might be on 'plain and natural' terms with everyone he met, and might further believe in free speech and free assembly, yet, following only these senses, could for example oppose universal suffrage, let alone government directed solely to the interests of the majority. The senses have in part been extended, in part moved away, from what was formerly and is probably still the primary sense of the character of political power.

No questions are more difficult than those of **democracy**, in any of its central senses. Analysis of variation will not resolve them, though it may sometimes clarify them. To the positive opposed senses of the socialist and liberal traditions we have to add, in a century which unlike any other finds nearly all political movements claiming to stand for **democracy** or **real democracy**, innumerable conscious distortions: reduction of the concepts of *election*, *representation* and *mandate* to deliberate formalities or merely manipulated forms; reduction of the concept of *popular power*, or government in the *popular interest*, to nominal slogans covering the rule of a bureaucracy or an oligarchy. It would sometimes be easier to believe in democracy, or to stand for it, if the C19 change had not happened and it were still an unfavourable or factional term. But that history has occurred, and the range of contemporary senses is its confused and still active record.

See CLASS, COMMON, EQUALITY, LIBERAL, MASSES, POPULAR, REPRESENTATIVE, SOCIALIST, SOCIETY

DETERMINE

Determine has a complex range of meanings in modern English, and within this range there is a special difficulty when the verb is associated with **determinant, determinism** and a particular use of **determined**. This special difficulty is important because it bears on several significant tendencies in modern thought.

Determine came into English in C14 from fw *determiner*, oF, *determinare*, L, rw *terminare*, L – to set bounds to. Several formations with the Latin prefix *de* are complicated in meaning, but in this case the sense of 'setting bounds' is dominant in all early uses. The difficulty and the later ambiguity arose when one of the applied senses, that of putting a limit and therefore an end to some process, acquired the significance of an absolute end. There are many processes with an ordinary limit or end, for which **determine** and its derivatives have been regularly used: a question or dispute is **determined** by some authority, and from this use, and the associated legal use in matters like leases, there is a more general sense which is equivalent to 'decide': e.g. 'on a date to be **determined**'. Associated with this is the sense which is equivalent to 'settle'; fixing by observation, calculation or definition. What is distinct about all these uses is that **determining** is some fixed point or act at the end of a process, and that this sense carries with it no necessary implication, and usually no implication at all, that the specific character of the ultimate decision or settlement or conclusion is inherent in the nature of the process. **Determination** resolves or completes a process; it does not prospectively control or predict it.

Yet clearly there is a possible overlap with the sense of a process so conditioned that its eventual or foreseeable **determination** can be held to define it. It is from this overlap that all the difficult modern senses derive. The main source of this emphasis is theological: God can be held (in a sense extended from the specific decision by an authority) to have **determined** the conditions of human life, including the inevitability of death, and in this sense to have **determined** human destiny. From eC16, for example in Tyndale, we have the scriptural '**determinat** counsell and foreknowledge of God'. There were of course prolonged and intricate arguments about the degree and character of such pre-ordained ends, and about their implications and consequences. In general, in these arguments, *predestination* (with the qualifying *free-will*) was much more often used than **determination**, but at times the two words were clearly associated. This is the main source of **determination** as something absolutely settled or fixed, but the absolute sense never completely took over, even in this area of use. Yet there was, obviously, plenty of room for confusion as this argument moved between the senses of conditions defining a process and of a process conditioned by its foreseen or known end.

When **determination** began to be used in science, from mC17, a corresponding range was established. **Determination** was occasionally the final or fundamental state of some substance, but in early physics (Boyle, 1660) it was in effect a definite tendency: 'others whose motion has an opposite determination'. Clarke in 1710 wrote: 'when a body moves any particular way, the Disposition that it has to move that way, rather than any other, is what we call its Determination'. Here the definite tendency is inherent in the character of the body, and thus the **determinants** of any process are still specific. It was in the subsequent formation of general laws, whether in science or, as earlier, in versions of the laws of God or of Nature, that the sense extended to an abstract principle: from a notion of specific effects and causes to a notion of 'inevitable' **determined** process. But it is very difficult, when this abstract sense has been reached, to make clear distinctions between versions of processes 'controlled' by some general law or laws and versions of consequence which, whether derived from some inherent or, as possibly, accidental element, are seen as inevitable. The difficulty is greatly increased when we realize that **determine** is used as often in prospect as in retrospect; the sense of inevitability which can be an observed consequence of retrospect becomes something different when it is projected into future events.

For several centuries various different kinds of argument have moved, often uneasily, around these senses of **determine**: in theology, in ethics, in physics and finally in social and economic

88

theory. The formation of **determinism**, in mC19, gave a special twist to all these arguments. In its most widely-used sense, **determinism** assumes pre-existing and commonly 'external' conditions which fix the course of some process or event. 'External' often means only external to the will or desire of the individuals caught up in such a process; the **determining** conditions are still inherent in the general process itself. But there is also a use, derived from the scale of some of these processes, in which the external determining quality is emphasized, often very strongly. Men have 'no control' over such **determinate** processes as, at one extreme, the solar system, or, intermediately, the processes of biological evolution and inheritance, or, at the other extreme, an economic system. **Determinism**, formerly (though not named as such) a theological or philosophical doctrine, was especially applied, from mC19, to biology and to economics, though its most confident use was still in physics. In the case of physics, the most limited meaning of **determinism** – wholly predictable events from known causes – became so conventional that observations of events which were inherently unpredictable or merely probable provoked the new negative **indeterminism**, which was then, from mC20, as rashly extended to other fields as had been the simple earlier **determinism**. It was by this period evident, in popular use, that **determinism** carried the sense not only of an inevitable but of a fundamentally external cause. This is why the extension of **indeterminism** from observed specific processes to the most general conditions of life was at once so rash and so interesting.

Determinism, that is to say, in its popular modern sense, had become attached to the most general conditions of life, whether biological or economic. These general processes might be within human knowledge but beyond human control; their courses were fixed. In fact, in all the relevant arguments, careful distinctions were attempted between **determination**, however absolute, and the old irrational sense embodied in *fate* (originally a *sentence* of the gods, rw *fari* – I speak; later an impersonal determining process and from C14 a determined end; acquiring, as especially from C17 in *fatal*, disastrous implications, while other determined ends were described as *fortune* – chance specializing to good luck – or *providence* – caring and loving control). Arguments for 'rational determinism' pointed to ability to understand the most general processes and, through such understanding, to gain some control over them, however limited. The sense is then more discriminating, in that it allows for the distinction, within general processes, between **determining** conditions or **determinants** – essential factors which, as in the earliest uses, set certain limits or exert certain pressures – and other accidental or unpredictable or voluntary factors. Most rational discussion of **determining conditions** or **determinants** depends on this distinction being made. Otherwise the observation of real determining factors – forces that set limits or exert pressures – can be quickly inflated into a *fatalism* (**determinism**) in which everything is already decided – **predetermined**, as it is often put for emphasis – and we have merely to wait for it to happen. Alternatively, a sense of the difficulties can depress us into a vague and indifferent state in which no necessary factors, not only hypothetically but practically, can be admitted to exist. This in real terms is a kind of madness, and only the specialized confidence of description of other views as **determinist** prevents its recognition. The argument has been especially important in Marxism, where absolute economic determination has often been urged, together with dependent political, social and cultural results – the laws of history and the law of *base* (the economic structure of society) and *superstructure* (all other social life) – while in other Marxist argument there has been a sense of certain **determinants** within which or in relation to which (and the distinction can be crucial) men act to make their own history. The more extreme POSITIVIST (q.v.) versions of a wholly or generally predictable process have produced correspondingly reductive versions of the 'play of events' which are called (with corresponding popular specialization of stricter meanings) EMPIRICISM or PRAGMATISM (qq.v.).

Matters of this degree of seriousness and complexity will not be settled by verbal definition but arguments about them can be thoroughly confused by insistent and pseudo-authoritative application of one fixed sense of this highly variable word and its derivatives. It is, after all, part of the history of the word that it contains quite another line of meaning, in which **determine**, **determined** and **determination** relate not to limits or ends, nor to any external cause, but specifically to acts of the will, as in 'I am **determined** to bring this about.' Initially this sense seems to derive from the early sense, already noted, of 'come to a decision'; several early uses are in the form of **determine** 'with oneself', as in the associated development of *resolve* and *resolution*. Perhaps nobody has yet said 'I am determined not to be determined', but this illustrates the actual range. From eC16 **determine** and **determined** are commonly used in this sense of a fixed or settled resolve, upon which someone has, on his own account, decided. The common derived sense, which does not ordinarily require further definition of an action – **determined** to do or not do something – is established by at latest C19 as a general adjective for 'unwavering' or 'persistent': a sense which is certainly not unconnected with the sense of a settled and 'inevitable' process but which, in actual use, must give an opposite kind of interpretation to human actions and events. For many general purposes the effective modern distinction between **determination** and **determinism** sustains, with sufficient clarity, this range of variation and opposition, but the distinction is much harder to realize in uses of **determine** and **determined**, as we can regularly observe.

See EMPIRICAL, EVOLUTION, PRAGMATIC

DIALECTIC

Dialectic appeared in English, from C14, in its accepted Latin sense to describe what we would now call *logic*. *Dialectique*, oF, *dialectica*, L, *dialektike*, Gk, were all, in their primary senses, the art of discussion and debate, and then, by derivation, the investigation of truth by discussion. Different glosses were given by different schools, and Plato's version has an important subsequent history: *dialektike* meant the art of defining *ideas* and, related to this, the method of determining the interrelation of ideas in the light of a single principle. These two senses would later be distinguished as *logic* and *metaphysics* respectively. In early English as in general medieval use **dialectic** was the art of formal reasoning: 'the seconde science is logyke whiche is called dyaletyque' (Caxton, 1481); 'Dialectike or Logike, which is to learn the truth of all things by disputation' (1586); 'Dialectick is the Art of Discourse, whereby we confirm or confute any thing by Questions and Answers of the Disputants' (Stanley, 1656). There was an extended sense of **dialectic**, **dialectics** and **dialectical**, from C17, to relate to argument in a more general way, and this extended sense has persisted.

There was then a special and influential use of **dialectic** in German idealist philosophy. This extended the notion of contradiction in the course of discussion or dispute to a notion of contradictions in reality. Through the intricacy of many subsequent arguments, this extended sense of **dialectic** (which has some relation to Plato's sense of determining the interrelation of ideas in the light of a single principle) has passed into fairly common if often difficult usage. For Kant, **dialectical** criticism showed the mutually contradictory character of the principles of knowledge when these were extended to metaphysical realities. For Hegel, such contradictions were surpassed, both in thought and in the world-history which was its objective character, in a higher and unified truth: the **dialectical** process was then the continual unification of opposites, in the complex relation of parts to a whole. A version of this process – the famous triad of thesis, antithesis and synthesis – was given by Fichte. It was then in Marxism that the sense of **dialectic** to indicate a progressive unification through the contradiction of opposites was given a specific reference in what Engels called **dialectical materialism.** Hegel's version of the dialectical process had made spirit primary and world secondary. This priority was reversed, and **dialectics** was then 'the science of the general laws of motion, both of the external world and of human thought – two sets of laws which are identical in their substance but differ in their expression' (Engels, *Essay on Feuerbach*). This was the 'materialist dialectic', later set out as **dialectical materialism,** and applied both to history and to nature (in *Dialectics of Nature*). The formal principles inherent in this process are seen as the transformation of quantity into quality, the identity of opposites and the negation of the negation; these are 'laws' of history and of nature.

There has been immense controversy about the relation of **dialectical materialism** to the thought of Marx, who did not use the term; to its idealist predecessors; and to the natural sciences. Some Marxists prefer the more specific *historical materialism*, not wishing to extend the **dialectical** description to *natural* processes, while others insist that the same basic laws apply to both. There are also forms of Marxist thought which reject the whole notion of **dialectical laws**, while retaining a looser sense of **dialectic** to describe the interaction of contradictory or opposite forces. This looser sense has passed into more general use, alongside the older sense of the process of argument or a method of argument. It is not often easy to see which of these various senses is being used, and with what implications, in the course of contemporary argument.

See MATERIALISM, SCIENCE

DOCTRINAIRE

Doctrinaire is an odd word, because it is now widely used, in a political context, to indicate a group or a person or an attitude which can be seen as based on a particular set of ideas; the implication, always unfavourable, is that political actions or attitudes so based are undesirable or absurd. This is a significant shift from the original sense of the term in politics. It was introduced in French, from c. 1815, to describe a party which attempted to reconcile two extreme positions, and the contempt in **doctrinaire** was an expression of what was felt to be the merely theoretical nature of this attempt, which included no practical understanding of the real interests and ideas of the opposing parties. It could be said that the original **doctrinaires** tried to intervene and bring about a reconciliation between what would now be called **doctrinaires**. The shift, which is difficult to trace but which was established by lC19 and has been especially common in mC20, probably depended on deterioration of the sense of **doctrine**, from a body of teaching (neutral or positive) to an abstract and inflexible position (cf. the related development of *dogma*, which now has the stronger negative sense). This occurred especially in relation to theological positions, and was largely transferred to politics in the course of C19. **Indoctrinate** and **indoctrination**, which had neutral or positive senses of teaching or instruction from C17, developed their significant negative senses from eC19 and are now, like **doctrinaire**, wholly negative. It is curious to read, from as late as 1868, in Mark Pattison: 'the philosophical sciences can only be indoctrinated by a master'. A distinction is now clearly made between our *teaching*, your **indoctrination**, with an associated but not defining sense of the exertion of pressure in the negative term. Meanwhile the modern sense of **doctrinaire** depends on its often explicit contrast with the specialized (usually self-applied) terms *sensible* and *practical*, and, significantly often, PRAGMATIC (q.v.).

The distinction between (my) *ideas* or *principles* and (your) *ideology* or *dogma* is closely related. The formation has become significant in politics since the development of movements and ideas based on positions and principles at variance with or opposed to those governing an existing social system. The charge of **doctrinaire** has been met by the similarly specialized use of a distinction between *principled* and *unprincipled* political programmes and actions.

See IDEOLOGY

DRAMATIC

Dramatic is one of an interesting group of words which have been extended, from their original and continuing application to some specific art, to much wider use as descriptions of actual events and situations. **Dramatic**, in the sense of an action or situation having qualities of spectacle and surprise comparable to those of written or acted drama, dates mainly from C18. So does *picturesque*: a view or costume or action as good to look at as, or having evident qualities in common with, a *picture*. *Theatrical*, to describe a certain exaggerated quality in some action, seems to date from C19. *Tragic*, to describe an event as calamitous as those commonly found in *tragedy*, probably dates from C16, but has become much more common since eC19. *Role*, a part or character in a play, has been extended to describe a social function, or a version of social function, in one dominant *idealist* school of sociology, and thence generally, since eC20. *Scenario*, from the plan of a dramatic action, especially in opera, has been extended in mC20 to describe a political forecast and, increasingly, a political programme.

The implications of the extensions of use evident in this group are controversial. Some, like *picturesque*, belong to a traceable habit of mind in which life is seen, or is claimed to be seen, through art. Others, like *dramatic* and *tragic*, seem to develop more naturally through habitual association. *Role*, though it is now widely repeated without particular implication, seems dependent on a particular abstract version of social action and organization, and especially, as in most uses of *scenario*, on a formalist version of social activity. *Theatrical* is unkind but is perhaps necessary.

The most important examples of this whole group are of course *person* and *personality*, which require separate discussion.

See PERSONALITY

E

EDUCATED

To **educate** was originally to rear or bring up children or animals, from rw *educere*, L – to lead forth (which led also to *educe*) and fw *educationem*, L, in the same general sense. The wide sense has never quite been lost but it has been specialized to organized teaching and instruction since eC17 and predominantly so since lC18. When a majority of children had no such organized instruction the distinction between **educated** and **uneducated** was reasonably clear, but, curiously, this distinction has been more common since the development of generally organized education and even of universal education. There is a strong class sense in this use, and the level indicated by **educated** has been continually adjusted to leave the majority of people who have received an education below it. The structure has probably been assisted by the surviving general sense of bringing-up, as in *properly brought-up* which can be made to mean anything a particular group wants it to mean. **Over-educated** and **half-educated** are mC19 and especially lC19 formations; they are necessary to preserve a specializing and distinguishing use of **educated** itself. This use interacts with the specialized use of *intelligent* to distinguish a particular level or form of a faculty from the common faculty which it originally indicated. It remains remarkable that after nearly a century of universal education in Britain the majority of the population should in this use be seen as **uneducated** or **half-educated**, but whether

95

educated people think of this with self-congratulation or self-reproach, or with impatience at the silliness of the usage, is for them to say.

See CULTURE, INTELLECTUAL

ELITE

Elite is an old word which since mC18 has been given a particular social meaning and since eC20 another, related but different, social meaning. **Elite** was originally the description of someone elected or formally chosen, from fw *elit*, oF, from *élire* – elect, from rw *eligere*, L – to choose, whence *electus*, L – chosen, and all the English group **elect, election, electoral**. **Elect** was extended, in C15, from persons formally chosen in some social process to the sense of specially chosen by God (**the elect** in theology and related social thought) and, in a different direction, to 'select' or 'choice', the most preferred and eminent persons. What in theology or social action had been some kind of formal choice was thus extended to a process of distinction or *discrimination* in which **elect** was often indistinguishable from 'best' or 'most important'. (Many of the words which describe these complicated and overlapping processes – *distinguished* and *preferred*, or *select* and *choice* (adjectives) – show the same complication and overlapping).

Elect was thus generally equivalent (beyond its specific use for the result of an **election**) to the post-mC18 use of **elite**, and for this general sense was almost invariably preferred. But probably as a result of its controversial theological use, which was specifically distinguished from both social choice and social eminence, the French form was readopted and eventually replaced *elect* in all its general senses as a noun. The verb of course remained, and **elected** and **the elected** came through to describe those formally chosen (except in the residual use of **Bishop-Elect, Professor-Elect** and the like).

Elite, from mC18 but more commonly from eC19, now expressed mainly social distinction by rank, but it was also available for distinction within a group. Compare Byron, 1823: 'With other Countesses of Blank, but rank; At once the "lie" and the "élite" of crowds' (*Don Juan*, XIII, where the implication is unfavourable and the word is still relatively novel, with some ambiguity about its English pronunciation); 'the élite of the Russian nobility' (in translation of a French book, 1848); and 'the élite of a comparatively civilized generation' (1880). As it developed along this line, **elite** became virtually equivalent with 'best' and was important within the general uncertainty, in the new conditions of C19 society, about other kinds of distinction as expressed in *rank*, *order* and CLASS (q.v.).

It is then not surprising that its emergence in a more specific modern sense is related to conscious arguments about class. This has two main elements: first, the sense that there has been a breakdown in old ways of distinguishing those best fitted to govern or exercise influence by rank or heredity, and a failure to find new ways of distinguishing such persons by formal (parliamentary or democratic) election; secondly, in response to socialist arguments about rule by classes, or about politics as conflict between classes, the argument that the effective formations of government and influence are not classes but **elites**. The first, less formal, sense is represented in C19 by many alternative words – Coleridge's *clerisy*, Mill's *the wisest*, Arnold's *the best* and *the remnant*. The significance in each case is the assumed distinction of such groupings from existing and powerful social formations. In general C20 usage, all these assumptions have found their way into **elite**, though it is characteristic that the word is still often avoided, because of some of its associations; (the abstract notions of *excellence* or STANDARDS (q.v.) are now most often used to express similar or related ideas). The second and more formal sense is effectively introduced in a tendency in social theory deriving from Pareto and Mosca. Pareto distinguished between governing and non-governing **elites**, but also insisted that revolution and other kinds of political change are the result of a former **elite** becoming inadequate or decadent and then being opposed and replaced or overthrown by the new real **elite**, who often claim that they are acting on behalf of a *class*. This conception of **elite** indicates a small effective group which remains an **elite** only by regular circulation and recruitment; the alternative continuities of rank or class prevent the formation or continued effectiveness of a genuine **elite**. The emergence and success of **elites** were seen by Mosca as necessary alternatives to revolutions. Remnants of class-struggle theory then combined with notions of an openly competitive society to produce the notion of **competitive elites**, who are either able groups representing and using competitive or antagonistic social interests, or, more neutrally, alternative able groups who compete for political power. Each of these versions has been applied to modern political parties, and each is a radical revision (not always made conscious) of the supposed general theory of DEMOCRATIC (q.v.) government and especially of REPRESENTATIVE (q.v.) democracy. Such **elites** do not *represent*; they either express or use other interests (whether for their own selfish purposes or not is of course controversial, because proponents of the theory claim that their real purposes, as **elites**, are the necessary best directions of the society as a whole).

Since 1945, attacks on this range of positions have produced the normally unfavourable descriptions **elitism** and **elitist**. Most contemporary uses of these words combine opposition to the informal sense of government or influence by 'the best' with opposition to the political and educational procedures designed to produce **elites** in a more formal sense. This is then either (i) opposition to government by a minority or education for a minority, including all the procedures and attitudes consistent with these processes, or (ii) a more general opposition to all kinds of social distinction, whether formally constituted and practised or not. There is often confusion between these senses, and this can be important in relations between ideas of an **elite** and ideas of a *class* or *ruling class*, where the real social argument seems to be centred. It is significant that there are alternative positive words for an effective political minority in *vanguard* and *cadres*. In some uses these overlap considerably with the more formal senses of **elite**, though there has been a distinction (related to ultimate purposes) between parties of the Right and of the Left (though compare *leadership*, as a group noun, which is used by both). Meanwhile the forgotten etymological association between **elite** and *elected* has a certain wry interest.

See CLASS, DEMOCRACY, REPRESENTATIVE, STANDARDS

EMPIRICAL

Empirical and the related **empiricism** are now in some contexts among the most difficult words in the language. **Empirical**

(with **empiric**) came into English in C16 from fw *empiricus*, L, *empeirikos*, Gk, from rw *empeiria*, Gk – experience, *empeiros*, Gk – skilled, *peira*, Gk – trial or experiment. But this general development was radically affected, in most early English uses, by a specialized use of the term within Greek medicine, where there were contending schools of *Empiriki*, *Dogmatiki* and *Methodiki*; the *Empiriki* had depended on observation and accepted methods, and were sceptical of theoretical explanations. This use was repeated in English, mostly in medical contexts, and in addition to its neutral sense gained a strong derogatory sense: 'mountebanks, quack-salvers, Empericks' (Browne, 1621). This derogatory sense was then extended to other activities, to indicate ignorance or imposture, and **empiricism** was first used, from C17, in this generally unfavourable sense.

The broader argument, which eventually affected the modern meanings of **empirical** and **empiricism**, is part of an exceptionally complex philosophical and scientific movement. The simplest general modern senses indicate a reliance on observed *experience*, but almost everything depends on how *experience* is understood. *Experience*, in one main sense, was until lC18 interchangeable with *experiment* (cf. modern French) from the common rw *experiri*, L – to try, to put to the test. *Experience*, from the present participle, became not only a conscious test or trial but a consciousness of what has been tested or tried, and thence a consciousness of an effect or state. From C16 it took on a more general meaning, with more deliberate inclusion of the past (the tried and tested), to indicate knowledge derived from real events as well as from particular observation. *Experiment*, a noun of action, maintained the simple sense of a test or trial.

The difficulty is that **empirical** and to some extent **empiricism** have been affected by and used over this complex and overlapping range of senses. Thus alongside the derogatory sense of **empiric** as quack there was a use which became especially important in the new medicine and new science of C17: 'empericall, that is to saie, that consisteth in practise, of experimentes' (1569); 'he had a laboratory, and knew of many empirical medicines' (1685). **Empiricals** was used of the materials of scientific experiment. In one important sense, of observation and experiment as the primary scientific procedure, **empirical** has remained normal in English to our own day.

But the word became complicated by two factors. First, the specialized sense of the *Empiriks*, and the derived English sense of untrained and ignorant, indicated not only a reliance on observation and experiment but a positive opposition or indifference to theory. Secondly, a complicated philosophical argument, about the relative contributions of *experience* and *reason* to the formation of ideas, produced as a description of one side of the argument the terms **empiricism** and **empiricist** to indicate theories of knowledge as derived wholly from the senses – that is from *experience* (not *experiment*) in a now special sense. There have been and continue to be many variations on this argument but in understanding the development of the word the crucial point is the range of indications, from the favourable 'direct observation' (cf. 'positive knowledge' and POSITIVISM (q.v.)) to the unfavourable 'mere' or 'random observation', without directing principle or theory. Specialized and intricate arguments in the theory of knowledge have led to one specific historical use, of the English **empirical** or **empiricist** philosophers from Locke to Hume. But the general modern use has less to do with the details of the philosophical argument than with the broad distinction between knowledge which is based on observation (*experience* and *experiment*) and knowledge which is based on the conscious application of directing principles or ideas, arrived at or controlled by reasoning. This difficult distinction sometimes leads to a loose use of **empirical** to mean atheoretical or antitheoretical, which interacts with the more common distinction between *practical* and THEORETICAL (q.v.).

It is difficult to read far in modern English without meeting confusing or at least difficult uses of **empirical** and **empiricism**. A theory or proposition is 'put to the test of empirical inquiry' (meaning, normally, put to the test of observation or practice, though here, precisely, it is a *theory* that is being tested). A report is 'crudely empirical', with a sense not far from the eC17 sense of untrained or ignorant but indicating mainly a lack of any (or any adequate) directing or controlling ideas or principles; whereas another report is 'empirically adequate' or 'empirically convincing', meaning that the knowledge is reliable or that a proposition has been proved. Some decisive issues are at stake in the arguments through which the words have developed, but these are usually masked rather than clarified by the now common use of **empirical** and **empiricism** as simple counters of praise and blame. When the words are further qualified by national adjectives – 'the English **empirical** bent', 'the notorious

Anglo-Saxon **empiricism'** – the argument usually goes beyond serious reach.

See POSITIVISM, RATIONAL, SCIENCE, THEORY

EQUALITY

Equality has been in regular use in English since eC15, from fw *équalité*, oF, *aequalitatem*, L, rw *aequalis*, L, from *aequus* – level, even, just. The earliest uses of **equality** are in relation to physical quantity, but the social sense of **equality**, especially in the sense of equivalence of rank, is present from C15 though more common from C16. **Equality** to indicate a more general condition developed from this but it represented a crucial shift. What it implied was not a comparison of rank but an assertion of a much more general, normal or normative, condition. This use is evident in Milton (*Paradise Lost*, XII, 26):

> . . . not content
> With faire equalitie, fraternal state.

But after mC17 it is not again common, in this general sense, until lC18, when it was given specific emphasis in the American and French revolutions. What was then asserted was both a fundamental condition – 'all men are created **equal**' – and a set of specific demands, as in **equality** before the law – that is to say, reform of previous statutory **inequalities**, in feudal and post-feudal ranks and privileges. In its bearings on social thought, **equality** has two main branches: (i) a process of **equalization**, from the fundamental premise that all men are naturally equal as human beings, though not at all necessarily in particular attributes; and (ii) a process of removal of inherent privileges, from the premise that all men should 'start equal', though the purpose or effect of this may then be that they become **unequal** in achievement or condition. There is of course considerable overlap between these two applications, but there is finally a distinction between (i) a process of continual equalization, in which any condition, inherited or newly created, which sets some men above others or gives them power over others, has to be removed or diminished in the name of the normative principle (which, as in Milton's use, brings **equality** and *fraternity* very close in meaning); and (ii) a process of abolishing or diminishing *privileges*, in which the moral notion of **equality** is on the whole limited to initial conditions, any subsequent inequalities being seen as either inevitable or right. The most common form of sense (ii) is **equality of opportunity**, which can be glossed as 'equal opportunity to become unequal'. (Compare the use of *underprivileged*, where privilege is the norm but some have less of it than others, to describe a poor or deprived or even oppressed group.) The familiar complaint against sense (i), that it wishes to bring everybody to a dead level, connects with the positive programme of economic equality which, in mC17 England, was the doctrine of the *Levellers*. There is a clear historical break, within both senses, between programmes limited to political and legal rights and programmes which also include economic equality, in any of its varying forms. It came to be argued, in eC19, that the persistence of economic inequalities, as in systems of landlord ownership or capitalist ownership of the means of production, made legal or political equality merely abstract.

Under the influence of arguments derived from the French Revolution, the older English form **equalitarian** was replaced, from mC19, by **egalitarian**, from the modern French form.

The persistence of **equal** in a physical sense, as a term of measurement, has obviously complicated the social argument. It is still objected to programmes of economic equality, and even to programmes of legal or political equality (though in these now less often) that men are evidently unequal in measurable attributes (height, energy, intelligence and so on). To this it is replied that what needs to be shown is that the measurable difference is relevant to the particular **inequality**, in a social sense: height would not be, though colour of skin has been held to be; energy or intelligence might be, and this is where most serious contemporary argument now centres. Measurable differences of this kind bear especially on sense (ii). They would usually be held, even where real and demonstrated, to be subordinate to sense (i), in which no difference between men would be allowed to give some men power over others.

See DEMOCRACY, ELITE

EVOLUTION

Evolution came from the sense of unrolling something and eventually indicated something being unrolled. It is now standard in two common senses, but in one of these, and in its specialized contrast with REVOLUTION (q.v.), this complexity of its history is significant.

Evolve is from fw *evolvere*, L – roll out, unroll, from rw *volvere*, L – to roll. It appeared in English, with **evolution**, in mC17. **Evolution** is from fw *évolution*, F, from *evolutionem*, L, which is recorded in the sense of unrolling a book. Its early uses were mainly physical and mathematical in the root sense, but it was soon applied, metaphorically, both to the divine creation and to the working-out, the developing formation, of Ideas or Ideal Principles. It is clear from the root sense and from these early applications that what is implied is the 'unrolling' of something that already exists. God comprehends 'the whole evolution of ages' (1667) in one eternal moment; there is an 'Evolution of Outward forms' (More, 1647); there is a 'whole Systeme of Humane Nature . . . in the evolution whereof the complement and formation of the Humane Nature must consist' (Hale, 1677).

An apparently modern sense is then indicated in biology. **Evolution** took the sense of development from rudimentary to mature organs, and the **theory of evolution**, as argued by Bonnet in 1762, was a description of development from an embryo which already contains, in rudimentary form, all the parts of the mature organism, and where the embryo itself is a development of a pre-existing form. The sense of 'unrolling' from something that already exists is thus still crucially present. However, in the course of description of various natural processes, **evolution** came to be used as virtually equivalent to *development* (mC18, from *develop*, C16 – to unfold, to lay open; C18 – to unfold fully, to complete). But it is still difficult to be sure whether any particular use carries the firm sense of something pre-existent or implicit, thus making the **evolution** natural or necessary. In the not particularly common but still standard contemporary use of the **evolution** of an argument or an idea, this sense of a necessary or rational *development* is still usually present.

What then happened in biology was a generalization of the sense of *development* (fully bringing out) from immature to mature forms, and especially the specialized sense of *development* from 'lower' to 'higher' organisms. From lC18 and eC19 this sense of a general natural process – a natural history over and above specific natural processes – was becoming known. It was explicit in Lyell on the evolution of land animals in 1832 and was referred to by Darwin in *The Origin of Species* (1859) as admitted 'at the present day' by 'almost all naturalists', 'under some form'. Herbert Spencer in 1852 defined a general **Theory of Evolution** from lower to higher forms of life and organization.

What Darwin did that was new was to describe some of the processes by which new species developed and to generalize these as *natural selection*. It is ironic that this radically new metaphor, in which NATURE (q.v.) was seen as discarding as well as developing various forms of life, was sustained within a continuing description of the process as **evolution**, with its sense of unrolling what already existed or maturing what was already preformed. Of course the metaphor of Nature *selecting* could be associated with a different sense of inherent design. A process shown in detail as generally material, environmental and in one sense accidental could be generalized as a process in which *Nature* had purpose or purposes. Nevertheless, as the new understanding of the origins of species spread, **evolution** lost, in biology, its sense of inherent design and became a process of natural historical development. It had happened because it had happened, and would go on happening because it was a natural process. The idea of necessary purpose became restricted to particular interpretations (**creative evolution**, Catholic biology and so on).

It was in the confusion of debate about **evolution** in this biological sense, and the even greater confusion of analogical applications from natural history to social history, that the contrast between **evolution** and *revolution* came to be made. REVOLUTION (q.v.) had now its developed sense of sudden and violent change, as well as its sense of the institution of a new order. **Evolution** in the sense of gradual development could readily be opposed to it, and the metaphors of 'growth' and of the ORGANIC (q.v.) had a simple association with this sense. Ironically, as can be seen in the development of Social Darwinism, the generalized natural history provided images for any imaginable kind of social action and change. Ruthless competition or mutual co-operation; slow change in the record of the rocks or sudden change in the appearance of mutations; violent change in the course of altered environment, or the disappearance of species in ruthless struggle: all could be and were adduced as the 'lessons' of nature to be applied or extended to society. To say that social change should be **evolutionary** might mean any or all of these things, from the slow development of new institutions to the wiping-out of former classes (species) and their replacement by higher forms. But in the contrast with *revolution* the earlier sense of **evolution** had primary effect. What was usually meant was the unrolling of something already implicitly formed (like a national *way of life*), or the *development* of something according to its inherent tendencies (like an existing constitution or economic system). (Cf. the conventional modern contrast between *developed* and *underdeveloped* societies, where the assumption of all societies as destined to become urban and industrial – not to say capitalist – is taken for granted, as if it were a technical term.) Radical change, which would include rejection of some existing forms or reversal of some existing tendencies, could then, within the metaphor, be described as 'unnatural' and, in the contrast with the specialized sense of *revolution*, be associated with sudden violence as opposed to steady growth.

In the real history of the last hundred years, in which the **evolution**/*revolution* contrast has become commonplace, the application has to be seen as absurd. It is carefully applied only to planned change, where in practice it is a distinction between a few slow changes controlled by what already exists and more and faster changes intended to alter much of what exists. The distinction is not really one of political process or method but of political affiliation. In 'unplanned' change – that is to say the **evolution** of forces and factors already inherent in a social order – there has, after all, been suddenness and violence enough, and the contrast with *revolution* seems merely arbitrary. But then the overlap and confusion between **evolution** as (i) inherent development, (ii) unplanned natural history and (iii) slow and conditioned change become matters for constant scrutiny.

See NATURE, ORGANIC, REVOLUTION

EXISTENTIAL

Existential, in contemporary English, ranges between a relatively old general meaning (probably from lC17, certainly from eC19) and a set of relatively new meanings derived from the philosophical tendency of **existentialism**. **Existence** has been in the language from C14, from fw *existence*, oF, *existentia*, mL – a state of being, from rw *ex(s)istere*, L – to stand out, to be perceptible, hence evidently to be. The relation between **existence** and the apparently alternative word **essence** (C14; fw *essence*, F, *essentia*, L – being) is far from clear in pre-C17 usage. Thus: 'God allone is be himself; of his awin natural existens' (1552); 'There is no essence mortal, That I can envie, but a plumpe cheekt foole' (Marston, 1602). But there was a theological use of **essence** as 'being', in the special context in which the three persons (beings) of the Trinity are one being (**essence**), and there was some consequent direction of the word towards the sense of fundamental or absolute being, or of the reality underlying appearances. This became the basis for an eventual contrast with **existence**, with its stress on evident and perceptible and therefore actual being (though it must be noted that **existence** also acquired the sense of continuity of being, which has some complicating effects). There was a distinction in lC17: 'I might believe its Existence, without meddling at all with its Essence' (More, 1667; of a spirit). **Essential** had been moving very strongly towards the sense of fundamental, intrinsic or necessary, but in many particular cases this had no necessary *contrast* with existence; indeed the contrast is only required in versions of idealist or metaphysical philosophy.

It was in this speculative context that **existential** began to be used from eC19, as when we find Coleridge asking 'whether God was existentially as well as essentially intelligent' or using the distinction in *The Friend* (III): 'the essential cause of fiendish guilt, when it makes itself existential and peripheric'. But there was also a more general use, expressing or predicating actuality: 'convention does not allow us to say "It executes" . . . But we can just as conveniently adopt the existential form "There was an execution"' (Venn, 1888).

C20 usage has been decisively affected by *Existenzphilosophie*, which we translate as **Existentialism**. The main currency of this term was from French influence after 1945, but the tendency was known from German thought from the 1920s and is usually traced back to Kierkegaard in mC19. Within this tendency, **existence** is a specifically human quality, as distinct from other things and (in most cases) creatures which may be said to **exist**. **Existence** is again contrasted with **essence**, but the major and minor signs are as it were transvalued. Where a definition of **essence** in the sense of something fundamental or intrinsic is still required, it is derived from the qualities of **existence**, that is of actual being. One use of this reversal is a critique of idealism and metaphysics: 'existence precedes essence': actual life is primary, and any **essential** characteristics are as it were distilled from it. But the main thrust of the new tendency (of which it was usually insisted that it was not a philosophical *system*) was towards a sense of uniqueness and unpredictability in any actual life, with a corresponding sense of rejection of DETER-MINATION (q.v.), or explanation by inherent forces. This condition of freedom to choose and to act in unique and unpredictable ways was accompanied by a sense of urgency and anxiety; in one common form, conventional or predictable or 'programmed' choices and acts are failures of **existence**, which implies taking responsibility for one's own life, with no possible certainty of any known outcome in the terms of some known scheme. But the conscious assumption of such responsibility, in the face of what is necessarily unknown and unpredictable (and in that special sense 'meaningless', a condition of the *absurd* in that now popular special sense), provoked an obvious anxiety (*angst*) which was at once terrifying and inevitable. Individuals who did not realize that this is how things are existed merely *in themselves*; to exist *for themselves* was to take conscious responsibility for this freedom within 'absurdity'.

There are many variants of this tendency, and there have been attempts to combine it with systems implying some degree of *determination*, such as Freudianism or Marxism. Several of these variants have controlled special uses of **existential**, with the implicit reference to a form of **existentialism**. But phrases like **existential awareness**, and the use of **existential** with a wide variety of nouns of feeling and of action, have become extended beyond any deliberate position. In their sense of process, actuality, or immediacy they can be seen as connected with earlier pre-existentialist senses, and indeed with the main history of the word. It is primarily in relation to senses of choice, anxiety and unpredictability that the philosophical tendency, however loosely in some cases, has given the contemporary word a special meaning. But this is not always distinguishable (and in some cases the lack of distinction is confusing) from simple descriptive uses for *living* or *actuality*. Thus 'the existential character of life in the modern city' may mean (i) the immediately observed day-to-day life of the inhabitants of a modern city, with no prior assumption of its necessary (**essential**) characteristics; or (ii) the strange, meaningless, alienated life of the inhabitants of the city, full of immediate occasions for unforeseen choices and full also of threat and anxiety; or (iii) the absurd condition of the modern city as a social form, with its inherent (? **essential**) conditions of strangeness and lack of purpose and connections. It is probably as well, whenever this now powerful word is used, to look for some early existential specification.

See DETERMINE, IDEALISM, INDIVIDUAL

F

FAMILY

Family has an especially significant social history. It came into English in lC14 and eC15, from fw *familia*, L – household, from rw *famulus* – servant. The associated adjective **familiar** appears to be somewhat earlier in common use, and its range of meanings reminds us of the range of meanings which were predominant in **family** before mC17. There is the direct sense of the Latin *household*, either in the sense of a group of servants or of a group of blood-relations and servants living together in one house. **Familiar** related to this, in phrases like **familiar angel**, **familiar devil** and the later noun **familiar**, where the sense is of being associated with or serving someone. There is also the common C15 and C16 phrase **familiar enemy**, to indicate an enemy within one's household, 'within the gates', and thence by extension an enemy within one's own people. But the strongest early senses of **familiar** were those which are still current in modern English: on terms of friendship or intimate with someone (cf. 'don't be too familiar'); well known, well used to or habitual (cf. 'familiar in his mouth as household words', *Henry V*). These uses came from the experience of people living together in a household, in close relations with each other and well used to each other's ways. They do not, and **familiar** still does not, relate to the sense of a blood-group.

Family was then extended, from at latest C15, to describe not a household but what was significantly called a *house*, in the sense of a particular lineage or kin-group, ordinarily by descent from a common ancestor. This sense was extended to indicate a people or group of peoples, again with a sense of specific descent from an ancestor; also to a particular religious sense, itself associated with previous social meanings, as in 'the Father of our Lord Jesus Christ, of whom the whole family in heaven and earth is named' (*Ephesians*, 1611). **Family** in the Authorized Version of the Bible (1611) was restricted to these wide senses: either a large kin-group, often virtually equivalent to *tribe* (*Genesis* 10:5; 12:3; *Jeremiah* 1:15; 31:1; *Ezekiel* 20:32) or the kin-group of a common father: 'and then shall he (a brother) depart from thee, both he and his children with him, and shall return unto his own family, and unto the possession of his fathers shall he return' (*Leviticus* 25:41; cf. *Numbers* 36:6). The lC16 and C17 sect of the **Family of Love** or **Familists** is interesting in that it drew on the sense of a large group, but made this open and voluntary through love.

In none of the pre-mC17 senses, therefore, can we find the distinctive modern sense of a small group confined to immediate blood relations. When this sense of relations between parents and children was required in A.V. *Genesis* it was rendered by *near kin*. Yet it is clear that between C17 and C19 the sense of the small kin-group, usually living in one house, came to be dominant: so dominant indeed that in C20 there has been an invention of terms to distinguish between this and the surviving subordinate sense of a larger kin-group: the distinction between **nuclear family** and **extended family**. It is very difficult to trace this evolution, which has a complicated social history. We can still read from 1631: 'his family were himself and his wife and daughters, two mayds and a man', where the sense is clearly that

Family

of *household*. This survived in rural use, with living-in farm servants who ate at the same table, until lC18 and perhaps beyond; the later distinction between **family** and *servants* was in this instance much resented. There was also a long influence from aristocratic use, in the sense of *lineage*, and this remained strong in the characteristic C18 **found a family**. Class distinction was expressed as late as C19 (and residually beyond it) in phrases like 'a person of no family', where the large kin-group is evidently in question but in the specialized sense of traceable lineage. Expressions like **the family** were still used to C20 to indicate a distinguishable upper-class group: 'the family is in residence', where the kin-group sense has clearly been separated from the household sense, since the servants are there in any case (but not 'in residence' even if 'resident').

The specialization of **family** to the small kin-group in a single house can be related to the rise of what is now called the **bourgeois family**. But this, with its senses of household and property, relates more properly, at least until C19, to the older sense. From eC19 (James Mill) we find this definition: 'the group which consists of a Father, Mother and Children is called a Family'; yet the fact that the conscious definition is necessary is in itself significant. Several lC17 and C18 uses of **family** in a small kin-group sense often refer specifically to children: 'but duly sent his family and wife' (Pope, *Bathurst*), where the sense of household, however, may still be present. **Family-way**, common since eC18, referred first to the sense of **familiar** but then, through the specific sense of children, to pregnancy. There was thus considerable overlap, between mC17 and lC18, of these varying senses of lineage, household, large kin-group and small kin-group.

The dominance of the sense of small kin-group was probably not established before eC19. The now predominant pressure of the word, and the definition of many kinds of feeling in relation to it, came in mC19 and later. This can be represented as the apotheosis of the **bourgeois family**, and the sense of the isolated family as a working economic unit is clearly stressed in the development of capitalism. But it has even stronger links to early capitalist production, and the C19 development represents, in one sense, a distinction between a man's *work* and his **family**: he works to support a **family**; the **family** is supported by his work. It is more probable, in fact, that the small kin-group definition, supported by the development of smaller separate houses and therefore households, relates to the new working class and lower-middle class who were defined by wage-labour: not **family** as lineage or property or as including these, and not family as *household* in the older established sense which included servants, but the near kin-group which can define its social relationships, in any positive sense, only in this way. **Family** or **family and friends** can represent the only immediately positive attachments in a large-scale and complex wage-earning society. And it is significant that class-feeling, the other major response to the new society, used *brother* and *sister* to express class affiliation, as in trade union membership, though there is also in this a clear religious precedent in certain related religious sects. It is significant also that this use of *brother* and *sister* came to seem artificial or comic in middle-class eyes. **Family**, there, combined the strong sense of immediate and positive blood-group relationships and the strong implicit sense of property.

It is a fascinating and difficult history, which can be only partly traced through the development of the word. But it is a history worth remembering when we hear that 'the **family**, as an institution, is breaking up' or that, in times gone by and still hopefully today, 'the **family** is the necessary foundation of all order and morality'. In these and similar contemporary uses it can be useful to remember the major historical variations, with some of their surviving complexities, and the sense, through these, of radically changing definitions of primary relationships.

See SOCIETY

FICTION

Fiction has the interesting double sense of a kind of IMAGIN-ATIVE (q.v.) LITERATURE (q.v.) and of pure (sometimes deliberately deceptive) invention. These senses have been in the English word from a very early period. It was introduced in C14 from fw *fiction*, F, *fictionem*, L, from rw *fingere*, L – to fashion or form; the same root produced *feign*, which had the sense of invent falsely or deceptively from C13. Caxton used the two words together: 'fyction and faynyng' (1483), but *ficcions* in the sense of imaginary works is recorded from 1398, and in lC16 there are *poeticall fiction* and *Ancient Fiction*. A general use, ranging between a consciously formed hypothesis ('mathematicall fictions', 1579) and an artificial and questionable assumption ('of his own fiction'), was then equally common and has remained active. **Fictitious**, from eC17, ranged from this to the sense of deceptive invention; the literary use required the later alternative **fictional**. The major development of the literary sense was from lC18: 'dramatic fiction' (1780); 'works of fiction' (1841). It was in C19 that the term became almost synonymous with *novels*. The popularity of novels led to a curious C20 back-formation, in library and book-trade use, in **non-fiction** (at times made equivalent to 'serious' reading; some public libraries will reserve or pay postage on any **non-fiction** but refuse these facilities for **fiction**; the sense of 'pure invention', or the conventional (and artificial) contrast between **fiction** and *fact*, from the other sense of the word, probably contributes to the confidence of this discrimination).

Novel, now so nearly synonymous with fiction, has its own interesting history. The two senses now indicated by the noun (prose fiction) and the adjective (new, innovating, whence *novelty*) represent different branches of development from rw *novus*, L – new: the former from fw *novella*, It, *novela*, Sp.; the latter from *novelle*, oF. Until eC18 *novel*, as a noun, carried both senses: (i) a tale; (ii) what we now call, with the same sense, *news*. Thus the tales of Boccaccio, Ariosto and others were called *novelles*: short tales, whether 'fictional' or HISTORICAL (q.v.): cf. 'in these histories (which by another term I call Novelles) he described the lives . . . of great princes' (Painter, 1566). On the other hand, in sense (ii): 'to hear novells of his devise' (Spenser, 1579); 'You promise in your clear aspect, some novel That may delight us' (Massinger, 1636). Even one of the 'fathers of the English novel', Fielding, wrote this exchange in one of his plays:

– What novel's this?
– Faith! it may be a pleasant one to you.

It was from this range of senses that *novelist* meant successively any kind of innovator (C17), a newsmonger (C18) and a writer of prose fiction (C18). Through C17 and part of C18 *novel* effectively alternated with the more familiar ROMANCE (q.v.), though it was generally held that the novel could be distinguished by being shorter (more like a *tale*) and by being more often related to real life. Milton referred (1643) to 'no mere amatorious novel', but by mC18 *novel* was becoming the standard word, though still with many deprecatory references, as in Goldsmith's 'those abilities that can hammer out a novel are fully sufficient for the production of a sentimental comedy' or the more persistent 'no Novel in the world can be more affecting, or more surprising, than this history' (Wesley, 1769). So complete, by eC19, was the development of *novel* as the standard term for a work of prose fiction that a new word for a short prose fiction was introduced: *novelette* (1820). Much of the opprobrium which *novel* had carried was transferred to this, as in *novelettish* (eC20). Indeed we can now sometimes say that *novelettes*, or bad novels, are pure fiction, while *novels* (serious fiction) tell us about real life.

See CREATIVE, IMAGE, MYTH, ROMANTIC

FORMALIST

Formalist is quite an old English word, but in C20 it has been widely used in a relatively new context, following uses of the corresponding word in Russian. Two senses of **formalist** appeared in English from eC17: (i) an adherent of the 'mere forms' or 'outward shows' of religion: 'formalists and time-servers' (1609); (ii) one who explains a matter from its superficial rather than its substantial qualities: 'it is a ridiculous thing . . . to see what shiftes theis Formalists have . . . to make superficies to seeme body, that hath depth and bulk' (Bacon, 1607–12). These uses, and some of the intricate confusions of more recent usage, can be understood only by reference to the complicated development of **form** itself. From fw *forme*, oF, *forma*, L – shape, *form* repeated in English the complications of its Latin development, of which two are principally relevant: (i), a visible or outward shape, with a strong sense of the physical body: 'an angel bi wai he mette, In mannes fourm' (c. 1325); 'forme is most frayle, a fading flattering showe' (1568); (ii), an essential shaping principle, making indeterminate material into a determinate or specific being or thing: 'the body was only mater, of which (the soul) were the fourme' (1413); 'according to the diversity of inward forms, things of the world are distinguished into their kinds' (Hooker, 1594). It is clear that in these extreme senses **form**

113

spanned the whole range from the external and superficial to the inherent and determining. **Formality** spanned the same range, from 'the attyre ... being a matter of meere formalitie' (Hooker, 1597), to 'those Formalities, wherein their Essence doth consist' (1672). In common use, **form** retained its full range but **formality**, **formalist** and (from mC19) **formalism** were predominantly used in negative or dismissive ways: 'the Ceremonies are Idols to Formalists' (1637); 'oh ye cold-hearted, frozen, formalists' (Young, 1742); 'useless formalism' (Kingsley, 1850); 'cant and formalism' (1878). Two examples have some relevance to the later specific development: 'Formalists who demand Explications of the least ambiguous Word' (1707); 'the formalist of dramatic criticism' (1814).

Given the complications of **form**, and the received implications of **formalist**, it is not surprising that the **formal method** and **formalist school** which can be distinguished, under those names, in Russian literary studies from about 1916, should have been so variously understood. Moreover, as **formalism** itself developed, it showed many different tendencies and emphases. Its predominant emphasis was on the specific, intrinsic characteristics of a literary work, which required analysis 'in its own terms' before any other kind of discussion, and especially social or ideological analysis, was relevant or even possible. The intricacies of the subsequent argument are extraordinary. There was a simple opposition (bringing into play a received distinction between *form* (i) and *content*) between a **formalism** limited to 'merely' AESTHETIC (q.v.) interests and a *Marxism* concerned with social content and ideological tendency. In the actual disposition and development of historical forces, it was this strongly negative sense of **formalism** which first became widely known in English, where it was used as if equivalent to ideas of 'art for art's sake'. At the same time, in some developments of **formalism**, notably in the idea of a quite separate category of 'poetic language', and in some tendency to deny the relevance of 'social content' or 'social meaning' at *any* stage, this was, quite often, the position really held. The debate (it is better to call it that than an argument) between these two schools (in the specialized senses of **formalist** and *Marxist*) dominated usage until c. 1950. The earlier English senses of 'outward show' and 'superficial appearance' undoubtedly compromised **formalist** in this stage. What was more interesting, but still extremely difficult, was the notion of **form** (ii) as a shaping principle, either in its widest sense (where it overlapped with *genre*) or in its most specific sense, where it was a discoverable organizing principle within a work (cf. 'no work of true genius dares want its appropriate form', Coleridge). With this sense of **form**, (ii) as distinct from (i), the *Marxist* emphasis could be reasonably described as a **formalism of content**, using the unfavourable sense (i) of 'outward show', and different questions could be asked about the real **formation** (form (ii)) of a work, which requires specific analysis of its elements in a particular organization. Moreover, as to some extent happened (though with much transfer and confusion of names) this kind of emphasis, allowing for or actually involving extension from the specific form to wider forms, and to forms of consciousness and relationship (*society*), was one of the tendencies within **formalism**. The point was confused by distinctions (involving deep disagreements which were not always fully articulated) between *intersubjective* and SOCIAL (q.v.) processes, and between *synchronic* and *diachronic* analyses: terms derived from a tendency in linguistics, and used either to express an absolute distinction between a self-sufficient system in language and a system as part of an historical process, or to express alternative emphases, now on the system, now on the process of development of which it is a moment, with real and dynamic relations between them. On the whole **formalism** (cf. *structuralism*) has followed the former (*intersubjective*, and the duality of *synchronic* and *diachronic*) rather than the latter emphasis, but while it is opposed only by a *Marxism* which treats **form** as the 'mere expression' or 'outward show' of *content*, its qualities of specification in analysis remain powerful. It has still to be seen whether the negative associations of the word will prevent general recognition of the important though partial redirection of emphasis which **formalism** and the **formalists** contributed.

See STRUCTURAL

G

GENETIC

Genetic sometimes presents difficulties because it has two senses: a general meaning, which has become relatively uncommon in English though it is still common, for example, in French, and a specialized meaning, in a particular branch of science, which has become well known. **Genetic** is an adjective from *genesis*, L, *genesis*, Gk – origin, creation, generation. It came into English in eC19, at first with the sense of a reference to origins, as in Carlyle: 'genetic Histories' (1831). It still had this main sense of origin in Darwin, where 'genetic connection' (1859) referred to a common origin of species. But **genetic** carried also the sense of development, as in 'genetic definitions' (1837) where the defined subject was 'considered as in the progress to be, as becoming', and this was present again in 'the genetic development of the parts of speech' (1860). In 1897 **genetics** was defined in distinction from *telics*, to describe a process of *development* rather than a fully developed or final state. Developments in eC20 biology showed the need for a new word. Bateson in 1905 referred to the 'Study of Heredity' and wrote: 'no word in common use quite gives this meaning . . . and if it were desirable to coin one, "Genetics" might do'. From this use the now normal scientific description became established: 'the physiology of heredity and variation . . . genetics' (*Nature*, 1906). But the older and more general sense of development was still active, as in 'genetic psychology' (1909), which we would now more often call *developmental* psychology, without reference to biological **genetics**. Moreover the earliest sense also survived, as in 'genetic fallacy' (1934) – the fallacy of explaining or discrediting something by reference to its original causes.

In normal English usage, **genetic** now refers to the facts of heredity and variation, in a biological context (**genetic inheritance**, **genetic code**, etc.). But in addition to the residual English uses **genetic** also often appears in translations, especially from French, where the sense is normally of formation and development.

Thus **genetic structuralism** (Goldmann) is distinguished from other forms of STRUCTURALISM (q.v.) by its emphasis on the historical (not biological) formation and development of *structures* (forms of consciousness). It is probable that in this translated use it is often misunderstood, or becomes loosely associated with biological **genetics**.

See FORMALIST, HISTORY, STRUCTURAL

H

HEGEMONY

Hegemony was probably taken directly into English from fw *egemonia*, Gk, rw *egemon*, Gk – leader, ruler, often in the sense of a state other than his own. Its sense of a political predominance, usually of one state over another, is not common before C19, but has since persisted and is now fairly common, together with **hegemonic**, to describe a policy expressing or aimed at political predominance. More recently **hegemonism** has been used to describe specifically 'great power' or 'superpower' politics, intended to dominate others; (indeed **hegemonism** has some currency as an alternative to IMPERIALISM (q.v.)).

There was an occasional early use in English to indicate predominance of a more general kind. From 1567 there is 'Aegemonie or Sufferaigntie of things growing upon ye earth', and from 1656 'the Supream or Hegemonick part of the Soul'. **Hegemonic**, especially, continued in this sense of 'predominant' or of a 'master principle'.

The word has become important in one form of C20 Marxism, especially from the work of Gramsci. In its simplest use it extends the notion of political predominance from relations between states to relations between social classes, as in **bourgeois hegemony**. But the character of this predominance can be seen in a way which produces an extended sense in many ways similar to

117

earlier English uses of **hegemonic**. That is to say, it is not limited to matters of direct political control but seeks to describe a more general predominance which includes, as one of its key features, a particular way of seeing the world and human nature and relationships. It is different in this sense from the notion of 'world-view', in that the ways of seeing the world and ourselves and others are not just intellectual but political facts, expressed over a range from institutions to relationships and consciousness. It is also different from IDEOLOGY (q.v.) in that it is seen to depend for its hold not only on its expression of the interests of a ruling class but also on its acceptance as 'normal reality' or 'commonsense' by those in practice subordinated to it. It thus affects thinking about REVOLUTION (q.v.) in that it stresses not only the transfer of political or economic power, but the overthrow of a specific **hegemony**: that is to say an integral form of class rule which exists not only in political and economic institutions and relationships but also in active forms of experience and consciousness. This can only be done, it is argued, by creating an alternative **hegemony** – a new predominant practice and consciousness. The idea is then distinct, for example, from the idea that new institutions and relationships will of themselves create new experience and consciousness. Thus an emphasis on **hegemony** and the **hegemonic** has come to include cultural as well as political and economic factors; it is distinct, in this sense, from the alternative idea of an economic *base* and a political and cultural *superstructure*, where as the *base* changes the *superstructure* is changed, with whatever degree of indirectness or delay. The idea of **hegemony**, in its wide sense, is then especially important in societies in which electoral politics and public opinion are significant factors, and in which social practice is seen to depend on consent to certain dominant ideas which in fact express the needs of a dominant class. Except in extreme versions of economic DETERMINISM (q.v.), where an economic *system* or STRUCTURE (q.v.) rises and falls by its own laws, the struggle for **hegemony** is seen as a necessary or as the decisive factor in radical change of any kind, including many kinds of change in the *base*.

See CULTURE, IMPERIALISM

HISTORY

In its earliest uses **history** was a narrative account of events. The word came into English from fw *histoire*, F, *historia*, L, from rw *istoria*, Gk, which had a basic sense of knowledge. In all these words the sense ranged from a *story* of events to a narrative of past events. In early English use, **history** and *story* (the alternative English form derived ultimately from the same root) were both applied to an account either of imaginary events or of events supposed to be true. The use of **history** for imagined events has persisted, in a diminished form, especially in novels. But from C15 **history** moved towards an account of past real events, and *story* towards a range which includes less formal accounts of past events and accounts of imagined events. **History** in the sense of organized knowledge of the past was from lC15 a generalized extension from the earlier sense of a specific written account. **Historian, historic** and **historical** followed mainly this general sense, although with some persistent uses referring to actual writing.

It can be said that this established general sense of **history** has lasted into contemporary English as the predominant meaning. But it is necessary to distinguish an important sense of **history** which is more than, though it includes, organized knowledge of the past. It is not easy either to date or define this, but the source is probably the sense of **history** as human self-development which is evident from eC18 in Vico and in the new kinds of **Universal Histories**. One way of expressing this new sense is to say that past events are seen not as specific **histories** but as a continuous and connected process. Various systematizations and interpretations of this continuous and connected process then become **history** in a new general and eventually abstract sense. Moreover, given the stress on human *self-development*, **history** in many of these uses loses its exclusive association with the past and becomes connected not only to the present but also to the future. In German there is a verbal distinction which makes this clearer: *Historie* refers mainly to the past, while *Geschichte* (and the associated *Geschichtsphilosophie*) can refer to a process including past, present and future. **History** in this controversial modern sense draws on several kinds of intellectual system:

notably on the Enlightenment sense of the progress and development of CIVILIZATION (q.v.); on the idealist sense, as in Hegel, of **world-historical** process; and on the political sense, primarily associated with the French Revolution and later with the socialist movement and especially with Marxism, of **historical forces** – products of the past which are active in the present and which will shape the future in knowable ways. There is of course controversy between these varying forms of the sense of process, and between all of them and those who continue to regard **history** as an account, or a series of accounts, of actual past events, in which no necessary design, or, sometimes alternatively, no necessary implication for the future, can properly be discerned. **Historicism**, as it has been used in mC20, has a neutral sense (i) of a method of study which relies on the facts of the past and traces precedents of current events, but also a controversial sense (ii), meant to discredit the general sense of **history** as a continuing process with definite implications for the future; (it has been most often used in attacks on Marxism but it would be relevant also to the Enlightenment and Idealist uses). It is not always easy to distinguish the attack on **historicism**, which centres mainly on the concept of a necessary or probable future, from a related attack on the notion of any *future* (in its specialized sense of a better, a more developed life) which uses the **lessons of history**, in a quite generalized sense, as an argument especially against hope. Though it is not always recognized or acknowledged as such, this latter use of **history** is probably a specific C20 form of **history** as general process, though now used, in contrast with the sense of achievement or promise of the earlier and still active versions, to indicate a general pattern of frustration and defeat.

It is then not easy to say which sense of **history** is currently dominant. **Historian** remains precise, in its earlier meaning. **Historical** relates mainly but not exclusively to this sense of the past, but **historic** is most often used to include a sense of process or destiny. **History** itself retains its whole range, and still, in different hands, *teaches* or *shows* us most kinds of knowable past and almost every kind of imaginable future.

See DETERMINE, EVOLUTION

HUMANITY

Humanity belongs to a complex group of words, including **human, humane, humanism, humanist, humanitarian**, which represent, in some or all of their senses, particular specializations of a root word for *man* (*homo, hominis*, L – man, of a man; *humanus*, L – of or belonging to men).

It is necessary first to understand the distinction between **human** and **humane**, which only became settled in its modern form from eC18. Before this **humane** was the normal spelling for the main range of meanings which can be summarized as the characteristic or distinct elements of *men*, in the general sense (cf. MAN) of the **human** species. (All men are **human**, or in the earlier spelling **humane**, but all **humans** are either *men* (in the specialized male sense) or *women* or *children*.) Early uses of **humane** referred to **human nature, human language, human reason** and so on, but there was also from eC16 a use of **humane** to mean kind, gentle, courteous, sympathetic. After eC18 the old spelling was specialized to the now distinct word **humane**, in this latter range of senses, while **human** became standard for the most general uses.

Humanity has a different but related development. First used in lC14, from fw *humanité*, F, it had an initial sense much closer to the specialized **humane** than to the general **human**. In medieval use it appears synonymous with courtesy and politeness, and this must be related to, though it is not identical with, the development of *umanità*, It., and *humanité*, F, from *humanitas*, L, which had contained a strong sense of *civility*. *Humanitas* had also an important specific sense of mental cultivation and a liberal education; it thus relates directly to the modern complex of *cultivation*, CULTURE and CIVILIZATION (qq.v.). From eC16, in English, the development is complex. The sense of courtesy and politeness is extended to kindness and generosity: 'Humanitie . . . is a generall name to those vertues, in whome semeth to be a mutuall concorde and love, in the nature of man' (Elyot, 1531). But there is also, from lC15, a use of **humanity** in distinction from *divinity*, and then, probably from lC16, a general use comparable with the general use of

human, which had been present in the adjective from lC14. There are two famous instances in Shakespeare:

I have thought some of Natures Jouerney-men had made men, and not made them well, they imitated Humanity so abhominably. (*Hamlet*)

I would change my Humanity with a Baboone. (*Othello*)

There is a strong sense in each of these uses of the physical form of man, though in the *Hamlet* instance other attributes are implicit. The use of **humanity** to indicate, neutrally, a set of human characteristics or attributes is not really common, in its most abstract sense, before C18, though thereafter it is very common indeed. There was the persistent sense ranging from courtesy to kindness, and there was also the sense, developing from *umanità* and *humanitas*, of a particular kind of learning. There were C15 and C16 uses of **humanity** as a kind of learning distinct from divinity, and Bacon defined 'three knowledges, Divine Philosophy, Natural Philosophy and Humane Philosophy, or Humanitie' (*Advancement of Learning*, II, v; 1605). Yet in academic use **Humanity** became equivalent to what we now call *classics*, and especially Latin (there are still residual uses in this sense). From C18 a French form, **the humanities** (*les humanités*) became steadily more common in academic and related usage, eventually adding modern literature and philosophy to the *classics*. This usage has remained normal in American English, as distinct from the more common English grouping of THE ARTS (q.v.).

Parts of this range are reflected in the development of **humanist** and eventually **humanism**. **Humanist** was probably taken directly from *umanista*, It., which from eC16 had been a significant Renaissance word. It had lC16 senses equivalent both to *classicist* and to the student of **human** as distinct from divine matters. This is a real complexity, related on the one hand to surviving distinctions between 'pagan' and 'Christian' learning, and on the other hand to distinctions between the 'learned' (defined as in classical languages) and others. There is also an ultimate relation to the double quality of the Renaissance: the 'rebirth' of classical learning; the new kinds of interest in *man* and in **human** activities. It is not surprising, given this complex, to find an eC17 use of **humanist** (Moryson, 1617) to describe someone interested in state affairs and history. The use of

Humanist to describe one of the group of scholars prominent in the Renaissance and the Revival of Learning seems to come later in C17, but has since been common.

Humanism, on the other hand, was probably taken direct from *humanismus*, a lC18 German formation which depended on the developed abstract sense of **humanity**. What was picked out from a complex argument, which belongs, essentially, with the contemporary development of CULTURE and CIVILIZATION (qq.v.), was the attitude to religion, and **humanism** in this sense (as a positive word preferred to the negative *atheism*) has become common. But a broader sense of **humanism**, related to post-Enlightenment ideas of HISTORY (q.v.) as human self-development and self-perfection, also became established in C19, and this overlapped with a new use of **humanism** to represent the developed sense of **humanist** and **the humanities**: a particular kind of learning associated with particular attitudes to CULTURE (q.v.) and **human** development or perfection.

Humanitarian appeared first, in eC19, in the context of arguments about religion: it described the position from which Christ was affirmed as a man and not a god. Moore (*Diary*, 1819) noted an acquaintance as 'more shocked as a grammarian at the word than as a divine at the sect'. The word took this particular form by analogy with *unitarian* and *trinitarian*. But this was soon left behind. By association with the developmental sense of **humanism**, but even more with new kinds of action and attitude belonging to the now specialized sense of **humane**, **humanitarian** became established from mC19 in the sense of a deliberately general exercise or consideration of WELFARE (q.v.). (There is one special and ironic sense in **humane killer** eC20.) It is interesting that through much of C19 the use of **humanitarian** was hostile or contemptuous (as in mC20 *do-gooder*). But it is now one of the least contentious of words. It was probably its conscious social generalization of what had been seen as local and individual acts and attitudes which attracted hostility (cf. *welfare* in C20).

It is necessary to add a final note on **human** in mC20 usage. It is of course now standard in general and abstract senses. It is also commonly used to indicate warmth and congeniality ('a very **human** person'). But there is also a significant use to indicate what might be called condoned fallibility ('human error', 'natural human error') and this is extended, in some uses, to indicate something more than this relatively neutral observation. 'He had a human side to him after all' need not mean only that some respected man was fallible; it can mean also that he was confused or, in some uses, that he committed various acts of meanness, deceit or even crime. The sense relates, obviously, to a traditional sense that it is **human** not only to err but to sin. But what is interesting about the contemporary use, especially in fashionable late bourgeois culture, is that 'sin' has been transvalued so that acts which would formerly have been described in this way as proof of the faults of **humanity** are now adduced, with a sense of approval that is not always either wry or covert, as proof of being **human** (and *likable* is not usually far away).

See CIVILIZATION, CULTURE, ISMS, MAN, WELFARE

I

IDEALISM

Idealism has two main modern senses: (i) its original philosophical sense, in which, though with many variations of definition, ideas are held to underlie or to form all reality; (ii) its wider modern sense of a way of thinking in which some higher or better state is projected as a way of judging conduct or of indicating action. One of the critical difficulties of sense (ii) is that, especially in some of its derived words, it is used, often loosely, for both praise and blame.

Idealism has been used in English from lC18, from fw *idealisme*, F, and especially *Idealismus*, G. It was preceded in this original philosophical sense by *idealist*, from eC18. The crucial reference back is to Greek thought, especially to Plato, and **idea** in this sense was present in English from mC15, though until lC16 its more common form was *idee*. The rw, *idea*, Gk, is from the verb 'to see', and has a range of meanings from appearance and form to the Platonic type or model. **Idea** (i) – ideal type, is common from C15; (ii) – figure, from C16; (iii) – thought or belief, from C17. A general noun for sense (iii), such as **ideation**

or **ideology**, did not develop until eC19, after the increasingly specialized uses of **idealism**.

The specific philosophical use has a predominant reference to German classical philosophy in lC18 and eC19, though with reference back not only to Plato but to such English philosophers as Berkeley. But in essentially the same period there was a complicated reversal of meaning in relation to art and social thought. **Idealism** in philosophy, in all its important variations, supposed ideas to be fundamental, whether these were the divine or universal Idea or Ideas, or the constitutive ideas of human consciousness. It was clearly from the reference to human consciousness that the reversal began. **Idealism** and **idealist** began to be used, from lC18 and especially eC19, to indicate not so much consciousness as a fundamental and formative activity but a special kind of consciousness, imaginatively conferring certain properties on an object (as opposed to the main sense of philosophical idealism, in which an object necessarily derived its properties from consciousness). The new verb **idealise**, from eC19, described, especially in its early uses, the processes of ART (q.v.). Its extension to a more general process of imaginative elevation was not common before mC19, when it also began to acquire the unfavourable implication of an accompanying falsification (**idealization**). The unfavourable senses of **idealism** and **idealist** were also C19 developments; by 1884 there was the now characteristic 'mere idealist'.

The subsequent complexities of meaning can be indicated by a pairing of opposites. There is **idealism** contrasted with MATERIALISM (q.v.): basically a philosophical opposition but in C20 especially extended, by the broadening of each term, to a distinction which is really that between altruism and selfishness: a distinction which whatever its other merits has nothing to do with the philosophical argument though it is often, in social polemic, confused with it. Then there is **idealism** contrasted with *realism*: again originally a philosophical distinction, and having some related development to describe types and processes of art, but in common use, from lC19 and especially in our own time, to indicate a contrast which is really that between impractical and practical, especially in the derived **idealistic** and REALISTIC (q.v.). Then there is also **idealism** as a positive social or moral sense contrasted either with self-seeking or indifference or with a general narrowness of outlook. Since all these current uses coexist with a continuing and important philosophical argument, itself now quite exceptionally complicated, **idealism** is obviously a word which needs the closest scrutiny whenever it is used.

See IDEOLOGY, MATERIALISM, NATURALISM, PHILOSOPHY, REALISM

IDEOLOGY

Ideology first appeared in English in 1796, as a direct translation of the new French word *idéologie* which had been proposed in that year by the rationalist philosopher Destutt de Tracy. Taylor (1796): 'Tracy read a paper and proposed to call the philosophy of mind, ideology'. Taylor (1797): '. . . ideology, or the science of ideas, in order to distinguish it from the ancient metaphysics'. In this scientific sense, **ideology** was used in epistemology and linguistic theory until lC19.

A different sense, initiating the main modern meaning, was introduced by Napoleon Bonaparte. In an attack on the proponents of democracy – 'who misled the people by elevating them to a sovereignty which they were incapable of exercising' – he attacked the principles of the Enlightenment as 'ideology'.

It is to the doctrine of the ideologues – to this diffuse metaphysics, which in a contrived manner seeks to find the primary causes and on this foundation would erect the legislation of peoples, instead of adapting the laws to a knowledge of the human heart and of the lessons of history – to which one must attribute all the misfortunes which have befallen our beautiful France.

This use reverberated throughout C19. It is still very common in conservative criticism of any social policy which is in part or in whole derived from social theory *in a conscious way*. It is especially used of democratic or socialist policies, and indeed, following Napoleon's use, **ideologist** was often in C19 generally equivalent to *revolutionary*. But **ideology** and **ideologist** and **ideological** also acquired, by a process of broadening from Napoleon's attack, a sense of abstract, impractical or fanatical theory. It is interesting in view of the later history of the word to read Scott (*Napoleon*, vi, 251): 'ideology, by which nickname the French ruler used to distinguish every species of theory, which, resting in no respect upon the basis of self-interest, could, he thought, prevail with none save hot-brained boys and crazed enthusiasts' (1827). Carlyle, aware of this use, tried to counter it: 'does the British reader . . . call this unpleasant doctrine of ours ideology?' (*Chartism*, vi, 148; 1839).

There is then some direct continuity between the pejorative sense of **ideology**, as it had been used in eC19 by conservative thinkers, and the pejorative sense popularized by Marx and Engels in *The German Ideology* (1845–7) and subsequently. Scott had distinguished ideology as theory 'resting in no respect upon the basis of self-interest', though Napoleon's alternative had actually been the (suitably vague) 'knowledge of the human heart and of the lessons of history'. Marx and Engels, in their critique of the thought of their radical German contemporaries, concentrated on its abstraction from the real processes of history. Ideas, as they said specifically of the ruling ideas of an epoch, 'are nothing more than the ideal expression of the dominant material relationships, the dominant material relationships grasped as ideas.' Failure to realize this produced **ideology**: an upside-down version of reality.

> If in all ideology men and their circumstances appear upside down as in a *camera obscura*, this phenomenon arises just as much from their historical life process as the inversion of objects on the retina does from their physical life process. (*German Ideology*, 47)

Or as Engels put it later:

> Every ideology . . . once it has arisen develops in connection with the given concept-material, and develops this material further; otherwise it would cease to be ideology, that is, occupation with thoughts as with independent entities, developing independently and subject only to their own laws. That the material life-conditions of the persons inside whose heads this thought process goes on in the last resort determines the course of this process remains of necessity unknown to these persons, for otherwise there would be an end to all ideology. (*Feuerbach*, 65–6)

Or again:

> Ideology is a process accomplished by the so-called thinker consciously indeed but with a false consciousness. The real

motives impelling him remain unknown to him, otherwise it
would not be an ideological process at all. Hence he imagines
false or apparent motives. Because it is a process of thought he
derives both its form and its content from pure thought,
either his own or his predecessors'. (*Letter to Mehring*, 1893)

Ideology is then abstract and false thought, in a sense directly
related to the original conservative use but with the alternative –
knowledge of real material conditions and relationships –
differently stated. Marx and Engels then used this idea critically.
The 'thinkers' of a ruling class were 'its active conceptive
ideologists, who make the perfecting of the illusion of the class
about itself their chief source of livelihood' (*German Ideology*, 65).
Or again: 'the official representatives of French democracy were
steeped in republican ideology to such an extent that it was only
some weeks later that they began to have an inkling of the
significance of the June fighting' (*Class Struggles in France*,
1850). This sense of **ideology** as illusion, false consciousness,
unreality, upside-down reality, is predominant in their work.
Engels believed that the 'higher ideologies' – philosophy and
religion – were more removed from material interests than the
direct ideologies of politics and law, but the connection, though
complicated, was still decisive (*Feuerbach*, 277). They were
'realms of ideology which soar still higher in the air . . . various
false conceptions of nature, of man's own being, of spirits,
magic forces, etc. . . . .' (*Letter to Schmidt*, 1890). This sense has
persisted.

Yet there is another, apparently more neutral sense of **ideology**
in some parts of Marx's writing, notably in the well-known
passage in the *Contribution to the Critique of Political Philosophy*
(1859):

The distinction should always be made between the material
transformation of the economic conditions of production . . .
and the legal, political, religious, aesthetic or philosophic
– in short, ideological – forms in which men become conscious
of this conflict and fight it out.*

This is clearly related to part of the earlier sense: the ideological
forms are expressions of (changes in) economic conditions of
production. But they are seen here as the forms in which men

*Marx's German reads: . . . *kurz, ideologischen Formen, worin sich die
Menschen diesen Konflikts bewusst werden. . .*

become *conscious* of the conflict arising from conditions and changes of condition in economic production. This sense is very difficult to reconcile with the sense of **ideology** as mere illusion.

In fact, historically, this sense of **ideology** as the set of ideas which arise from a given set of material interests has been at least as widely used as the sense of **ideology** as illusion. Moreover, each sense has been used, at times very confusingly, within the Marxist tradition. There is clearly no sense of illusion or false consciousness in a passage such as this from Lenin:

> Socialism, insofar as it is the ideology of struggle of the proletarian class, undergoes the general conditions of birth, development and consolidation of an ideology, that is to say it is founded on all the material of human knowledge, it presupposes a high level of science, demands scientific work, etc. . . . In the class struggle of the proletariat which develops spontaneously, as an elemental force, on the basis of capitalist relations, socialism is *introduced* by the ideologists. (*Letter to the Federation of the North*)

Thus there is now 'proletarian ideology' or 'bourgeois ideology', and so on, and **ideology** in each case is the system of ideas appropriate to that class. One ideology can be claimed as correct and progressive as against another ideology. It is of course possible to add that the other ideology, representing the class enemy, is, while a true expression of their interests, false to any general human interest, and something of the earlier sense of illusion or false consciousness can then be loosely associated with what is primarily a description of the class character of certain ideas. But the neutral sense of **ideology**, which usually needs to be qualified by an adjective describing the class or social group which it represents or serves, has in fact become common in many kinds of argument. At the same time, within Marxism but also elsewhere, there has been a standard distinction between **ideology** and SCIENCE (q.v.), in order to retain the sense of illusory or merely abstract thought. This develops the distinction suggested by Engels, in which ideology would end when men realized their real life-conditions and therefore their real motives, after which their consciousness would become genuinely *scientific* because they would then be in contact with reality. This attempted distinction between Marxism as *science* and other social thought as **ideology** has of course been controversial, not least among Marxists. In a very much broader area of the 'social sciences', comparable distinctions between **ideology** (speculative systems) and *science* (demonstrated facts) are commonplace.

Meanwhile, in popular argument, **ideology** is still mainly used in the sense given by Napoleon. Sensible people rely on *experience*, or have a *philosophy*; silly people rely on **ideology**. In this sense **ideology**, now as in Napoleon, is mainly a term of abuse.

See DOCTRINAIRE, IDEALISM, PHILOSOPHY, SCIENCE

IMAGE

The earliest meaning of **image** in English was, from C13, a physical figure or likeness. This was also the earliest meaning of the rw *imago*, L, which however also developed the senses of phantom and of conception or idea. There is a probable root relation to the development of *imitate*, but as in many words describing these processes (cf. *vision* and *idea*) there is a deep tension between ideas of 'copying' and ideas of **imagination** and the **imaginary**. Each of these has throughout, in English, referred to mental conceptions, including a quite early sense of seeing what does not exist as well as what is not plainly visible. The unfavourable sense, however, was not common until C16.

The physical sense of **image** was predominant until C17, but from C16 the wider sense, with a predominantly mental reference, was established and from C17 there was an important specialized use in discussions of literature, to indicate a 'figure' of writing or speech. The physical sense is still available in contemporary English, but has acquired some unfavourable connotations overlapping with *idol*. The general sense of a mental conception (compare **the image of** . . . a characteristic or representative type) is still normal, and the specialized use in literature is common.

But it sometimes seems that all these uses have been overtaken by a use of **image** in terms of publicity, which can be seen to depend on the earlier senses of conception or characteristic type but which in practice means 'perceived reputation', as in the commercial **brand image** or a politician's concern with his **image**. This is in effect a jargon term of commercial advertising and public relations. Its relevance has been increased by the growing importance of visual media such as television. The sense of **image** in literature and painting had already been developed to describe the basic units of composition in film. This technical sense in practice supports the commercial and manipulative processes of **image** as 'perceived' reputation or character. It is interesting that the implications of **imagination** and especially **imaginary** are kept well away from the mC20 use of **image** in advertising and politics.

See FICTION, IDEALISM, REALISM

IMPERIALISM

Imperialism developed as a word during the second half of C19. **Imperialist** is much older, from eC17, but until lC19 it meant the adherent of an emperor or of an imperial form of government. **Imperial** itself, in the same older sense, was in English from C14; fw *imperialis*, L; rw *imperium*, L – command or supreme power.

Imperialism, and **imperialist** in its modern sense, developed primarily in English, especially after 1870. Its meaning was always in some dispute, as different justifications and glosses were given to a system of organized colonial trade and organized colonial rule. The argument within England was sharply altered by the evident emergence of rival imperialisms. There were arguments for and against the military control of colonies to keep them within a single economic, usually protectionist system. There was also a sustained political campaign to equate imperialism with modern CIVILIZATION (q.v.) and a 'civilizing mission'.

Imperialism acquired a new specific connotation in eC20, in the work of a number of writers – Kautsky, Bauer, Hobson, Hilferding, Lenin – who in varying ways related the phenomenon of modern imperialism to a particular stage of development of CAPITALIST (q.v.) economy. There is an immense continuing literature on this subject. Its main effect on the use of the word has been an evident uncertainty, and at times ambiguity, between emphases on a political system and on an economic system. If **imperialism**, as normally defined in lC19 England, is primarily a political system in which colonies are governed from an imperial centre, for economic but also for other reasons held to be important, then the subsequent grant of independence or self-government to these colonies can be described, as indeed it widely has been, as 'the end of imperialism'. On the other hand, if **imperialism** is understood primarily as an economic system of external investment and the penetration and control of markets and sources of raw materials, political changes in the status of colonies or former colonies will not greatly affect description of the continuing economic system as **imperialist**. In current political argument the ambiguity is often confusing. This is especially the case with 'American imperialism', where the primarily political reference is less relevant, especially if it carries the C19 sense of direct government from an imperial centre, but where the primarily economic reference, with implications of consequent indirect or manipulated political and military control, is still exact. **Neo-imperialism** and especially **neo-colonialism** have been widely used, from mC20, to describe this latter type of imperialism. At the same time, a form of the primarily political sense has been revived in counter-descriptions of 'Soviet imperialism', as a way of describing the current political status of Eastern Europe. Thus the same powerful word, now used almost universally in a negative sense, is employed to indicate radically different and consciously opposed political and economic systems. But as in the case of DEMOCRACY (q.v.), which is used in a positive sense to describe, from particular positions, radically different and consciously opposed political systems, **imperialism**, like any word which refers to fundamental social and political conflicts, cannot be reduced, semantically, to a single proper meaning. Its important historical and contemporary variations of meanings point to real processes which have to be studied in their own terms.

See HEGEMONY, NATIVE

IMPROVE

Improve is an interesting example of the development of a general meaning from a more specific meaning. It came into English, at first with many variations of spelling, from fw *en preu*, oF, rw *pros* – profit. In its earliest uses it referred to operations for monetary profit, where it was often equivalent to *invest*, and especially to operations on or connected with land, often the enclosing of common or waste land. From C16 to lC18 the predominant meaning was that of profitable operations in connection with land; in C18 it was a key word in the development of a modernizing agrarian capitalism. The sense of 'using to make a profit' is retained in surviving phrases such as 'improve the occasion' and 'improve the hour'. The wider meaning of 'making something better' developed from C17 and became established, often in direct overlap with economic operations, in C18. From mC18 there is the characteristic 'improve oneself', and such phrases as 'improving reading' followed. Jane Austen was aware of the sometimes contradictory senses of **improvement**, where economic operations for profit might not lead to, or might hinder, social and moral refinement. In *Persuasion* (ch. v), a landowning family was described as 'in a state of alteration, perhaps of improvement'. The separation of the general meaning from the economic meaning is thereafter normal, but the complex underlying connection between 'making something better' and 'making a profit out of something' is significant when the social and economic history during which the word developed in these ways is remembered. We can compare the corresponding development of *interest*.

See INTEREST

INDIVIDUAL

Individual originally meant indivisible. That now sounds like paradox. 'Individual' stresses a distinction from others; 'indivisible' a necessary connection. The development of the modern meaning from the original meaning is a record in language of an extraordinary social and political history.

The immediate fw *individualis*, mL, is derived from *individuus*, L, C6, a negative (*in-*) adjective from rw *dividere*, L – divide. *Individuus* was used to translate *atomos*, Gk – not cuttable, not divisible. Boethius, C6, defined the meanings of *individuus*:

Something can be called individual in various ways: that is called individual which cannot be divided at all, such as unity or spirit (i); that which cannot be divided because of its hardness, such as steel, is called individual (ii); something is called individual, the specific designation of which is not applicable to anything of the same kind, such as Socrates (iii). (*In Porphyrium commentarium liber secundus*)

Individualis and **individual** can be found in the sense of essential indivisibility in medieval theological argument, especially in relation to the argument about the unity of the Trinity (the alternate form, *indivisible*, was also then used). Thus: 'to the . . . glorie of the hye and indyvyduall Trynyte' (1425). Sense (i) continued in more general use into C17: '*Individuall*, not to bee parted, as man and wife' (1623); '. . . would divide the individuall Catholicke Church into severall Republicks' (Milton, 1641). Sense (ii), in physics, was generally taken over by *atom*, from C17. It is sense (iii), indicating a single distinguishable person, which has, from eC17, the most complicated history.

The transition is best marked by uses of the phrase 'in the individuall' as opposed to 'in the general'. Many of these early uses can be read back in a modern sense, for the word is still complex. Thus: 'as touching the Manners of learned men, it is a thing personal and individual' (Bacon, *Advancement of Learning*, I, iii; 1605). In the adjective the first developing sense is 'idiosyncratic' or 'singular': 'a man should be something that men are not, and individuall in somewhat beside his proper nature' (Browne, 1646). The sense is often, as here, pejorative. The word was used in the same kind of protest that Donne made against the new 'singularity' or 'individualism':

For every man alone thinks he hath got
To be a Phoenix, and that then can be
None of that kind of which he is but he.
(*First Anniversarie*, 1611).

In this form of thought, the ground of human nature is common; the 'individual' is often a vain or eccentric departure from this. But in some arguments the contrast between 'in the general' and 'in the individual' led to the crucial emergence of the new noun. It was almost there in Jackson (1641): 'Peace . . . is the very supporter of Individualls, Families, Churches, Commonwealths', though 'individualls' is here still a class. It was perhaps not till Locke (*Human Understanding*, III, vi; 1690) that the modern social sense emerged, but even then still as an adjective: 'our Idea of any individual Man'.

The decisive development of the singular noun was indeed not in social or political thought but in two special fields: logic, and, from C18, biology. Thus: 'an individual . . . in Logick . . . signifies that which cannot be divided into more of the same name or nature' (Phillips, 1658). This formal classification was set out in Chambers (1727–41): 'the usual division in logic is made into genera . . . those genera into species, and those species into individuals'. The same formal classification was then available to the new biology. Until C18 **individual** was rarely used without explicit relation to the group of which it was, so to say, the ultimate indivisible division. This is so even in what reads like a modern use in Dryden:

That individuals die, his will ordains;
The propagated species still remains.
(Dryden, *Fables Ancient and Modern*, 1700)

It is not until lC18 that a crucial shift in attitudes can be clearly seen in uses of the word: 'among the savage nations of hunters and fishers, every individual . . . is . . . employed in useful labour' (Adam Smith, *Wealth of Nations*, i, Introd., 1776). In the course of C19, alike in biology and in political thought, there was a remarkable efflorescence of the word. In evolutionary biology there was Darwin's recognition (*Origin of Species*, 1859) that 'no one supposes that all the individuals of the same species are cast in the same actual mould'. Increasingly the phrase 'an individual' – a single example of a group – was joined and overtaken by 'the individual': a fundamental order of being.

The emergence of notions of **individuality**, in the modern sense, can be related to the break-up of the medieval social, economic and religious order. In the general movement against feudalism there was a new stress on a man's personal existence over and above his place or function in a rigid hierarchical society. There was a related stress, in Protestantism, on a man's direct and individual relation to God, as opposed to this relation MEDIATED (q.v.) by the Church. But it was not until lC17 and C18 that a new mode of analysis, in logic and mathematics, postulated the individual as the substantial entity (cf. Leibniz's 'monads'), from which other categories and especially collective categories were derived. The political thought of the Enlightenment mainly followed this model. Argument began from individuals, who had an initial and primary existence, and laws and forms of society were derived from them: by submission, as in Hobbes; by contract or consent, or by the new version of natural law, in liberal thought. In classical economics, trade was described in a model which postulated separate individuals who decided, at some starting point, to enter into economic or commercial relations. In utilitarian ethics, separate individuals calculated the consequences of this or that action which they might undertake. Liberal thought based on 'the individual' as starting point was criticized from conservative positions – 'the individual is foolish . . . the species is wise' (Burke) – but also, in C19, from socialist positions, as most thoroughly in Marx, who attacked the opposition of the abstract categories 'individual' and 'society' and argued that the individual is a social creation, born into relationships and DETERMINED (q.v.) by them.

The modern sense of **individual** is then a result of the development of a certain phase of scientific thought and of a phase of political and economic thought. But already from eC19 a distinction began to be made within this. It can be summed up in the development of two derived words: **individuality** and **individualism**. The latter corresponds to the main movement of liberal political and economic thought. But there is a distinction indicated by Simmel: 'the individualism of uniqueness – *Einzigheit* – as against that of singleness – *Einzelheit*'. 'Singleness' – abstract individualism – is based, Simmel argued, on the quantitative thought, centred in mathematics and physics, of C18. 'Uniqueness', by contrast, is a qualitative category, and is a concept of the Romantic movement. It is also a concept of evolutionary biology, in which the species is stressed and the individual related to it, but with the recognition of uniqueness within a kind. Many arguments about 'the individual' now confuse the distinct senses to which **individualism** and **individuality** point. **Individuality** has the longer history, and comes out of the complex of meanings in which **individual** developed, stressing both a unique person and his (indivisible) membership of a group. **Individualism** is a C19 coinage: 'a novel expression, to which a novel idea has given birth' (tr. Tocqueville, 1835): a theory not only of abstract individuals but of the primacy of individual states and interests.

See MAN, PERSONALITY, SOCIALISM, SOCIETY, SUBJECTIVE

INDUSTRY

There are two main senses of **industry**: (i) the human quality of sustained application or effort; (ii) an institution or set of institutions for production or trade. The two senses are neatly divided by their modern adjectives **industrious** and **industrial**.

Industry has been in English since C15, from fw *industrie*, F, rw *industria*, L – diligence. Elyot wrote in 1531: 'industrie hath nat ben so longe tyme used in the englisshe tonge as Providence; wherfore it is the more straunge, and requireth the more plaine exposition', and he went on to define it as quick perception, fresh invention and speedy counsel. Yet there were uses, contemporary with this, in contrast to sloth and dullness; as a synonym for diligence; and, in a specialized use, as a working method or device. **Industrious**, meaning either skilful or assiduous, was the common derived adjective from mC16, but there was also a C16 appearance of **industrial**, in a distinction between cultivated (*industriall*) and *natural* fruits. **Industrial** is then rare or absent until lC18, when it began the development which made it common by mC19, perhaps in a new borrowing from French.

It was from C18 that the sense of **industry** as an institution or set of institutions began to come through. There was mention of a 'College of Industry for all useful Trades and Husbandry' in 1696, and of subsequent 'schools of industry' associated with Sunday Schools. But the most widespread C18 use was in 'House of Industry', the workhouse, where the ideas of forced application and useful work came together. Then, in Adam Smith, there was a modern generalizing use: '. . . funds destined for the maintenance of industry' (*Wealth of Nations*, II, iii; 1776). By the 1840s, at latest, this use was common: Disraeli – 'our national industries' (1844); Carlyle – 'Leaders of Industry' (1843). **Industry** as a human quality rather than an institution, while continuing to be used, was on the whole subordinate after this period, and survives mainly in different kinds of patronizing reference.

The sense of **industry** as an institution was radically affected, from the period of its main early uses, by two further derivations: **industrialism**, introduced by Carlyle in the 1830s to indicate a new order of society based on organized mechanical production,

137

and the phrase **industrial revolution**, which is now so central a term. **Industrial revolution** is especially difficult to trace. It is usually recorded as first used by Arnold Toynbee, in lectures given in 1881. But there were much earlier uses in French and German. Bezanson (1922) traced several French associations of *révolution* and *industrielle* between 1806 and the 1830s, but analysis of these depends on understanding the ways in which both REVOLUTION (q.v.) and **industrial** were shifting, in both English and French. Most of the early uses referred to technical changes in production – a common later meaning of **industrial revolution** itself – and this was still the primary sense as late as 'Grande Révolution Industrielle' (1827). The key transition, in the developed sense of *revolution* as instituting a new order of society, was in the 1830s, notably in Lamartine: 'le 1789 du commerce et de l'industrie', which he described as the real revolution. Wade (*History of the Middle and Working Classes*, 1833) wrote in similar terms of 'this extraordinary revolution'. This sense of a major social change, amounting to a new order of life, was contemporary with Carlyle's related sense of **industrialism**, and was a definition dependent on a distinguishable body of thinking, in English as well as in French, from the 1790s. The idea of a new social order based on major industrial change was clear in Southey and Owen, between 1811 and 1818, and was implicit as early as Blake in the early 1790s and Wordsworth at the turn of the century. In the 1840s, in both English and French ('a complete industrial revolution', Mill, *Principles of Political Economy*, III, xvii; 1848 – revised to 'a sort of industrial revolution'; 'l'ère des révolutions industrielles', Guilbert, 1847) the phrase became more common. But the decisive uses were probably by Blanqui (*Histoire de l'économie politique*, II, 38; 1837): 'la fin du dix-huitième siècle . . . Watt et Arkwright . . . la révolution industrielle se mit en possession de l'Angleterre'; and by Engels (*Condition of the Working Class in England*; written in German, 1845): 'these inventions . . . gave the impulse to an industrial revolution, a revolution which at the same time changed the whole of civil society'. Though the phrase was not in common use in English until lC19, the idea was common from mC19 and was clearly forming in eC19. It is interesting that it has survived in two distinct (though overlapping) senses: of the series of technical inventions (from which we can speak of *Second* or *Third Industrial Revolutions*); and of a wider but also more historically specific social change – the institution of **industrialism** or **industrial capitalism**. (It must be noted also that the relations between **industrialism** and *capitalism* are problematic, and that this is sometimes masked by the terms. In one use, **industrialism** is euphemistic for *capitalism*, but problems of 'socialist' **industrialization** have elements in common with the **industrial capitalist** history.)

From eC19, association with organized mechanical production, and the series of mechanical inventions, gave **industry** a primary reference to productive institutions of that type, and distinctions like **heavy industry** and **light industry** were developed in relation to them. **Industrialists** – employers in this kind of institution – were regularly contrasted not only with *workpeople* – their employees, but with other kinds of employer – *merchants*, *landowners*, etc. This contrast between **industry** as factory production and other kinds of organized work was normal to mC20 and is still current. Yet since 1945, perhaps under American influence, **industry** has again been generalized, along the line from effort, to organized effort, to an institution. It is common now to hear of the **holiday industry**, the **leisure industry**, the **entertainment industry** and, in a reversal of what was once a distinction, the **agricultural industry**. This reflects the increasing capitalization, organization and mechanization of what were formerly thought of as **non-industrial** kinds of service and work. But the development is not complete: **industrial workers**, for example, still primarily indicates factory workers, as distinct from other kinds of worker, and the same is true of **industrial areas**, **industrial town** and **industrial estate**.

See CAPITALISM, CLASS, LABOUR, REVOLUTION, WORK

INSTITUTION

Institution is one of several examples (cf. CULTURE, SOCIETY, EDUCATION) of a noun of action or process which became, at a certain stage, a general and abstract noun describing something apparently objective and systematic; in fact, in the modern sense, an **institution**. It has been used in English since C14, from fw *institution*, oF, *institutionem*, L, from rw *statuere*, L – establish, found, appoint. In its earliest uses it had the strong sense of an act of origin – something **instituted** at a particular point in time –

but by mC16 there was a developing general sense of practices established in certain ways, and this can be read in a virtually modern sense: 'in one tonge, in lyke maners, institucions and lawes' (Robinson's translation of More's *Utopia*, 1551); 'many good institutions, Lawes, maners, the art of government' (Ashley, 1594). But there was still, in context, a strong sense of custom, as in the surviving sense of 'one of the institutions of the place'. It is not easy to date the emergence of a fully abstract sense; it appears linked, throughout, with the related abstraction of SOCIETY (q.v.). By mC18 an abstract sense is quite evident, and examples multiply in C19 and C20. At the same time, from mC18, **institution** and, later, **institute** (which had carried the same general senses as **institution** from C16) began to be used in the titles of specific organizations or types of organization: 'Charitable Institutions' (1764) and several titles from lC18; **Mechanics' Institutes**, **Royal Institute of British Architects**, and comparable organizations from eC19, here probably imitated from the *Institut National*, created in France in 1795 in consciously modern terminology. **Institute** has since been widely used for professional, educational and research organizations; **institution** for charitable and benevolent organizations. Meanwhile the general sense of a form of social organization, specific or abstract, was confirmed in mC19 development of **institutional** and **institutionalize**. In C20 **institution** has become the normal term for any organized element of a society.

See SOCIETY

INTELLECTUAL

Intellectual as a noun to indicate a particular kind of person or a person doing a particular kind of work dates effectively from eC19, though there were some isolated earlier uses. **Intelligence** as a general faculty of understanding dates from C14, but the interesting development of **intelligent** and **intelligence** as terms of comparison between people seems to date primarily from C16: among clear uses we can cite 'some learned Englishman of good intelligence' (Grafton, 1568) where **intelligence**, however, can be read as knowledge, information (as still in **intelligence service**). There was an earlier use of 'man devoyde of intelligence' (? 1507). 'The more intelligent', in a distinctive sense, is recorded from 1626; there is also 'grave and intelligent persons' (Clarendon) from 1647. There appears to be some association between these distinctions, of relative and absolute intelligence, and arguments about the nature of government. Several of the defining and separating uses of **intelligent** and **intelligence** in C17 and lC18 and C19 were associated with conservative political positions, in a kind of argument that has remained familiar: that the more or most **intelligent** should govern. It is in any case significant that **intellectual**, as a noun, followed a different course. It had been an ordinary adjective, from C14, for **intelligence** in its most general sense, and it became a noun to indicate the faculties or processes of **intelligence**. Then from eC19 there was an interesting use of the plural, **intellectuals**, to indicate a category of persons, often unfavourably: 'I wish I may be well enough to listen to these intellectuals' (Byron, 1813). Though **intellectual** as an adjective retained a neutral general use, there was a distinct formation of unfavourable implications around **intellectuals** in the new sense. **Intellectualism** had been a simple alternative to **rationalism**. Partly from this, but also for more general reasons, it acquired implications of coldness, abstraction and, significantly, ineffectiveness. **Intelligence** and **intelligent** retained their general and mainly positive senses, while several negative senses gathered around **intellectual**. The reasons are complicated but almost certainly include opposition to social and political arguments based on theory or on rational principle. This often connects, curiously, with the distinguishing use of **the more** or **the most intelligent** as a governing class, and with opposition, as in Romanticism, to a 'separation' of 'head' and 'heart', or 'reason' and 'emotion'. Nor can we overlook a crucial kind of opposition to groups engaged in **intellectual** work, who in the course of social development had acquired some independence from established institutions, in the church and in politics, and who were certainly seeking and asserting such independence through lC18, C19 and C20. Eventually, under the influence of these developments, **intellectual** and **intelligent** could be offered as terms of contrast, and by lC19 there was the characteristic formation 'so-called **intellectuals**'. From eC20 the new group term **intelligentsia** was borrowed from Russian. This source is significant, for the sense of a distinct and self-conscious group had, for good social reasons, been important in Russia from mC19.

Until mC20 unfavourable uses of **intellectuals, intellectualism** and **intelligentsia** were dominant in English, and it is clear that such uses persist. But **intellectuals**, at least, is now often used neutrally, and even at times favourably, to describe people who do certain kinds of **intellectual** work and especially the most general kinds. Within universities the distinction is sometimes made between *specialists* or *professionals*, with limited interests, and **intellectuals**, with wider interests. The social tensions around the word are significant and complicated, ranging from an old kind of opposition to a group of people who use theory or even organized knowledge to make judgments on general matters, to a different but sometimes related opposition to ELITES (q.v.), who claim not only specialized but directing kinds of knowledge. The argument about the relation of **intellectuals** to an established social system, and therefore about their relative independence or incorporation in such a system, is crucially relevant in this. However, to the degree that people now argue about the social STATUS (q.v.) or social *function* of **intellectuals**, the word itself has clearly entered a new and more general phase of its history, supported by comparable uses in other languages and cultures. The increasing commonness of **anti-intellectual**, to describe positions opposed to organized thought and learning, is part of this same movement, drawing on an older and wider sense.

Though **intelligence** and **intelligent** continue in wide and general senses, the distinguishing comparative use of both is perhaps more common than it has ever been ('Haven't you got any **intelligence**?'; 'it would soon be clear to any **intelligent** person'). Meanwhile, description of **high** or **low intelligence** has been reinforced by a controversial system of apparently objective measurement, the **intelligence quotient** or **I.Q.**, which has passed into common use. An old tension is still evident, however, even in this, when the measurable abstract quality is compared and sometimes contrasted with a sense of **intelligent** that draws, however tacitly, on ideas of *experience* and *information* as well as on abstract ability.

See EDUCATED, ELITE, THEORY

INTEREST

Interest is a significant example (cf. IMPROVE) of a word with specialized legal and economic senses which, within a particular social and economic history, has been extended to a very general meaning. The word **interest** is etymologically very complicated, especially in relation to the earlier *interess* with which it alternates and overlaps until C17. The rw was *interesse*, L – to be between, to make a difference, to concern, but the fw were *interesse*, mL – a compensation for loss, and the derived *interesse*, oF, and *interest*, mF, which ranged from compensation for loss to a transitive use for investment with a right or share. Most uses of **interest** before C17 referred to an objective or legal share of something, and the extended use, to refer to a natural share or common concern, was at first usually a conscious metaphor:

Ah so much interest have (I) in thy sorrow
As I had Title in thy Noble Husband. (*Richard III*)

It is exceptionally difficult to trace the development of **interest**, first to a common name for a general or natural concern, and beyond this to something which first 'naturally' and then just 'actually' attracts our attention. But **interesting** and **interestingly** in their most general modern senses were not clear before mC18. **Interest** in the sense of general concern or having the power to attract concern was also a mC18 development. **Interest** in the now predominant sense of general curiosity or attention, or having the power to attract curiosity or attention, is not clear before C19. But the problem is that the sense of objective concern and involvement, derived from the formal and legal uses, is not always easy to distinguish from these later more SUBJECTIVE (q.v.) and voluntary senses. The distinction is now formalized in the negatives: **disinterested** retains its early sense of 'impartial' – that is, not affected by objective involvement in a matter, while **uninterested** and **uninteresting**, which were formerly equivalent to the senses of **disinterested**, expressed from C19 the senses of being not attracted to something or having no power to attract. (**Disinterested** is still used, with what are intended to be positive implications, to express a personal habit not only of 'unbiased' but 'undogmatic' concern. It is also being

143

used, increasingly often, to mean simply not interested, and this gives substantial offence to those to whom the former sense is still important.)

As a formal term in matters of money, **interest** has another significant history. In medieval use it was distinguished from *usury*; **interest** or **interess** was compensation for default on a debt (a specialized application of the earliest meaning) whereas *usury* was taking what we would now call **interest** for a deliberate loan. **Interest** in the modern financial sense appeared from C16, when the laws affecting moneylending were revised, and when profit from the use of money, as distinct from compensation for default on a debt, became accepted practice.

It remains significant that our most general word for attraction or involvement should have developed from a formal objective term in property and finance. It is not difficult to understand the extended sense of an objective general share or concern, which resumes the range of the original Latin and which was applied in phrases like **having an interest, taking an interest, being interested**. More significant, perhaps, is the extension and projection of this power to concern or attract attention and curiosity, when we say that people, things or events are **interesting**. The question is whether this sense of an object generating such **interest** is related to the active sense of **interest** – of money generating money – after its distinction from the sin of *usury* and the formerly static, retrospective and compensatory, sense of **interest** itself. It seems probable that this now central word for attention, attraction and concern is saturated with the experience of a society based on money relationships.

See IMPROVE

ISMS

There have been **isms**, and for that matter **ists**, as far back as we have record. *Ism* and *ist* are Greek suffixes. **Ism** was used in English to form a noun of action (*baptism*); of a kind of action (*heroism*); and of actions and beliefs characteristic of some group (*Atticism, Judaism*) or tendency (*Protestantism, Socialism*) or school (*Platonism*). **Ist** was used to form various agent-nouns (*psalmist*) and also nouns to indicate an adherent of some system or teacher (*altruist, Thomist*). There was an extensive formation of new Latin words of this type in the medieval period, and there were English forms from C13. From C16 they multiplied and became common. What was probably new from lC18 and eC19 was the reaction expressed in the isolation of **isms** and **ists** as separate words: 'you would soon squabble about Socianism, or some of those isms' (Walpole, 1789); 'he is nothing – no "ist", professes no "-ism" but superbism and irrationalism' (Shelley, 1811); 'neither Pantheist nor Pot-theist, nor any Theist or Ist whatsoever, having a decided contempt for all such manner of system-builders or sect-founders' (Carlyle, 1835); 'ists and isms are rather growing a weariness' (Emerson, 1841); 'that class of untried social theories which are known by the name of *isms*' (Lowell, 1864).

This development expressed several tendencies. There was, first, the impatience with theological controversy; most of the early examples are of this kind. Second, there was the impatience with theory (as in the Carlyle example) which can be more easily and contemptuously expressed in this form than in any other. Third, there was the significant transfer from theological to political controversy, which by the time of the Lowell example was predominant. **Isms** and **ists** are still used, wittily or contemptuously (often with a sense of rapturous originality) but usually from orthodox and conservative positions, and even by *scientists, economists* and those professing *patriotism*.

L

LABOUR

Among the two earliest examples of the use of **labour** in English are 'bigin a laboure . . . and make a toure' and 'quit o labur, and o soru' (both c. 1300). These two senses, of work and of pain or trouble, were already closely associated in fw *labor*, oF, *laborem*, L; the rw is uncertain but may be related to slipping or staggering under a burden. As a verb **labour** had a common sense of ploughing or working the land, but it was also extended to other kinds of manual work and to any kind of difficult effort. A **labourer** was primarily a manual worker: 'a wreched laborer that lyveth by hys hond' (c. 1325). The sense of **labour** as pain was applied to childbirth from C16. The general sense of hard work and difficulty was well summed up in Milton's

So he with difficulty and labour hard
Mov'd on, with difficulty and labour hee. (*Paradise Lost*, II)

In the Authorized Version of the Bible, both senses were active:

For thou shalt eat the labour of thine
hands: happy shalt thou be . . . (*Psalm* 128:2)

The days of our years are threescore and ten;
and if by reason of strength they be
fourscore years, yet is their strength labour
and sorrow. (*Psalm* 90:10)

From C17, except in the special use for childbirth, **labour** gradually lost its habitual association with pain, though the general and applied senses of difficulty were still strong. The sense of **labour** as a general social activity came through more clearly, and with a more distinct sense of abstraction. Locke produced a defence of private property on the fact (in its context and bearings highly abstract) of having mixed our **labour** with the earth; (those who most visibly bore the stains of this mixing usually had, in fact, no property). **Labour** was personified, as in Goldsmith's *The Traveller* (1764): 'Nature . . . Still grants her bliss at Labour's earnest call.' But the most important change was the introduction of **labour** as a term in political economy: at first in an existing general sense, 'the annual labour of every nation' (Adam Smith, *Wealth of Nations*, Intro.) but then as a measurable and calculable component: 'Labour . . . is the real measure of the exchangeable value of all commodities' (*ibid* I, i). Where **labour**, in its most general use, had meant all productive work, it now came to mean that element of production which in combination with capital and materials produced commodities. This new specialized use belongs directly to the systematized understanding of CAPITALIST (q.v.) productive relationships. Phrases like the 'price of labour' (Malthus, 1798) and the 'supply of labour' took on more precise and more specialized meanings. The effect was well summed up, later, by Beatrice Webb:

> With the word labour I was, of course, familiar. Coupled mysteriously with its mate capital, this abstract term was always turning up in my father's conversation, and it occurred and reoccurred in the technical journals and reports of companies which lay on the library table. 'Water plentiful and labour docile', 'The wages of labour are falling to their natural level' . . . were phrases which puzzled me . . . I never visualized labour as separate men and women of different sorts and kinds . . . labour was an abstraction, which seemed to denote an arithmetically calculable mass of human beings, each individual a repetition of the other . . . (*My Apprenticeship*, Ch. 1)

Yet, as the two phrases she quotes make clear, **labour** had by this time developed two modern senses: first the economic abstraction of the activity; secondly the social abstraction of that class of people who performed it. The first sense, as we have seen, is earlier. **Labour** was an abstracted component of production: between the **labourer** and the object of his **labour**, as in the older uses, *capital* had been isolated as a productive component and **labour** in the specialized and measurable sense was part of the same abstraction. This is the sense of Mrs Webb's second phrase: 'the wages of labour'. But her first phrase, 'labour docile', is clearly a description of a class.

It is not easy to trace the precise emergence of this class description (cf. CLASS). Obviously the habit of referring to the 'supply of labour' prepared the ground for it. But the broad social use in response to this kind of assumption may well belong equally, or more, to the defenders of labour, especially from the 1820s. Thus we find *Labour Defended Against the Claims of Capital* (1825), by 'A Labourer' (Thomas Hodgskin), where one 'component' was set against the other but in terms which identified both as social classes. *Labour Rewarded* (Thompson, 1827) was still, in its title, the activity, but J. F. Bray's lectures of the 1830s, published as *Labour's Wrongs and Labour's Remedies*, had the full sense of a social class. This use was to become common, from this period. While **labour**, both as a component to be hired and as a 'pool' of persons available to be hired (cf. mC19 **labour market**), was habitually used in capitalist descriptions, this was increasingly countered by a self-conscious and self-styled **Labour Movement.** There were many complex interactions with the more common word *trades* (which in that older sense gave us *trade unions*) and with the complex senses of *work, worker* and *working class* (see WORK and CLASS), but the most general sense of a political and economic interest and movement came through in English as **Labour.** It was most specifically defined in Britain in the **Labour Representation League** (1869), the **Labour Electoral Committee** (1887), the **Independent Labour Party** (1893) and eventually, under its present name, the **Labour Party** (1906).

It is interesting to watch the effects of these modern developments on the old general senses of **labour.** The special use in childbirth has continued, but otherwise the word is not often used outside its specific modern contexts. It survives in rather self-conscious phrases ('rest from my labours') and whenever used is at once understood. **Laborious** retains its old general sense. But the specializations of the capitalist period have come to predominate: **labour costs, labour market, labour relations** from one side; **labour movement** and the titular **Labour Party** from the other. **Labourer,** however, is still current, as a particular kind of *worker,* while *work,* with all its difficulties, has taken over almost all other general senses.

See CAPITALISM, CLASS, WORK

LIBERAL

Liberal has, at first sight, so clear a political meaning that some of its further associations are puzzling. Yet the political meaning is comparatively modern, and much of the interesting history of the word is earlier.

It began in a specific social distinction, to refer to a class of free men as distinct from others who were not free. It came into English in C14, from fw *liberal,* oF, *liberalis,* L, rw *liber,* L – free man. In its use in **liberal arts** – 'artis liberalis' (1375) – it was predominantly a class term: the skills and pursuits appropriate, as we should now say, to men of independent means and assured social position, as distinct from other skills and pursuits (cf. MECHANICAL) appropriate to a lower class. But there was a significant development of a further sense, in which the pursuits had their own independence: 'Liberal Sciencis . . . (fre scyencis, as gramer, arte, fisike, astronomye, and otheris' (1422). Yet as with any term which distinguishes some free men from others, a tension remained. The cultivated ideal of the **liberal arts** was matched by the sense of **liberal** as generous ('in giffynge liberal', 1387), but at the same time this was flanked by the negative sense of 'unrestrained'. **Liberty**, though having an early general sense of freedom, had a strong sense from C15 of formal permission or privilege; this survives in the naval phrase **liberty boat** and, though often not noticed as such, in the conservative phrase **liberties of the subject**, where **liberty** has no modern sense but the old sense of certain rights granted within an unquestionable subjection to a particular sovereignty. The other word for such a formal right was *licence*, and the play of feeling, towards the sense of 'unrestrained', can be clearly seen in the development, from C16, of *licentious*. **Liberal**, as well as being widely used in the stock phrase *lyberal arbytre* (C15) – free will, was close to *licentious* in such uses as Shakespeare's

> Who hath indeed most like a liberall villaine
> Confest the vile encounters they have had.
> (*Much Ado About Nothing*, IV, i)

A weaker but related form of this sense is clear in the development, from lC18, of the sense of 'not rigorous', which could be taken either as 'not harsh' or as 'not disciplined'.

The affirmation of **liberal**, in a social context quite different from that of a special class of free men, came mainly in lC18 and eC19, following the strong general sense of **Liberty** from mC17. It was used in the sense of 'open-minded', and thence of 'unorthodox', from lC18: 'liberal opinions' (Gibbon, 1781). The adjective is very clear in a political sense in an example from 1801: 'the extinction of every vestige of freedom, and of every liberal idea with which they are associated'. This led to the formation of the noun as a political term, proudly and even defiantly announced in the periodical title, *The Liberal* (1822). But, as often since, this term for an unorthodox political opinion was given, by its enemies, a foreign flavour. There was talk of the 'Ultras' and 'Liberals' of Paris in 1820, and some early uses were in a foreign form: *Liberales* (Southey, 1816); *Liberaux* (Scott, 1826). The term was applied in this sense as a nickname to advanced Whigs and Radicals by their opponents; it was then consciously adopted and within a generation was powerful and in its turn orthodox. **Liberality**, which since C14 had carried the sense of generosity, and later of open-mindedness, was joined by political **Liberalism** from eC19.

In the established party-political sense, **Liberal** is now clear enough. But **liberal** as a term of political discourse is complex. It has been under regular and heavy attack from conservative positions, where the senses of lack of restraint and lack of discipline have been brought to bear, and also the sense of a (weak and sentimental) generosity. The sense of a lack of rigour has also been drawn on in intellectual disputes. Against this kind of attack, **liberal** has often been a group term for PRO-GRESSIVE or RADICAL (qq.v.) opinions, and is still clear in this sense, notably in USA. But **liberal** as a pejorative term has also been widely used by socialists and especially Marxists. This use shares the conservative sense of lack of rigour and of weak and sentimental beliefs. Thus far it is interpreted by **liberals** as a familiar complaint, and there is a special edge in their reply to socialists, that they are concerned with political freedom and that socialists are not. But this masks the most serious sense of the socialist use, which is the historically accurate observation that **liberalism** is a doctrine based on INDIVI-DUALIST (q.v.) theories of man and society and is thus in fundamental conflict not only with SOCIALIST (q.v.) but with most strictly SOCIAL (q.v.) theories. The further observation, that **liberalism** is the highest form of thought developed within BOURGEOIS (q.v.) society and in terms of CAPITALISM (q.v.), is also relevant, for when **liberal** is not being used as a loose swear-word, it is to this mixture of liberating and limiting ideas that it is intended to refer. **Liberalism** is then a doctrine of certain necessary kinds of freedom but also, and essentially, a doctrine of possessive individualism.

See ART, INDIVIDUAL, PROGRESSIVE, RADICAL, SOCIALIST, SOCIETY

LITERATURE

Literature is a difficult word, in part because its conventional contemporary meaning appears, at first sight, so simple. There is no apparent difficulty in phrases like **English literature** or

contemporary literature, until we find occasion to ask whether all books and writing are **literature** (and if they are not, which kinds are excluded and by what criteria) or until, to take a significant example, we come across a distinction between **literature** and *drama* on the grounds, apparently, that drama is a form primarily written for spoken performance (though often also to be read). It is not easy to understand what is at stake in these often confused distinctions until we look at the history of the word.

Literature came into English, from C14, in the sense of polite learning through reading. Its fw, *littérature*, F, *litteratura*, L, had the same general sense. The rw is *littera*, L – letter (of the alphabet). Thus a man of **literature**, or of *letters*, meant what we would now describe as a man of wide reading. Thus: 'hes nocht sufficient literatur to undirstand the scripture' (1581); 'learned in all literature and erudition, divine and humane' (Bacon, 1605). It can be seen from the Bacon example that the noun of condition – being well-read – is at times close to the objective noun – the books in which a man is well-read. But the main sense can be seen from the normal adjective, which was **literate**, from C15, rather than **literary**, which appeared first in C17 as a simple alternative to **literate** and only acquired its more general meaning in C18. As late as Johnson's *Life of Milton*, this original usage was still normal: 'he had probably more than common literature, as his son addresses him in one of his most elaborate Latin poems' (1780).

Literature, that is to say, corresponded mainly to the modern meanings of **literacy**, which, probably because the older meaning had then gone, was a new word from lC19. It meant both an ability to read and a condition of being well-read. This can be confirmed from the negatives. **Illiterate** usually meant poorly-read or ill-educated: 'Judgis illitturate' (1586); 'my illeterate and rude stile' (1597); and as late as Chesterfield (1748): 'the word *illiterate*, in its common acceptance, means a man who is ignorant of those two languages' (Greek and Latin). Even more clearly there was the now obsolete **illiterature**, from lC16: 'the cause . . . ignorance . . . and . . . illiterature' (1592). By contrast, from eC17, the **literati** were the highly-educated.

But the general sense of 'polite learning', firmly attached to the idea of printed books, was laying the basis for the later specialization. Colet, in C16, distinguished between **literature** and what he called **blotterature**; here the sense of inability to write clear letters is extended to a kind of book which was below the standards of polite learning. But the first certain signs of a general change in meaning are from C18. **Literary** was extended beyond its equivalence to **literate**: probably first in the general sense of well-read but from mC18 to refer to the practice and profession of writing: 'literary merit' (Goldsmith, 1759); 'literary reputation' (Johnson, 1773). This appears to be closely connected with the heightened self-consciousness of the profession of authorship, in the period of transition from patronage to the bookselling market. Where Johnson had used **literature** in the sense of being highly literate in his *Life of Milton*, in his *Life of Cowley* he wrote, in the newly objective sense: 'an author whose pregnancy of imagination and elegance of language have deservedly set him high in the ranks of literature'. Yet **literature** and **literary**, in these new senses, still referred to the whole body of books and writing; or if distinction was made it was in terms of falling below the level of polite learning rather than of particular kinds of writing. A philosopher such as Hume quite naturally described his 'Love of literary Fame' as his 'ruling passion'. All works within the orbit of polite learning came to be described as **literature** and all such interests and practices as **literary**.

What has then to be traced is the attempted and often successful specialization of **literature** to certain kinds of writing. This is difficult just because it is incomplete; a **literary editor** or a **literary supplement** still deals generally with all kinds of books. But there has been a specialization to a sense which is sometimes emphasized (because of the remaining uncertainty) in phrases like **creative literature** and **imaginative literature** (cf. CREATIVE and IMAGINATIVE as descriptions of kinds of writing; cf. also FICTION). In relation to the past, **literature** is still a relatively general word: Carlyle and Ruskin, for example, who did not write novels or poems or plays, belong to **English literature**. But there has been a steady distinction and separation of other kinds of writing – philosophy, essays, history, and so on – which may or may not possess **literary merit** or be of **literary interest** (meaning that 'in addition to' their intrinsic interest as philosophy or history or whatever they are 'well written') but which are not now normally described as **literature**, which may be understood as well-written books but which is even more clearly understood as well-written books of an *imaginative* or *creative* kind. The teaching of English, especially in universities, is understood as the teaching of **literature**, meaning mainly poems and plays and novels; other kinds of 'serious' writing are described as *general* or *discursive*. Or there is **literary criticism** – judgment of how a (*creative* or *imaginative*) work is written – as distinct, often, from discussion of 'ideas' or 'history' or 'general subject-matter'. At the same time many, even most poems and plays and novels are not seen as **literature**; they fall below its level, in a sense related to the old distinction of *polite learning*; they are not 'substantial' or 'important' enough to be called **works of literature**. A new category of **popular literature** or the **sub-literary** has then to be instituted, to describe works which may be *fiction* but which are not *imaginative* or *creative*, which are therefore devoid of AESTHETIC (q.v.) interest, and which are not ART (q.v.).

Clearly the major shift represented by the modern complex of **literature**, *art*, *aesthetic*, *creative* and *imaginative* is a matter of social and cultural history. **Literature** itself must be seen as a late medieval and Renaissance isolation of the skills of reading and of the qualities of the book; this was much emphasized by the development of printing. But the sense of *learning* was still inherent, and there were also the active arts of *grammar* and *rhetoric*. Steadily, with the predominance of print, *writing* and *books* became virtually synonymous; hence the subsequent confusion about *drama*, which was writing for speech (but then Shakespeare is obviously **literature**, though with the *text* proving this). Then **literature** was specialized towards *imaginative writing*, within the basic assumptions of Romanticism. It is interesting to see what word did service for this before the specialization. It was, primarily, *poetry*, defined in 1586 as 'the arte of making: which word as it hath alwaies beene especially used of the best of our English Poets, to expresse the very faculty of speaking or wryting Poetically' (note the inclusion of *speaking*). Sidney wrote in 1581: 'verse being but an ornament and no cause to Poetry: sith there have been many most excellent Poets, that never versified.' The specialization of *poetry* to metrical composition is evident from mC17, though this was still contested by Wordsworth: 'I here use the word "Poetry" (though against my own judgment) as opposed to the word "Prose", and synonymous with metrical composition' (1798). It is probable that this specialization of *poetry* to verse, together with the increasing importance of prose forms such as the NOVEL (q.v.), made **literature** the most available general word.

But this was in its turn affected by an emphatic definition of appropriate subject-matter. *Poetry* had been the high skills of writing and speaking in the special context of high imagination; the word could be moved in either direction. **Literature**, in its C19 sense, repeated this, though excluding speaking. But it is then problematic, not only because of the further specialization to *imaginative* and *creative* subject-matter (as distinct from *imaginative* and *creative* writing) but also because of the new importance of many forms of writing for speech (*broadcasting* as well as *drama*) which the specialization to books seemed by definition to exclude.

Significantly in recent years **literature** and **literary**, though they still have effective currency in post-C18 senses, have been increasingly challenged, on what is conventionally their own ground, by concepts of *writing* and *communication* which seek to recover the most active and general senses which the extreme specialization had seemed to exclude. Moreover, in relation to this reaction, **literary** has acquired two unfavourable senses, as belonging to the printed book or to past literature rather than to active contemporary writing and speech; or as (unreliable) evidence from books rather than 'factual inquiry'. This latter sense touches the whole difficult complex of the relations between *literature* (poetry, *fiction, imaginative* writing) and real or *actual* experience. Meanwhile **literacy** and **illiteracy** have become key social concepts, in a much wider perspective than in the pre-C19 sense. **Illiteracy** was extended, from C18, to indicate general inability to read and write, and **literacy**, from lC19, was a new word invented to express the achievement and possession of what were increasingly seen as general and necessary skills.

See AESTHETIC, ART, CREATIVE, FICTION, IMAGE, MYTH, NOVEL

M

MAN

There is an important and interesting use of **Man**, in the singular and with a capital letter, to describe the whole human race, the human species or **mankind**. The identity of **man** (human) with **man** (male) has persisted in English longer than in most European languages. The abstract use in English is interesting in that it has no article (cf. *l'homme, der Mensch*): 'the anatomy of man and the ape'. In descriptions of the physical species, **Man** presents few problems; only the sexual specialization is difficult in some contexts (cf. a recent title *The Descent of Woman*). Sexual specialization has also made the word problematic in some general social and philosophical theory (cf. Paine's *Rights of Man* (human) and Wollstonecraft's *Rights of Woman* (feminine)). But it is the singular use, apart from sexual specialization, that is most interesting in other than physical contexts. There are some obvious applied and extended uses, as in 'the future of man on this planet', which raise no real problems. But in some other uses the singular raises, and as often conceals, problems. It was simpler when **Man** was a generalization distinguished from *God*, as in 'man purposith and god disposith' (1450); the one singular depended on the other, and the creation and control of **Man** (**Man-kind**) by *God* was assumed. What is interesting is that this assumed common condition – spiritual and metaphysical – continued to be expressed in the same singular form when universal moral and social qualities were being described, as in the Enlightenment. The singular universal then stood on its own. The use continued, moreover, even into periods when the emphasis was on human self-development (*Man Makes Himself*) and was remarkably common even within a deliberate historical and cultural relativism. It is then very difficult to distinguish generic assumptions from what are really social and cultural propositions, as in the range from 'Man has invented the wheel, the compass and the internal combustion engine' to 'Man is naturally a hunter' and 'Man has now entered the critical period of industrial civilization.' All these uses are possible, but it is usually important to be aware of the implications of the capitalized singular (with its assumptions of universality), and indeed of the often similar implications of the abstract **Men** used in the same sense. If the uses were confined to metaphysical, universalist or historically unilinear contexts, the problem would be smaller; but the habits of these assumptions are now embedded in the language, so that there is persistence even when actual historical and cultural variation is being stressed. The uses in Marxism, where there was an original and significant and perhaps unresolved difficulty about the concept of 'species-being', require special attention for just this reason.

See HUMANITY

MANAGEMENT

When we now speak of negotiations between **management** and *men*, we are expressing, in both terms, a particular version of social and economic relationships. The word **manage** seems to have come into English directly from *maneggiare*, It. – to handle and especially to handle or train horses. Its earliest English uses were in this context. The fw is *manidiare*, vL – to handle, from rw *manus*, L – hand. **Manage** was quickly extended to operations of war, and from eC16 to a general sense of taking control, taking charge, directing. Its subsequent history is affected by confusion with *ménager*, F – to use carefully, from *ménage* – household, which goes back to *mansionaticum*, vL and rw *mansionem*, L – a dwelling (which led directly to *maison*, F – house). There is ample evidence from lC17 and C18 of overlap between **manage** and **menage**, expressed in variations of spelling. This affected the senses of **manager**, from trainer and director (*maneggiare*) to careful housekeeper (*ménager*). This range is still active in the language, with applications from sport to business to housekeeping (**a good manager**).

Management was originally a noun of process for any of these activities. It seems to have been first specialized to the idea of a collective body of men, and thence a controlling or directing institution, in the theatre, where **the management** is still a live phrase. This was from mC18, but **manage** and **manager** were in the same period being increasingly used for financial and business activities. **Management** as a collective noun was extended in C19 to the running of newspapers. **The managers**, in an institutional sense, was steadily extended from mC18 to describe those in charge of or directing a public institution (workhouse, school). In business, **manager** was still not clearly distinguished from *agent* and from the special use equivalent to *receiver* (one who manages a business which has passed into the control of the courts). As the term was extended in business there was still a clear distinction between owners and directors on the one hand and managers on the other; **manager** as *agent* was in this sense still relevant.

The increasingly general C20 sense of **management** is related to two historical tendencies. First, there was the increasing employment of a body of paid agents to administer increasingly large business concerns; these became, with a new emphasis, **the managers** or **the management**, as distinct from public agents who were called (from residual reference to the monarchy) *civil servants* or, more generally, the BUREAUCRACY (q.v.). This class of public officials is still distinguished from **management**, even where their actual activities are identical; this follows the received and ideologically affected distinction between public and private business. The polite term for semi-public institutions has been *the administration* (though this is also used as a political synonym for *government*). The second historical tendency was in effect a mystification of capitalist economic relationships. There used to be negotiations (C19) between *masters* and *men*. Increasingly, in C20, the softer word *employers* was substituted for *masters*, and is still often used. But in mC20 **the management** has been increasingly preferred; it is an abstract term, and implies abstract and apparently disinterested criteria. It is worth noting that there is still lively controversy over what has been called the **managerial revolution**, in which, within capitalism, paid **managers** are said to have taken over effective control of large companies from their legal owners or shareholders. If this were true (and the facts are extremely complicated) the **management** would now be the *employers*, and the abstract and apparently neutral term would still have ideological effect. Where *directors* fit into this process is of course part of the central argument.

The description of negotiations between **management** and *men* often displaces the real character of negotiations between *employers* and *workers* and further displaces the character of negotiations about relative shares of the labour product to a sense of dispute between the general 'requirements' of a process (the abstract **management**) and the 'demands' of actual individuals (*men*). The internal laws of a particular capitalist institution or system can then be presented as general, abstract or technical laws, as against the merely selfish desires of individuals. This has powerful ideological effects.

Meanwhile one example of the older sense of **manage** (from *maneggiare*) can be found in the common phrase **man-management**. This began in the army, and had direct relations with the earlier training and control of horses. In mC20 it has been widely extended as an operative phrase in many kinds of employment and direction of labour, and is widely used in **management-training** courses, not always with full consciousness of what it implies. The more negotiable because more abstract phrase is **personnel management**, where the human beings on each side of the process have been fully generalized and abstracted.

See BUREAUCRACY, LABOUR, MAN

MASSES

Mass is not only a very common but a very complex word in social description. **The masses**, while less complex, is especially interesting because it is ambivalent: a term of contempt in much conservative thought, but a positive term in much socialist thought.

Terms of contempt for the majority of a people have a long and abundant history. In most early descriptions the significant sense is of *base* or *low*, from the implicit and often explicit physical model of a society arranged in successive stages or layers. This physical model has determined much of the vocabulary of social description; compare *standing, status, eminence, prominence* and the description of social *levels, grades, estates* and *degrees*. At the same time more particular terms of description of certain 'low' groups have been extended: *plebeian* from Latin *plebs*; *villein* and *boor* from feudal society. COMMON (q.v.) added the sense of 'lowness' to the sense of mutuality, especially in the phrase 'the common people'. *Vulgar* by C16 had lost most of its positive or neutral senses and was becoming a synonym for 'low' or 'base'; a better derived sense was preserved in *vulgate*. *The people* itself became ambiguous, as in C17 arguments which attempted to distinguish the 'better sort' of people from the *meaner* or *basest*. The grand ratifying phrase, *the people*, can still be applied, according to political position, either generally or selectively.

Terms of open political contempt or fear have their own history. In C16 and C17 the key word was *multitude* (see Christopher Hill: 'The Many-Headed Monster' in *Change and Continuity in Seventeenth-century England*; 1974). Although there was often reference to *the vulgar* and *the rabble*, the really significant noun was *multitude*, often with reinforcing description of numbers in *many-headed*. There were also *base multitude*, *giddy multitude*, *hydra-headed monster multitude* and *headless multitude*. This stress on large numbers is significant when compared with the later development of **mass**, though it must always have been an obvious observation that the most evident thing about 'the common people' was that there were so many of them.

Base is an obvious sense, ascribing lowness of social condition and morality. *Idiot* and *giddy* may have originally overlapped, from 'ignorant' and 'foolish' to the earlier sense of *giddy* as 'crazed' (it had signified, originally, possession by a god). But the sense of *giddy* as 'unstable' became historically more important; it is linked with the Latin phrase *mobile vulgus* – the unstable common people, which by lC17 was being shortened to English *mob* (though still under protest in eC18, among others from Swift, who condemned it, nicely, as a *vulgarism*). The common C16 and C17 *multitude* was steadily replaced, from C18, by *mob*, though with continuing support from the usual battery of *vulgar*, *base*, *common* and *mean*. *Mob* has of course persisted into contemporary usage, but it has been since eC19 much more specific: a particular unruly crowd rather than a general condition. The word that then came through, for the general condition, was **mass**, followed by **the masses**.

Mass had been widely used, in a range of meanings, from C15, from fw *masse*, F and *massa*, L – a body of material that can be moulded or cast (the root sense was probably of kneading dough) and by extension any large body of material. Two significant but alternative senses can be seen developing: (i) something amorphous and indistinguishable; (ii) a dense aggregate. The possible overlaps and variations are obvious. There was the use in *Othello*: 'I remember a masse of things, but nothing distinctly'. There is the significant use in Clarendon's *History of the Rebellion*, on the edge of a modern meaning: 'like so many atoms contributing jointly to this mass of confusion now before us'. Neutral uses of **mass** were developing in the physical sciences, in painting and in everyday use to indicate bulk. (The religious **mass** was always a separate word, from *missa*, L – sent, dismissed, and thence a particular service.) But the social sense can be seen coming through in lC17 and eC18: 'the Corrupted Mass' (1675); 'the mass of the people' (1711); 'the whole mass of mankind' (1713). But this was still indeterminate, until the period of the French Revolution. Then a particular use was decisive. As Southey observed in 1807: 'the levy in mass, the telegraph and the income-tax are all from France.' Anna Seward had written in 1798: 'our nation has almost risen in mass'. In a period of revolution and open social conflict many of the things that had been said, during the English Revolution, about *the multitude* were now said about **the mass**, and by the 1830s, at latest, **the masses** was becoming a common term, though still sometimes needing a special mark of novelty. A sense of the relation of the term to the INDUSTRIAL REVOLUTION (qq.v.) appears to be evident in Gaskell's 'the steam engine has drawn together the population into dense masses' (*The Manufacturing Population of England*, 6; 1833). Moore in 1837 wrote: 'one of the few proofs of good Taste that "the masses", as they are called, have yet given', and Carlyle, in 1839: 'men . . . to whom millions of living fellow-creatures . . . are "masses", mere "explosive masses for blowing down Bastilles with"', for voting at hustings for *us*'. These two examples neatly illustrate the early divergence of implication. Moore picked up the new word, in a cultural context, to indicate 'lowness' or 'vulgarity' as distinct from TASTE (q.v.). Carlyle was aware of the precise historical reference to the revolutionary *levée en masse* but was also sufficiently aware of the established usage in physical science to carry through the metaphor of explosion. He also, significantly, linked the revolutionary usage, which he condemned as manipulative, with the electoral or parliamentary usage – 'voting at hustings for *us*' – which was given the same manipulative association.

The senses are thus very complex, for there is a persistence of the earlier senses (i) and (ii) of **mass**. Sense (i), of something amorphous and indistinguishable, persisted especially in the established phrase **in the mass**, as in Rogers (1820): 'we condemn millions in the mass as vindictive'; or Martineau (1832): 'we speak of society as one thing, and regard men in the mass', where what is implied is a failure to make necessary distinctions. Increasingly, however, though less naturally in English than in either French or German, the positive sense (ii), of a dense aggregate, was given direct social significance, as in the directly comparable *solidarity*. It was when the people acted together, 'as one man', that they could effectively change their condition. Here what had been in sense (i) a lack of necessary distinction or discrimination became, from sense (ii), an avoidance of un- necessary division or fragmentation and thus an achievement of unity. Most English radicals continued to use *the people* and its variations – *common people, working people, ordinary people* – as their primary positive terms, but **the masses** and its variants – **the broad masses, the working masses, the toiling masses** – have continued to be specifically used (at times in imperfect translation) in the revolutionary tradition.

In the modern social sense, then, **masses** and **mass** have two distinguishable kinds of implication. **Masses** (i) is the modern word for *many-headed multitude* or *mob*: low, ignorant, unstable. **Masses** (ii) is a description of the same people but now seen as a positive or potentially positive social force. The distinction became critical in many of the derived and associated forms. **Mass meeting**, from mC19, was sense (ii): people came together for some common social purpose (though the derogatory **like a mass meeting** is significant as a reaction). But sense (i), as in 'there are very few original eyes and ears; the great mass see and hear as they are directed by others' (S. Smith, 1803), has come through in C20 in several formations: **mass society, mass sug- gestion, mass taste**. Most of these formations have been relatively sophisticated kinds of criticism of DEMOCRACY (q.v.), which, having become from eC19 an increasingly respectable word, seemed to need, in one kind of thought, this effective alternative. **Mass-democracy** can describe a manipulated political system, but it more often describes a system which is governed by un- instructed or ignorant preferences and opinions: the classical complaint against *democracy* itself. At the same time several of these formations have been influenced by the most popular among them: **mass production**, from USA in the 1920s. This does not really describe the process of *production*, which in fact, as originally on an assembly line, is multiple and serial.

What it describes is a process of *consumption* (cf. CONSUMER), the **mass market**, where **mass** is a variation of sense (i), *the many-headed multitude* but now a *many-headed multitude* with purchasing power. **Mass market** was contrasted with *quality market*, retaining more of sense (i), but by extension **mass production** came to mean production in large numbers. The deepest difficulty of C20 uses of **mass** is then apparent: that a word which had indicated and which still indicates (both favourably and unfavourably) a solid aggregate now also means a very large number of things or people. The sense of a very large number has on the whole predominated. **Mass communication** and the **mass media** are by comparison with all previous systems not directed at **masses** (persons assembled) but at numerically very large yet in individual homes relatively isolated members of audiences. Several senses are fused but also confused: the large numbers reached (*the many-headed multitude* or *the majority of the people*); the mode adopted (*manipulative* or *popular*); the assumed taste (*vulgar* or *ordinary*); the resulting relationship (*alienated and abstract* or a *new kind of social communication*).

The most piquant element of the **mass** and **masses** complex, in contemporary usage, is its actively opposite social implications. To be engaged in **mass work**, to belong to **mass organizations**, to value **mass meetings** and **mass movements**, to live wholly in the service of **the masses**: these are the phrases of an active revolutionary tradition. But to study **mass taste**, to use the **mass media**, to control a **mass market**, to engage in **mass observation**, to understand **mass psychology** or **mass opinion**: these are the phrases of a wholly opposite social and political tendency. Some part of the revolutionary usage can be understood from the fact that in certain social conditions revolutionary intellectuals or revolutionary parties do not come from *the people*, and then see 'them', beyond themselves, as **masses** with whom and for whom they must work: **masses** as object or **mass** as material to be worked on. But the active history of the *levée en masse* has been at least as influential. In the opposite tendency, **mass** and **masses** have moved away from the older simplicities of contempt (though in the right circles, and in protected situations, the *mob* and *idiot multitude* tones can still be heard). The C20 formations are mainly ways of dealing with large numbers of people, on the whole indiscriminately perceived but crucial to several operations in politics, in commerce and in culture.

The **mass** is assumed and then often, ironically, divided into parts again: *upper* or *lower* ends of the **mass market**; the *better kind* of **mass entertainment**. **Mass society** would then be a society organized or perceived in such ways; but, as a final complication, **mass society** has also been used, with some relation to its earlier conservative context, as a new term in radical and even revolutionary criticism. **Mass society, massification** (usually with strong reference to the **mass media**) are seen as modes of disarming or incorporating the *working class*, the *proletariat*, **the masses**: that is to say, they are new modes of alienation and control, which prevent and are designed to prevent the development of an authentic *popular* consciousness. It is thus possible to visualize, or at least hope for, a **mass uprising** against **mass society**, or a **mass protest** against the **mass media**, or **mass organization** against **massification**. The distinction that is being made, or attempted, in these contrasting political uses, is between **the masses** as the SUBJECT (q.v.) and **the masses** as the *object* of social action.

It is in the end not surprising that this should be so. In most of its uses **masses** is a cant word, but the problems of large societies and of collective action and reaction to which, usually confusingly, it and its derivatives and associates are addressed, are real enough and have to be continually spoken about.

See COMMON, DEMOCRACY, POPULAR

MATERIALISM

Materialism and the associated **materialist** and **materialistic** are complex words in contemporary English because they refer (i) to a very long, difficult and varying set of arguments which propose **matter** as the primary substance of all living and non-living things, including human beings; (ii) to a related or consequent but again highly various set of explanations and judgments of mental, moral and social activities; and (iii) to a distinguishable set of attitudes and activities, with no necessary philosophical and scientific connection, which can be summarized as an overriding or primary concern with the production or acquisition of things and money. It is understandable that opponents of the views indicated in senses (i) and (ii) often take advantage of, or are themselves confused by, sense (iii) and its associations. Indeed in certain phases of sense (ii) there are plausible connections with elements of sense (iii), which can hardly, however, be limited to proponents of any of the forms of senses (i) and (ii). The loose general association between senses (i) and (ii) and sense (iii) is in fact an historical residue, which the history of the words does something to explain.

The central word, **matter**, has a suitably material primary meaning. It came into English, in varying forms, from fw *matere*, oF, from rw *materia*, L – a building material, usually *timber* (with which the word may be etymologically associated, as also with *domestic*); thence, by extension, any physical substance considered generally, and, again by extension, the substance of anything. In English this full range of meanings was established very early, though the most specific early sense was never important and was quickly lost. Among early established uses, **matter** was regularly distinguished from FORM (q.v.) which it was held was required to bring **matter** into *being*. There was a related distinction between **material** and *formal*, but the most popular distinction was between **material** and *spiritual*, where *spirit* was the effective theological specialization of *form*. **Matter** was also contrasted, from lC16, with *idea*, but the important modern **material**/*ideal* and **materialist**/ *idealist* contrasts, from eC18, were later than the **material**/*formal* and **material**/*spiritual* contrasts. It is this latter contrast which has most to do with the specific meanings of **material** and **materialist** in sense (iii). It is not easy to trace these, but there was a tendency to associate **material** with 'worldly' affairs and an associated distinction, of a class kind, between people occupied with **material** activities and others given to *spiritual* or LIBERAL (q.v.) pursuits. Thus Kyd (1588): 'not of servile or materiall witt, but . . . apt to studie or contemplat'; Dryden (1700): 'his gross material soul'. This tendency would probably have developed in any event, but it was to be crucially affected by the course and context of the philosophical argument.

Philosophical positions that we would now call **materialist** are at least as old as C5, BC, in the Greek atomists, and the fully developed Epicurean position was widely known through Lucretius. It is significant that in addition to simply physical explanations of the origins of nature and of life, this doctrine had connected explanations of civilization (the development of natural human powers within a given environment), of society (a contract for security against others), and of morality (a set of conventions which lead to happiness and which may be altered if they do not, there being no pre-existing values where the only natural force is self-interest). The key moment in English **materialism**, though still not given this name, was in Hobbes, where the fundamental premise was that of physical bodies in motion – MECHANICS (q.v.) – and where deduction was made from the laws of such bodies in motion to individual human behaviour (sensation and thought being forms of motion) and to the nature of society – human beings acting in relation to each other (and submitting to sovereignty for necessary regulation). In C18 France, for example in Holbach, it was comparably argued that all causal relationships were simply the laws of the motion of bodies, and, with a new explicitness, that alternative causes and especially the notion of God or any other kind of metaphysical creation or direction were false. It was from mC17 that doctrines of this kind became known as **materialist** and from mC18 as **materialism**. The regular association between physical explanations of the origins of nature and of life, and CONVENTIONAL or MECHANICAL (qq.v.) explanations of morality and society, had the understandable effect, much sharpened when they became explicit denials of religion, of transferring **materialism** and **materialist** in one kind of popular use to the sense of mere attitudes and forms of behaviour. In the furious counter-attack, by those who would give religious and traditional explanations of nature and life, and thence other kinds of cause in moral behaviour and social organization, **materialism** and **materialist** were joined to the earlier sense of **material** (worldly) to describe not so much the antecedent reasoning as the deduced moral and social positions, and then, in a leap of controversy, to transfer the notion of self-interest as the only natural force to 'selfishness' as a supposedly recommended or preferred way of life. It hardly needs to be pointed out that both the *conventional* and the *mechanical* forms of **materialist** moral argument had been concerned with how this force – 'self-interest' – might be or actually was regulated for mutual benefit. In C18 the usage was still primarily philosophical; by eC19 the rash and polemical extension from a proposition to a recommendation had deeply affected the senses of **materialism** and **materialist**, and the suitably looser **materialistic** followed from mC19.

So complex an argument cannot be resolved by tracing the

development of the words. Some people still assert that a selfish worldliness is the inevitable even if unintended consequence of the denial of any primary moral force, whether divine or human. Some read this conclusion back to qualify the physical arguments; others accept, explicitly or implicitly, the physical arguments but introduce new terms for social or moral explanation. In religious and quasi-religious usage, **materialism** and its associates have become catchwords for description and free association of anything from physical science to capitalist society, and also, significantly often, the socialist revolt against capitalist society. The arbitrary character of this popular association has to be seen both critically and historically. But what has also to be seen, for it bears centrally on this argument, is the later development of philosophical materialism. Thus Marx's critique, of the materialism hitherto described, accepted the physical explanations of the origin of nature and of life but rejected the derived forms of social and moral argument, describing the whole tendency as *mechanical* materialism. This form of materialism had isolated objects and had neglected or ignored *subjects* (see SUBJECTIVE) and especially human activity as *subjective*. Hence his distinction between a received **mechanical materialism** and a new **historical materialism**, which would include human activity as a primary force. The distinction is important but it leaves many questions unresolved. Human economic activity – men acting on a physical environment – was seen as primary, but in one interpretation all other activity, social, cultural and moral, was simply derived from (cf. DETERMINED by) this primary activity. (This allows, incidentally, a new free association within the popular sense of **materialism**: economic activity is primary, therefore **materialists** are primarily interested in activities which make money – which is not at all what Marx meant.) Marx's sense of interaction – men working on physical things and the ways they do this, and the relations they enter into to do it, working also on 'human nature', which they make in the process of making what they need to subsist – was generalized by Engels as DIALECTICAL (q.v.) **materialism**, and extended to a sense of laws, not only of historical development but of all natural or physical processes. In this formulation, which is one version of Marxism, **historical materialism** refers to human activity, **dialectical materialism** to universal processes. The point that matters, in relation to the history of the words, is that **historical materialism** offers explanations of the causes of sense (iii)

materialism – selfish preoccupation with goods and money – and so far from recommending it describes social and historical ways of overcoming it and establishing cooperation and mutuality. This is of course still a **materialist** reasoning as distinguished from kinds of reasoning described, unfavourably, as IDEALIST (q.v.) or *moralistic* or *utopian*. But it is, to take the complex senses of the words, a **materialist** argument, an argument based on **materialism**, against a **materialistic** society.

See DIALECTIC, IDEALISM, MECHANICAL, REALISM

MECHANICAL

Mechanical now appears to be derived from *machine* and to carry its main senses and implications. But this is misleading. **Mechanical** was earlier in English than *machine*, and has long had certain separable senses. The rw, as in Latin *machina*, had the sense of any contrivance, and **mechanical** (from fw *mechanicus*, L) was used from C15 to describe various mechanical arts and crafts; in fact the main range of non-agricultural productive work. For social reasons **mechanical** then acquired a derogatory class sense, to indicate people engaged in these kinds of work and their supposed characteristics: 'mechanicall and men of base condition' (1589); 'most Mechanicall and durty hand' (2 *Henry IV*, v); 'mean mechanical parentage' (1646). From eC17 there was a persistent use of **mechanical** in the sense of routine, unthinking activity. This may now be seen as an analogy with the actions of a machine, and the analogy is clear from mC18. But in the earliest uses the social prejudice seems to be at least as strong.

Machine, from C16, indicated any structure or framework, but from C17 began to be specialized to an apparatus for applying power and from C18 to a more complex apparatus of interrelated and moving parts. The distinction from *tool*, and the distinction between *machine-made* and *handmade*, belong to this phase, especially from lC18. But meanwhile **mechanical** had taken on a new and influential meaning, primarily from the new science of **mechanics**. Boyle wrote in 1671:

I do not here take the term, *Mechanicks*, in that stricter and more proper sense, wherein it is wont to be taken, when 'tis used onely to signifie the Doctrine about the Moving Powers (as the Beam, the Leaver, the Screws, and the Wedg) and of framing Engines to multiply Force; but . . . in a larger sense, for those Disciplines that consist of the Applications of pure Mathematicks to produce or modifie motion in inferior bodies.

In moving from a body of theory about specific practices to general theories about the laws of motion, **mechanics** began to interact with various religious theories and in practice often overlapped with MATERIALISM (q.v.). Thus we hear by lC17 of 'the Mechanical Atheist', and this led to lC18 **mechanism** – in which everything in the universe was seen as produced by mechanical forces. (**Mechanism**, from C17, had previously meant mainly a mechanical contrivance.) Thus **mechanical**, **the mechanical philosophy**, **mechanical doctrine** were identified as forms of materialist philosophy and were used sometimes descriptively, sometimes abusively, by religious and idealist thinkers to describe their main opponents. Eventually, from mC19, there was a distinction within MATERIALISM (q.v.) between **mechanical** and *historical* or *dialectical*.

This main development is not especially difficult to understand, but **mechanical** became exceptionally complicated from eC19, as a result of interaction with the new sense of *machine* and its extension to such descriptions as a **mechanical civilization**. This can mean a civilization which uses or depends on *machines* in the modern sense: an INDUSTRIAL (q.v.) *society*, as we now also say. But from eC19, in some kinds of thinking, there was an association or fusion or confusion of this sense (as in Coleridge and Carlyle) with the sense in which **mechanical** was opposed to *spiritual*, *metaphysical* or *idealist*. It was in the same period that there was a significant distinction between **mechanical** and ORGANIC (q.v.), which had previously been very close in meaning. The new *machines*, started up to work 'on their own', 'replacing human labour', suggested an association with an idea of the universe without a God or divine directing force, and also an association with the older (and socially affected) sense of routine, unthinking activity – thus action without consciousness.

The complexity of the word, whenever it is used beyond the descriptive sense directly related to machines, has remained difficult, even where some of the early associations and fusions have, as such, been discarded. Both the real sources of these senses of the word, and the various implied oppositions, need continual examination.

See INDUSTRY, MATERIALISM, ORGANIC

MEDIA

Medium, from *medium*, L – middle, has been in regular use in English from lC16, and from at latest eC17 has had the sense of an intervening or intermediate agency or substance. Thus Burton (1621): 'To the Sight three things are required, the Object, the Organ, and the Medium'; Bacon (1605): 'expressed by the Medium of Wordes'. There was then a conventional C18 use in relation to newspapers: 'through the medium of your curious publication' (1795), and this was developed through C19 to such uses as 'considering your Journal one of the best possible mediums for such a scheme' (1880). Within this general use, the description of a newspaper as a **medium** for advertising became common in eC20. The mC20 development of **media** (which had been available as a general plural from mC19) was probably mainly in this context. **Media** became widely used when broadcasting as well as the press had become important in COMMUNI-CATIONS (q.v.); it was then the necessary general word. MASS (q.v.) **media, media people, media agencies, media studies** followed.

There has probably been a convergence of three senses: (i) the old general sense of an intervening or intermediate agency or substance; (ii) the conscious technical sense, as in the distinction between print and sound and vision as **media**; (iii) the specialized capitalist sense, in which a newspaper or broadcasting service – something that already exists or can be planned – is seen as a **medium** for something else, such as advertising. It is interesting that sense (i) depended on particular physical or philosophical ideas, where there had to be a substance intermediate between a sense or a thought and its operation or expression. In most modern science and philosophy, and especially in thinking about language, this idea of a **medium** has been dispensed with; thus language is not a **medium** but a primary practice, and writing (for print) and speaking or acting (for broadcasting) would also be practices. It is then controversial whether print and broadcasting, as in the technical sense (ii), are **media** or, more strictly, material *forms* and sign systems. It is probably here that specific social ideas, in which writing and broadcasting are seen as DETERMINED (q.v.) by other ends – from the relatively neutral 'information' to the highly specific 'advertising' and 'propaganda' – confirm the received sense but then confuse any modern sense of COMMUNI-CATION (q.v.). The technical sense of **medium**, as something with its own specific and *determining* properties (in one version taking absolute priority over anything actually said or written or shown), has in practice been compatible with a social sense of **media** in which the practices and institutions are seen as agencies for quite other than their primary purposes.

It might be added that in its rapid popularization since the 1950s **media** has come often to be used as a singular (cf. *phenomena*).

See COMMUNICATION, MEDIATION

MEDIATION

Mediation has long been a relatively complex word in English, and it has been made very much more complex by its uses as a key term in several systems of modern thought. It came into English in C14, from fw *mediacion*, oF, *mediationem*, lL, from rw *mediare*, L – to divide in half, to occupy a middle position, to act as an intermediary. These three very different senses of the Latin word have all been present in English uses of **mediation** and of the verb **mediate** which was later formed from the noun and from the intervening adjective **mediate**. Thus two of the earliest examples of the use of **mediation** in English, both from Chaucer, carry two of the three main senses which became established: (i) interceding between adversaries, with a strong sense of reconciling them – 'By the popes mediacion . . . they been acorded' (*Man of Law's Tale*, c. 1386); (ii) a means of transmission, or agency as a medium – 'By mediacion of this litel tretis, I purpose to teche . . .' (*Astrolabe*, c. 1391). From c. 1425 the third early sense, now obsolete, is recorded: (iii), division or halving – 'mediacion is a takyng out of halfe a nombre out of a holle nombre'.

In general use senses (i) and (ii) became common. Sense (i)

was repeatedly used of the intercession of Christ between God and Man, and politically of the act of reconciling, or attempting to reconcile, adversaries. Sense (ii) covered intermediate agency, from material things – 'not to be touched but by the mediation of a sticke' (1615) – to mental acts – 'the understanding receives things by the mediation, first of the externall sences, then of the fancy' (1646). Meanwhile **mediate** as a verb carried both these senses, while **mediate** as an adjective carried not only the senses of intermediary and intermediate but of an indirect or dependent relationship of this kind, as which **mediate** was regularly contrasted with **immediate**. Thus: 'the Immediate Cause of Death, is the Resolution or Extinguishment of the Spirits . . . the Destruction or Corruption of the Organs is but the Mediate Cause' (Bacon, 1626); 'Perception is either immediate or mediate . . . Mediate, as when we perceive how (ideas) are related to each by comparing them both to a third' (Norris, 1704); 'all truth is either mediate . . . derived from some other truth . . . or immediate and original' (Coleridge, 1817).

There was thus a complex of senses ranging from reconciling to intermediate to indirect. It was into this complex that various specific uses, in certain modern systems of thought, were inserted by translation, usually of the German word *Vermittlung*. Sense (i), of reconciliation, was strongly present in Idealist philosophy: between God and Man, between Spirit and World, between Idea and Object, between Subject and Object. In its developed uses, three stages of this process can be distinguished: (a) finding a central point between two opposites, as in many political uses; (b) describing the interaction of two opposed concepts or forces within the totality to which they are assumed to belong, or do really belong; (c) describing such interaction as in itself substantial, with forms of its own, so that it is not the neutral process of the interaction of separate forms, but an active process in which the form of the mediation alters the things mediated, or by its nature indicates their nature.

The political sense of **mediation** as reconciliation has remained strong, but most modern philosophical uses depend on the idea of a substantial rather than a merely neutral or instrumental mediator. How this is defined of course varies. In idealist thought, the apparently separate entities were already parts of a totality; thus their mediation shared its laws. A different use of *totality*, in the Marxist tradition, emphasized irresolvable contradictions within what was nevertheless a total society: **mediation** then

171

sometimes took on the sense already present in English as indirect connection. It is still often used in an unfavourable sense, in a contrast between *real* and **mediated** relations, **mediation** being then one of the essential processes not only of consciousness but of IDEOLOGY (q.v.). This use of **mediation** has chimed with the modern use of MEDIA or MASS MEDIA (q.v.), where certain social agencies are seen as deliberately interposed between reality and social consciousness, to prevent an understanding of reality. A similar sense of the indirect, the devious or the misleading is present in some psychoanalytical thought, in which UNCONSCIOUS (q.v.) content undergoes **mediation** into the conscious mind. These uses depend on an assumed dualism, of reality and consciousness, or of unconscious and conscious: **mediation** acts between them, but indirectly or misleadingly. Yet there is also, in addition to these uses derived mainly from sense (b) above, a variety of uses which depend on sense (c). These are now perhaps the most important. **Mediation** is here neither neutral nor 'indirect' (in the sense of devious or misleading). It is a direct and necessary activity between different kinds of activity and consciousness. It has its own, always specific forms. The distinction is evident in a comment by Adorno: 'mediation is in the object itself, not something between the object and that to which it is brought. What is contained in communications, however, is solely the relationship between producer and consumer' (*Theses on the Sociology of Art*, 1967). All 'objects', and in this context notably works of art, are **mediated** by specific social relations but cannot be reduced to an abstraction of that relationship; the **mediation** is positive and in a sense autonomous. This is related, if controversially, to FORMALIST (q.v.) theory, in which the *form* (which may or may not be seen as a **mediation**) supersedes questions of the relationships which lie on either side of it, among its 'producers' or its 'consumers'.

The complexity of **mediation**, in current use, is then very apparent. Its most common, but conflicting, uses are: (1) the political sense of intermediary action designed to bring about reconciliation or agreement; (2) the dualist sense, of an activity which expresses, either indirectly or deviously and misleadingly, (and thus often in a falsely reconciling way) a relationship between otherwise separated facts and actions and experiences; (3) the formalist sense, of an activity which directly expresses otherwise unexpressed relations. It can be said that each of these senses has a better word: (1) *conciliation*; (2) IDEOLOGY or RATION-ALIZATION (qq.v.) (3) *form*. But in the real historical development of mediation as a concept it has been the relations between these distinct senses which, understandably, have been the subject of prolonged inquiry and argument, and especially the relations between (2) and (3). The long and intricate inquiries and arguments have left their varying marks on the word, which in its most thoughtful uses recalls, if it cannot solve, the inevitable and important difficulties.

See DIALECTIC, IDEALISM, MEDIA

MEDIEVAL

Medieval (originally spelled *mediaeval*) has been used since eC19 to indicate a period between the *ancient* and MODERN (q.v.) 'worlds'. It was preceded by *the middle Ages* (eC18) and *Middle Age* (eC17), following C16 Latin equivalents (*media aetas, medium aevum*). One mC18 definition (Chambers) named the period between Constantine and the fall of Constantinople. The *Ancient* and *Modern* contrast had developed in the Renaissance and was in English by lC16. The insertion of another or middle period came in C16 thought, but its emphasis depended on the revaluation of **medieval** art and life which occurred mainly from lC18 and especially from eC19, when the favourable contrast with *modern* (and especially with *modern industrial* or *modern commercial*) began to be made. The *Middle Ages* then took on their full capitalized definition, and **mediaeval** (from *medius*, L – middle, *aevum*, L – age) became the normal adjective. **Medievalism** and **medievalist** followed in mC19, but all three words divided into (i) the historical reference to the Middle Ages; (ii) advocacy of certain aspects of medieval life, religion, architecture and art (as variously in Cobbett, Pugin, Ruskin, Morris). In reaction to sense (ii), **medieval** acquired from mC19 a persistent unfavourable use, comparable with the unfavourable sense of *primitive* or with antiquated. Though dispute continues about the dating of the Middle Ages, which have indeed been sub-divided in several ways, the historical sense is now predominant.

See MODERN

MODERN

Modern came into English from fw *moderne*, F, *modernus*, lL, from rw *modo*, L – just now. Its earliest English senses were nearer our *contemporary*, in the sense of something existing now, just now. (*Contemporary*, or the equivalent – till mC19 – *cotemporary*, was mainly used, as it is still often used, to mean 'of the same period', including periods in the past, rather than 'of our own immediate time'.) A conventional contrast between *ancient* and **modern** was established in the Renaissance; a middle or MEDIEVAL (q.v.) period was not fully defined until C17. **Modern** in this comparative and historical sense was common from lC16. **Modernism**, **modernist** and **modernity** followed, in C17 and C18; the majority of pre-C19 uses were unfavourable, when the context was comparative. **Modernize**, from C18, had initial special reference to buildings (Walpole, 1748: 'the rest of the house is all modernized'); spelling (Fielding, 1752: 'I have taken the liberty to modernize the language'); and fashions in dress and behaviour (Richardson, 1753: 'He scruples not to modernize a little'). We can see from these examples that there was still a clear sense of a kind of alteration that needed to be justified.

The unfavourable sense of **modern** and its associates has persisted, but through C19 and very markedly in C20 there was a strong movement the other way, until **modern** became virtually equivalent to IMPROVED (q.v.) or satisfactory or efficient. **Modernism** and **modernist** have become more specialized, to particular tendencies. **Modernize**, which had become general by mC19 (cf. Thackeray (1860): 'gunpowder and printing tended to modernize the world'), and **modernization** (which in C18 had been used mainly of buildings and spelling) have become increasingly common in C20 argument. In relation to INSTITUTIONS (q.v.) or INDUSTRY (q.v.) they are normally used to indicate something unquestionably favourable or desirable. As catchwords of particular kinds of change the terms need scrutiny. It is often possible to distinguish **modernizing** and **modernization** from **modern**, if only because (as in many such actual programmes) the former terms imply some local alteration or improvement of what is still, basically, an old institution or system. Thus a

174

modernized democracy would not necessarily be the same as a **modern democracy**.

See IMPROVE, PROGRESSIVE

MONOPOLY

Monopoly can be difficult because it has a common literal meaning but also a rather wider meaning which has been historically important. It came into English in C16 from fw *monopolium*, lL, *monopolion*, Gk, from rw *monos*, Gk – alone, only, single, and *polein*, Gk – sell. Two senses appear in the early English examples: (i) the exclusive possession of trade in some article; (ii) the exclusive privilege granted by licence of selling some commodity. Thus, in sense (i):

Who knoweth not that Monopoly is, when one engrosseth some commodite into his owne handes, that none may sell the same but himself or from him (1606);

Monopoly is a kind of Commerce, in buying, selling, changing or bartering, usurped by a few, and sometimes but by one person, and forestalled from all others (1622).

And in sense (ii):

Monopolie ... a licence that none shall buy or sell a thing, but one alone (1604);
Monopolies of Sope, Salt, Wine, Leather, Sea-Cole ... (1641).

This privileged or licensed **monopoly** was especially important in eC17. The main sense that came through, however, was sense (i).

The difficulty arises when the literal meaning – exclusive single selling, which has some historical basis and can be a contemporary fact – is insisted upon as against uses of **monopoly** to mean effective domination of a market. The 1622 example shows that the word was used for possession by 'a few' as well as 'by one person', and there is an earlier mC16 example (from the translation of More's *Utopia*) which supports this:

Suffer not thies ryche men to bye up all, to ingrosse and forstalle, and with their monopolye to keep the market alone as please them.

This is clearly a description of the activity not of an individual but of a class. It is in this sense that we can understand the otherwise confusing use in the modern phrase **monopoly capitalism**, which became popular in eC20 to describe a phase of CAPITAL- ISM (q.v.) in which the market was either (a) organized by cartels and the like or (b) dominated by increasingly large corporations. Either use can be criticized from the literal sense of **monopoly**, which would suggest that large corporations, with or without formal cartels, do not compete in selling: i.e., that there is only one seller. Since this is manifestly not true, and since there are strict **monopolies** in state industries or utilities, especially the latter, the term **monopoly capitalism** can appear loose. Trade unions are then accused of being **monopolies**, controlling the terms and conditions of the selling of labour. But the range has been historically wide. The mC16 example from *Utopia* could be quite reasonably applied to the conditions that socialists now call capitalist **monopoly**.

See CAPITALISM

MYTH

Myth came into English as late as eC19, though it was somewhat preceded by the form *mythos* (C18) from fw *mythos*, lL, *mythos*, Gk – a fable or story or tale, later contrasted with *logos* and *historia* to give the sense of 'what could not really exist or have happened'. **Myth** and **mythos** were widely preceded in English by **mythology** (from C15) and the derived words (from eC17) **mythological, mythologize, mythologist, mythologian**. These all had to do with 'fabulous narration' (1609) but **mythology** and **mythologizing** were most often used with a sense of interpreting or annotating the fabulous tales. We have **mythological inter- pretation** from 1614, and there is a title of Sandys in 1632: *Ovid's Metamorphosis Englished, Mythologiz'd, and Represented in Figures*, with the same sense.

Two tendencies can be seen in the word in eC19. Coleridge used **mythos** in a sense which has become common: a particular imaginative construction (*plot* in the most extending sense). Meanwhile the rationalist *Westminster Review*, in perhaps the first use of the word, wrote in 1830 of 'the origin of myths' and of seeking their 'cause in the circumstances of fabulous history'.

Each of these references was retrospective, and **myth** alternated with *fable*, being distinguished from *legend* which, though perhaps unreliable, was related to history and from *allegory* which might be fabulous but which indicated some reality. However, from mC19, the short use of **myth** to mean not only a fabulous but an untrustworthy or even deliberately deceptive invention became common, and has widely persisted.

On the other hand, **myth** acquired in an alternative tradition a new and would-be positive sense, or rather senses. Before C19 **myths** had either been dismissed as mere fables (often as *pagan* or *heathen* fables), or treated as allegories or confused memories of origins and pre-history. But several new intellectual approaches were now defined. Myths were related to a 'disease of language' (Muller) in which a confusion of names led to personifications; to an animistic stage of human culture (Lang); and to specific rituals, which the myths gave access to (Frazer, Harrison; the popular association of 'myth and ritual' dates from this lC19 and eC20 work). With the development of anthropology, both this last sense, of accounts of rituals, and a different sense, in which myth, as an account of origins, was an active form of social organization, were strongly developed. From each version (which in varying forms have continued to contend with each other as well as with efforts to RATIONALIZE (q.v.) myths in such a way as to discredit them or to reveal their true (other) causes or origins) a body of positive popular usage has developed. **Myth** has been held to be a truer (deeper) version of reality than (secular) history or realistic description or scientific explanation. This view ranges from simple irrationalism and (often post-Christian) supernaturalism to more sophisticated accounts in which myths are held to be fundamental expressions of certain properties of the human mind, and even of basic mental or psychological human organization. These expressions are 'time-less' (permanent) or fundamental to particular periods or cultures. Related attempts have been made to assimilate this **mythic** function to the more general CREATIVE (q.v.) functions of art and literature, or, in one school, to assimilate art and literature to this view of **myth**. The resulting internal and external controversies are exceptionally intricate, and **myth** is now both a very significant and a very difficult word. Coming into the language only in the last hundred-and-fifty years, in a period of the disintegration of orthodox religion, it has been used negatively as a contrast to fact, HISTORY (q.v.) and SCIENCE (q.v.); has become involved with the difficult modern senses of *imagination*, *creative* and *fiction*; and has been used both to illustrate and to analyse 'human nature' in a distinctively post-Christian sense (though the mode of various schools using **myth** in this sense has been assimilated to Christian restatement and apology). Meanwhile, outside this range of ideas, it has the flat common sense of a false (often deliberately false) belief or account.

See CREATIVE, FICTION, HISTORY, IMAGE, RATIONAL

N

NATIONALIST

Nation (from fw *nation*, F, *nationem*, L – breed, race) has been in common use in English from lC13, originally with a primary sense of a racial group rather than a politically organized grouping. Since there is obvious overlap between these senses, it is not easy to date the emergence of the predominant modern sense of a political formation. Indeed the overlap has continued, in relation to such formations, and has led on the one hand to particularizing definitions of the **nation-state** and on the other hand to very complex arguments in the context of **nationalist** and **nationalism**. Clear political uses were evident from C16 and were common from lC17, though *realm*, *kingdom* and *country* remained more common until lC18. There was from eC17 a use of **the nation** to mean the whole people of a country, often in contrast, as still in political argument, with some group within it. The adjective **national** (as now in **national interest**) was used in this persuasive unitary sense from C17. The derived noun **national**, which is clearly political, is more recent and still alternates with the older *subject*. **Nationality**, which had been used in a broad sense from lC17, acquired its modern political sense jn lC18 and eC19.

    Nationalist appeared in eC18 and **nationalism** in eC19. Each became common from mC19. The persistent overlap between racial grouping and political formation has been important, since claims to be a **nation**, and to have **national** rights, often envisaged the formation of a **nation** in the political sense, even against the will of an existing political **nation** which included and claimed the loyalty of this grouping. It could be and is still often said, by opponents of **nationalism**, that the basis of the group's claims is *racial*. (*Race*, of uncertain origin, had been used in the sense of a common stock from C16. *Racial* is a C19 formation. In most C19 uses *racial* was positive and favourable, but discriminating and arbitrary theories of *race* were becoming more explicit in the same period, generalizing **national** distinctions to supposedly radical *scientific* differences. *Racial* was eventually affected by criticism of these kinds of thinking, and acquired both specific and loose negative senses. *Racialism* is a C20 formation to characterize, and usually to criticize, these explicit distinctions and discriminations.) It was also said that the claims were 'selfish', as being against the interests of **the nation** (the existing large political group). In practice, given the extent of conquest and domination, **nationalist** movements have been as often based on an existing but subordinate political grouping as upon a group distinguished by a specific language or by a supposed *racial* community. **Nationalism** has been a political movement in subjected countries which include several 'races' and languages (as India) as well as in subjected countries or provinces or regions where the distinction is a specific language or religion or supposed *racial* origin. Indeed in **nationalism** and **nationalist** there is an applied complexity comparable with that of NATIVE (q.v.). But this is often masked by separating **national feeling** (good) from **nationalist feeling** (bad if it is another's country, making claims against one's own), or by separating **national interest** (good) from **nationalism** (the asserted national interest of another group). The complexity has been increased by the usually separable distinction between **nationalism** (selfish pursuit of a nation's interests as against others) and **internationalism** (co-operation between nations). But **internationalism**, which refers to relations between **nation-states**, is not the opposite of **nationalism** in the context of a subordinate political group seeking its own distinct identity; it is only the opposite of selfish and competitive policies between existing political nations.

    Nationalize and **nationalization** were eC19 introductions to express the processes of making a nation or making something distinctively national. The modern economic sense emerged in mC19 and was not common before lC19, at first mainly in the context of the proposed **nationalization** of land. In the course of political controversy each word has acquired specific tones, so that it may be said without apparent difficulty that it either is or is not in the **national interest** to **nationalize.**

See NATIVE, STATUS

NATIVE

Native is one of those interesting words which, while retaining a substantial unity of meaning, are applied in particular contexts in ways which produce radically different and even opposite senses and tones. **Native** came into English as an adjective from C14 and as a noun from C15, from fw *natif*, F, which had earlier taken the form *naif* (giving English *naive* in the sense of artless and simple), from *nativus*, L – an adjective meaning innate or natural and *nativus*, mL – a noun formed from this. The root was the past participle of *nasci*, L – to be born.

Most of the early uses of **native** as an adjective were of a kind we would still recognize: innate, natural, or of a place in which one is born (cf. the related *nation*). A positive social and political sense, as in **native land, native country,** was strong from C16 onwards. But political conquest and domination had already produced the other and negative sense of **native,** in both noun and adjective, where it was generally equivalent to bondman or villein, born in bondage. Though the particular social usage became obsolete, the negative use of **native** to describe the inferior inhabitants of a place subjected to alien political power or conquest, or even of a place visited and observed from some supposedly superior standpoint, became general. It was particularly common as a term for 'non-Europeans' in the period of colonialism and imperialism, but it was also used of the inhabitants of various countries and regions of Britain and North America, and (in a sense synonymous with the disparaging use of *locals*) of the inhabitants of a place in which some superior person had settled. Yet all the time, alongside this use, **native** remained a very positive word when applied to one's own place or person.

The negative use, especially for 'non-Europeans', has become politically difficult, and the noun in this sense, though not yet the adjective, is probably disappearing. *Indigenous* has served both as a euphemism and as a more neutral term; it is fortunately more difficult to use in the sense which converts all others to inferiors (*to go indigenous* is obviously less plausible than **to go native**).

See NATION, PEASANT

NATURALISM

Naturalism is now primarily a critical term of literature or of art, but it is a more complex word, as its history indicates, than is usually now realized. **Naturalism** first appeared in English, from eC17, as a term in religious and philosophical argument. It had been preceded by **naturalist**, in the same context, from lC16. It followed a particular sense of NATURE (q.v.) in which there was a contrast with *God* or *spirit*. To study the **natural causes** of events, or to explain or justify morality from *nature* or *human nature*, was to be a **naturalist** and to propound **naturalism**, although the actual terms seem to have been conferred by their opponents. Thus: 'those blasphemous truth-opposing Heretikes, and Atheisticall naturalists' (1612); 'atheists or men who will admit of nothing but Morality, but Naturalismes, and humane reason' (1641). The implied opposite of **naturalism** in this original sense was thus **supernaturalism**, and this has remained true, though with many more negotiable alternative terms, in moral and ethical argument. But there was also the sense of the study of physical nature, and though this at times, for obvious reasons, overlapped with the moral sense, it also came through on its own. **Naturalist** was a common C17 term for **natural philosopher**, or as we should now say SCIENTIST (q.v.): in practice those whom we would now call *physicists* or *biologists*. As late as mC19 these senses of **naturalism** and **naturalist** (either (i) opposition to **supernaturalism** or (ii) the study of **natural history** – now mainly biology) were predominant.

The developments in relation to art and literature are complicated. There was first the effect of one of the senses of **natural**, as in 'simple and natural manner of writing' (mC18). This clearly affected one of the earliest new uses: 'the earliest prominent example of a naturalism without afterthought in the whole of Italian poetry' (Rossetti, 1850). Then, second, there was the effect of the sense of **natural history,** in its special characteristic of close and detailed observation: 'Fielding was a naturalist in the sense that he was an instinctive and careful observer.' Each of these senses, but especially the second, survives into the developed C20 term. But what is usually left out, in its history and critical discussion, is the third effect, from **naturalism** in the general philosophical and scientific sense, itself much influenced by the new and controversial developments in geology and biology and especially by Darwin's theory of **natural selection** in EVOLUTION (q.v.). The school of **naturalisme** in France was especially affected, as in Zola, by the idea of the application of scientific method in literature: specifically the study of heredity in the story of a family, but also, more generally, in the sense of describing and interpreting human behaviour in strictly **natural** terms, excluding the hypothesis of some controlling or directing force outside human nature. This **naturalism** was the basis of a major new kind of writing, and the philosophical position was explicitly argued: cf. Strindberg: 'the naturalist has abolished guilt by abolishing God'; 'the summary judgments on men given by authors . . . should be challenged by naturalists, who know the richness of the soul-complex, and recognize that "vice" has a reverse side very much like virtue' (*Preface to Lady Julie*, 1888). A new importance was given to the *environment* of characters and actions. (*Environment* in its special and now primary sense of the conditions, including the physical conditions, within which someone or something lives and develops, was an associated mC19 development from the earlier general sense of surroundings.) Character and action were seen as affected or determined by *environment*, which especially in a social and social-physical sense had then to be accurately described as an essential element of any account of a life. This connected with the sense of careful and detailed observation, from natural history, but it was not (as was later supposed) detailed description for its own sake, or for some conventional plausibility; rather it rested on the new and properly **naturalist** sense of the determining or decisive or influential effect of an environment on a life; (in the variations between *determining* and *influential* much of the subsequent development can be understood). There were also two specialized applications.

First, **naturalism** implied a critical searching-out of elements of the social environment which had hitherto and especially recently been excluded from literature; this explains the response recorded from the *Daily News* in 1881: 'that unnecessarily faithful portrayal of offensive incidents for which M. Zola has found the new name of "Naturalism" '. This is caricature but also characteristic. Second, there was a specialized application of a version of **natural selection,** as in Social Darwinism, to struggle and conflict in human relationships: 'true naturalism, which seeks out those points in life where the great conflicts occur' (Strindberg, *Preface to Lady Julie,* 1888). From each of these tendencies, but also from the older and more fundamental denial of supernaturalism, there was a conservative reaction which has continued, though often implicitly, to influence critical uses of **naturalism** as a term.

However, these uses combined with the sense of detailed and accurate observation coming through both from biological **naturalism** and from the older sense of **natural.** There was a complicated and often confused interaction between **naturalism** and REALISM (q.v.). In painting especially, **naturalism** and the new mC19 **naturalistic** were used to describe not only close observation but detailed 'reproduction' of natural objects: 'our modern school of **naturalistic** landscape painters'. The real complication is that, subsequently, further studies of *nature* and of *human nature,* in what were still in the older sense wholly **naturalist** terms, discovered processes and effects which were either not immediately available to visual observation or not representable in static external appearances. The thrust of what had been **naturalism** found other names for its processes and its methods, and **naturalism** itself was increasingly specialized to a style of accurate external representation. That is what the term now primarily means, but because of the specialization several crucial parts of the original argument have been left behind. One of the results is that various IDEALIST (q.v.) and **super-naturalist** versions of nature and of man have drawn apparent (and confusing) support from artistic methods (*impressionism, expressionism* and the like) which, in a broader view, can be seen as continuing, often quite directly and explicitly, the original **naturalist** impulse. At the same time there has been an interaction of **naturalism** with EMPIRICISM and MATERIALISM (qq.v.) in which the crucial argument affecting the sense of **naturalism** (with some support from *environmental* methods in description and explanation) has been about the relation between the observing SUBJECT (q.v.) and the observed (**natural** or **naturalistic**) *objects.*

Given the complexity of this history, **naturalism** is a very much more difficult word than most of its current uses suggest.

See EMPIRICAL, MATERIALISM, NATURE, POSITIVIST, REALISM

NATURE

Nature is perhaps the most complex word in the language. It is relatively easy to distinguish three areas of meaning: (i) the essential quality and character *of* something; (ii) the inherent force which directs either the world or human beings or both; (iii) the material world itself, taken as including or not including human beings. Yet it is evident that within (ii) and (iii), though the area of reference is broadly clear, precise meanings are variable and at times even opposed. The historical development of the word through these three senses is important, but it is also significant that all three senses, and the main variations and alternatives within the two most difficult of them, are still active and widespread in contemporary usage.

Nature comes from fw *nature*, oF and *natura*, L, from a root in the past participle of *nasci*, L – to be born (from which also derive *nation, native, innate*, etc.). Its earliest sense, as in oF and L, was (i) the essential character and quality *of* something. **Nature** is thus one of several important words, including *culture*, which began as descriptions of a quality or process, immediately defined by a specific reference, but later became independent nouns. The relevant L phrase for the developed meanings is *natura rerum* – the nature of things, which already in some L uses was shortened to *natura* – the constitution of the world. In English sense (i) is from C13, sense (ii) from C14, sense (iii) from C17, though there was an essential continuity and in senses (ii) and (iii) considerable overlap from C16. It is usually not difficult to distinguish (i) from (ii) and (iii); indeed it is often habitual and in effect not noticed in reading.

In a state of *rude* nature there is no such thing as a people . . .

The idea of a people . . . is wholly artificial; and made, like all other legal fictions, by common agreement. What the particular nature of that agreement was, is collected from the form into which the particular society has been cast.

Here, in Burke, there is a problem about the first use of **nature** but no problem – indeed it hardly seems the same word – about the second (sense (i)) use. Nevertheless, the connection and distinction between senses (i), (ii) and (iii) have sometimes to be made very conscious. The common phrase **human nature**, for example, which is often crucial in important kinds of argument, can contain, without clearly demonstrating it, any of the three main senses and indeed the main variations and alternatives. There is a relatively neutral use in sense (i): that it is an essential quality and characteristic of human beings to do something (though the something that is specified may of course be controversial). But in many uses the descriptive (and hence verifiable or falsifiable) character of sense (i) is less prominent than the very different kind of statement which depends on sense (ii), the directing inherent force, or one of the variants of sense (iii), a fixed property of the material world, in this case 'natural man'.

What has also to be noticed in the relation between sense (i) and senses (ii) and (iii) is, more generally, that sense (i), by definition, is a specific singular – the **nature of** something, whereas senses (ii) and (iii), in almost all their uses, are abstract singulars – the **nature of** all things having become singular **nature** or **Nature**. The abstract singular is of course now conventional, but it has a precise history. Sense (ii) developed from sense (i), and became abstract, because what was being sought was a single universal 'essential quality or character'. This is structurally and historically cognate with the emergence of *God* from *a god* or *the gods*. Abstract **Nature**, the essential inherent force, was thus formed by the assumption of a single prime cause, even when it was counterposed, in controversy, to the more explicitly abstract singular cause or force *God*. This has its effect as far as sense (iii), when reference to the whole material world, and therefore to a multiplicity of things and creatures, can carry an assumption of something common to all of them: either (a) the bare fact of their existence, which is neutral, or, at least as commonly, (b) the generalization of a common quality which is drawn upon for statements of the type, usually explicitly sense (iii), '**Nature** shows us that . . .'. This reduction of a multiplicity to a singularity, by the structure and history of the critical word, is then, curiously, compatible either with the assertion of a common quality, which the singular sense suits, or with the general or specific demonstration of differences, including the implicit or explicit denial of a common effective quality, which the singular form yet often manages to contain.

Any full history of the uses of **nature** would be a history of a large part of human thought. But it is possible to indicate, in outline, some of the critical uses and changes. There is, first, the very early and surprisingly persistent personification of singular **Nature**: Nature the goddess, 'nature herself'. This singular personification is critically different from what are now called 'nature gods' or 'nature spirits': mythical personifications of particular natural forces. 'Nature herself' is at one extreme a literal goddess, a universal directing power, and at another extreme (very difficult to distinguish from some non-religious singular uses) an amorphous but still all-powerful creative and shaping force. The associated 'Mother Nature' is at this end of the religious and mythical spectrum. There is then great complexity when this kind of singular religious or mythical abstraction has to coexist, as it were, with another singular all-powerful force, namely a monotheistic God. It was orthodox in medieval European belief to use both singular absolutes but to define God as primary and Nature as his minister or deputy. But there was a recurrent tendency to see Nature in another way, as an absolute monarch. It is obviously difficult to separate this from the goddess or the minister, but the concept was especially used to express a sense of fatalism rather than of providence. The emphasis was on the power of natural forces, and on the apparently arbitrary or capricious occasional exercise of these powers, with inevitable, often destructive effects on men.

As might be expected, in matters of such fundamental difficulty, the concept of **nature** was usually in practice much wider and more various than any of the specific definitions. There was then a practice of shifting use, as in Shakespeare's *Lear*:

Allow not nature more than nature needs,
Man's life's as cheap as beast's . . .

    . . . one daughter
Who redeems nature from the general curse
Which twain have brought her to.

That nature, which contemns its origin,
Cannot be border'd certain in itself . . .

 . . . All shaking thunder
Crack nature's moulds, all germens spill at once,
That make ungrateful man . . .

 . . . Hear, nature hear; dear goddess, hear . . .

In these examples there is a range of meanings: from nature as
the primitive condition before human society; through the sense
of an original innocence from which there has been a fall and a
curse, requiring redemption; through the special sense of a
quality of birth, as in the rootword; through again a sense of the
forms and moulds of nature which can yet, paradoxically, be
destroyed by the natural force of thunder; to that simple and
persistent form of the goddess, Nature herself. This complexity
of meaning is possible in a dramatic rather than an expository
mode. What can be seen as an uncertainty was also a tension:
nature was at once innocent, unprovided, sure, unsure, fruitful,
destructive, a pure force and tainted and cursed. The real
complexity of natural processes has been rendered by a complexity within the singular term.

There was then, especially from eC17, a critical argument
about the observation and understanding of nature. It could
seem wrong to inquire into the workings of an absolute monarch,
or of a minister of God. But a formula was arrived at: to understand the creation was to praise the creator, seeing absolute
power through contingent works. In practice the formula became
lip-service and was then forgotten. Paralleling political changes,
nature was altered from an absolute to a constitutional monarch,
with a new kind of emphasis on natural laws. Nature, in C18
and C19, was often in effect personified as a constitutional
lawyer. The laws came *from* somewhere, and this was variously
but often indifferently defined; most practical attention was
given to interpreting and classifying the laws, making predictions
from precedents, discovering or reviving forgotten statutes,
and above all shaping new laws from new cases: nature not as
an inherent and shaping force but as an accumulation and
classification of cases.

This was the decisive emergence of sense (iii): **nature** as the
material world. But the emphasis on discoverable laws –

> Nature and Nature's laws lay hid in night;
> God said, Let Newton be! and all was light! (Pope)

– led to a common identification of Nature with Reason: the object of observation with the mode of observation. This provided a basis for a significant variation, in which Nature was contrasted with what had been made of man, or what man had made of himself. A 'state of nature' could be contrasted – sometimes pessimistically but more often optimistically and even programmatically – with an existing state of society. The 'state of nature', and the newly personified idea of Nature, then played critical roles in arguments about, first, an obsolete or corrupt society, needing redemption and renewal, and, second, an 'artificial' or 'mechanical' society, which learning from **Nature** must cure. Broadly, these two phases were the Enlightenment and the Romantic movement. The senses can readily be distinguished, but there was often a good deal of overlapping. The emphasis on law gave a philosophical basis for conceiving an ideal society. The emphasis on an inherent original power – a new version of the much older idea – gave a basis for actual regeneration, or, where regeneration seemed impossible or was too long delayed, an alternative source for belief in the goodness of life and of humanity, as counterweight or as solace against a harsh 'world'.

Each of these conceptions of Nature was significantly static: a set of laws – the constitution of the world, or an inherent, universal, primary but also recurrent force – evident in the 'beauties of nature' and in the 'hearts of men', teaching a singular goodness. Each of these concepts, but especially the latter, has retained currency. Indeed one of the most powerful uses of nature, since lC18, has been in this selective sense of goodness and innocence. **Nature** has meant the 'countryside', the 'unspoiled places', plants and creatures other than man. The use is especially current in contrasts between town and country: **nature** is what man has not made, though if he made it long enough ago – a hedgerow or a desert – it will usually be included as **natural**. **Nature-lover** and **nature poetry** date from this phase.

But there was one further powerful personification yet to come: nature as the goddess, the minister, the monarch, the lawyer or the source of original innocence was joined by nature the selective breeder: natural selection, and the 'ruthless' competition apparently inherent in it, were made the basis for seeing nature as both historical and active. Nature still indeed had laws, but they were the laws of survival and extinction: species rose and flourished, decayed and died. The extraordinary accumulation of knowledge about actual evolutionary processes, and about the highly variable relations between organisms and their environments including other organisms, was again, astonishingly, generalized to a singular name. **Nature** was doing this and this to species. There was then an expansion of variable forms of the newly scientific generalization: 'Nature teaches . . .', 'Nature shows us that . . .'. In the actual record what was taught or shown ranged from inherent and inevitable bitter competition to inherent mutuality or co-operation. Numerous **natural** examples could be selected to support any of these versions: aggression, property, parasitism, symbiosis, co-operation have all been demonstrated, justified and projected into social ideas by selective statements of this form, normally cast as dependent on a singular **Nature** even while the facts of variation and variability were being collected and used.

The complexity of the word and the concept are hardly surprising, given the fundamental importance of the processes to which they refer. But since **nature** is a word which carries, over a very long period, many of the major variations of human thought, often, in any particular use, only implicitly yet with powerful effect on the character of the argument, it is necessary to be especially aware of its difficulty.

See COUNTRY, CULTURE, EVOLUTION, NATURALISM, SCIENCE

O

ORGANIC

Organic has a specific meaning in modern English, to refer to the processes or products of life, in human beings, animals or plants. It has also an important applied or metaphorical meaning, to indicate certain kinds of relationship and thence certain kinds of society. In this latter sense it is an especially difficult word, and its history is in any case exceptionally complicated.

Organ first appeared in English, from C13, to signify a musical instrument; something like the modern **organ**, in this context, appeared from C14. It had fw *organe*, oF, from *organum*, L, rw *órganon*, Gk – an instrument, engine or tool, with two derived senses: the abstract 'instrument' – agency, and musical instrument. There was a later applied sense of *órganon*, which was repeated in all the derived words: the eye as a 'seeing instrument', the ear a 'hearing instrument' and so on, whence **organ** as a part of the body, in English from eC15. But the full range of meanings – musical instrument, engine, instrument (**organ of opinion**) and part of the body – was present in English in C16. **Organic**, appearing from C16, followed first the sense of engine or tool. North, translating Plutarch in 1569, wrote 'to frame instruments and Engines (which are called mechanicall, or organicall)'. This is instructive in view of the later conventional contrast between **organic** and *mechanical*.

It is from the sense of **organ** as instrument or agency that **organize** and **organization** in their modern senses eventually developed, mainly from lC18 and eC19 (compare the developments of *society* and *civilization*). But each word was used earlier with the distinct physical reference, as, from C17, was **organism**.

Organic followed a different course, and indeed by C19 could be used in contrast with **organized**. The source of its common specific modern meaning is the major development of natural history and biology in C18, when it acquired a dominant reference to things living and growing. **Organic chemistry** was defined in eC19, acquiring the later more specialized sense of the chemistry of compounds of carbon from c. 1860. It was this development in biology and the 'life sciences' which laid the basis for the distinction between the former synonyms **organic** and MECHANICAL (q.v.).

The distinction was made in the Romantic movement, probably first in German, among the Nature Philosophers. Coleridge distinguished between **organic** and **inorganic** bodies or systems; in the **organic** 'the whole is everything and the parts are nothing', while in the **inorganic** 'the whole is nothing more than a collection of the individual parts'. This has obvious connections with the developing sense of **organized** and of **organism**, but the distinction was profoundly influenced by the contrast with *mechanical*, in opposition to *mechanical* philosophy and, unquestionably, to the new significance of machines in the Industrial Revolution. When applied to social organization, **organic** moved towards a contemporary specialization of *natural*: an **organic** society was one that has 'grown' rather than been 'made'. This acquired early relevance in criticism of revolutionary societies or proposals as *artificial* and against the 'natural order' of things. It later acquired relevance to contrasts between primarily agricultural and primarily INDUSTRIAL (q.v.) societies. Carlyle still had the complex sense in mind when he wrote of 'taming' the French Revolution, 'so that its intrinsic purpose can be made good, that it may become organic, and be able to live among other organisms and formed things.' Yet Burke, on the same subject, had used an opposite sense: comparing the English of 1688 with the French of 1789 he wrote: 'they acted by the ancient organized states in the shape of their old organization, and not by the organic moleculae of a disbanded people.' *Moleculae*, here, reminds us of a developing sense of *atomistic* to indicate relatively disorganized or disintegrating forms of society and social thought.

Through C19 and to mC20 **organic** was often used in social thought, mainly of a conservative kind. Leavis and Thompson, in *Culture and Environment* (1932) contrasted the ' "organized" modern state' with the 'Old England . . . of the organic community'. R. J. White, in *The Conservative Tradition* (1954), argued that 'it were better that a state should be a tree than an engine' and that 'diffusion of power is the characteristic of organic life, just as concentration of power is the characteristic of mechanism.' Bertrand Russell, in a different tradition, argued in *The Prospects of Industrial Civilization* (1923) that 'a machine is essentially organic, in the sense that it has parts which co-operate to produce a single useful result, and that the separate parts have little value on their own account' (the latter distinction recalling that made by Coleridge) and that, consequently, 'when we are exhorted to make society "organic" it is from machinery that we shall necessarily derive our imaginative models, since we do not know how to make society a living animal.' At some points, behind the modern controversy, the old metaphor of society as a *body*, with *members*, and hence an **organism** in an applied biological sense, seems to have some influence. But the fundamental overlap of meanings, and the difficult modern relationship between **organic**, **organized**, **organization** and **organism**, can tempt one to say that all societies are **organic** but that some are more **organic** – instrumentally planned or naturally evolving – than others.

Two other senses of **organic** still have effect. There is the modern specialized use of farming and of food, with a stress on *natural* rather than *artificial* fertilizers or growing and breeding methods. This is linked with general criticism of *industrial* society. There is also the wider sense, to describe a kind of relationship rather than, as in explicit social theory, a kind of society. **Organic** has been widely used in discussions of art and literature to indicate a significant relationship and interrelationship between parts of a work: **organic relation** or **organic connection**. This use, to indicate significantly or 'integrally' connected or related, is evident in descriptions not so much of societies as wholes but of specific internal relationships: 'an **organic** connection with the local community'. The word is easier but still not easy to use in this more specific sense.

See EVOLUTION, INDUSTRY, MECHANICAL, NATURE, SOCIETY

ORIGINALITY

Originality is a relatively modern word. It came into common use in English from lC18. It depends, of course, on a particular sense of **original**, which, with **origin** (from fw *origine*, F, *originem*, L – rise, beginning, source, from rw *oriri*, L – to rise) had been in the language from C14. In all its early uses **origin** had a static sense, of some point in time or some force or person from which subsequent things and conditions have arisen. But while **origin** has kept this inherently retrospective sense, **original** developed additional senses, so that **original sin** and **original law** and **original text** were joined by **original** in the sense of an authentic work of art (as distinct from a copy) and in the sense of a *singular* individual (where the eventual distinction between *singularity* and **originality** was to be crucial). In the case of works of art there was a transfer from the retrospective sense of **original** (the first work and not the copy) to what was really a sense close to *new* (not like other works). This happened mainly in

C17: 'of this Treatise, I shall only add, 'tis an Original' (Dryden, 1683). **An Original** was common in C18, in the sense of something singular or rare but also in a sense related to a new theory of art (cf. *genius*, which, after its root sense of spirit, was changing from 'characteristic disposition' and 'innate capacity' to 'exalted ability' in the same period). Young wrote in 1759: 'an Original . . . rises spontaneously from the vital root of genius; it *grows*, it is not made; Imitations are often a sort of *manufacture*, wrought up by those *mechanics*, *art* and *labour*, out of pre-existent materials not their own' (*Conjectures on Original Composition*, 12). Here an unusual number of key words in a new philosophy of art, nature and society are used together and interact. It is interesting that what has happened is a metaphorical extension from the older use of an **original** and its *imitations* (copies) to the new use of a kind of work distinguished by *genius, growing* not *made* and therefore not *mechanical*, taking its material from itself and not from others, and not merely a product of ART (q.v., but here still 'skill') and *labour* (effort). **Originality** then became a common term of praise of art and literature, not always with all Young's associations, but usually with most of them. A work was good not by comparison with others, or by a standard, but 'in its own terms'.

An original had also followed another course, in descriptions of persons. Wycherley wrote in *The Plain Dealer* (1676): 'I hate imitation, to do anything like other people. All that know me do me the honour to say, I am an original.' This is ambiguous in tone, and in application to persons the tone remained ambivalent, meaning an *eccentric* or at least an unusual INDIVIDUAL (q.v.) more often than it meant something interestingly new or, as in art, *authentic*. Yet by lC18 Hawkins wrote in his *Life* of Johnson: 'of singularity it may be observed, that, in general, it is originality; and therefore not a defect'. The transition from **an original** to **originality** seems to have confirmed the favourable sense, and this was subsequently predominant, producing the damning opposite of a person or writer of **no originality**.

As **originality** settled into the language it lost virtually all contact with **origin**; indeed the point is that it has no **origin** but itself. **Original**, however, has maintained both senses: the retrospective use and the description of something that is new and (usually) significant.

See ART, CREATIVE, INDIVIDUAL, MECHANICAL, ORGANIC

P

PEASANT

Peasant came from fw *paisant*, oF, (rw *pagus*, Rom, – country district, whence in another development *pagan*). It was in common use in English from C15, often distinguishable from *rustic* (fw *rusticus*, L – countryman; rw *rus*, L – country) in that **peasant** usually meant working on the land as well as living in the country. The collective noun **peasantry** came in C16. **Peasant** continued in its traditional sense in English until our own century, though increasingly in literary usage only. The social and economic transformation of English agriculture, from C16 to C19, created a special difficulty in uses of the word. The class of small working landholders in feudal or semi-feudal relationships to a landowning aristocracy, as found in pre-revolutionary France or Russia, and often described by this primarily French word, had virtually ceased to exist in England by lC18, and had been replaced by the new capitalist relationships of landlord, tenant and labourer. From this period, in English, **peasant** and **peasantry** have been either declining LITERARY (q.v.) words or, in social description, in effect re-imports from other languages, mainly French and Russian. There has also been a specialized use, again imitated from French and Russian, in which **peasant** is a loose term of abuse – in English usually very self-conscious and exaggerated – of 'uneducated' or 'common' people.

See COMMON, COUNTRY, EDUCATED, MASSES

PERSONALITY

Personality was something we all once had. In its earliest English sense it was the quality of being a person and not a thing, and this, from lC14, lasted at least until eC19: 'these capacities

194

constitute personality, for they imply consciousness and thought' (Paley, 1802). This is not its present day meaning, but the development is part of a significant process. **Person** came into English in C13 from fw *persone*, oF, *persona*, L. *Persona* had already gone through a remarkable development, from its earliest meaning of a mask used by a player, through a character in a play and a part that a man acts, to a general word for human being. (We have separated some of these senses out again, in variant forms, as in **personage** and the psychological use of **persona**.) The implicit metaphor can still haunt us. But in English, though there were early uses of **person** for a character played or assumed, the sense of an individual was equally early (C13), and between C14 and C16 this gathered, especially in **personal**, the senses we would now recognize as INDIVIDUAL and PRIVATE (qq.v.). *Personalitas*, L, had two senses, especially in medieval development: the general quality of being a person and not a thing (a complex term in scholastic argument about the Trinity but also a generalizing term for humanity), and the sense of personal belongings, which was taken into English as **personalty**. (A related reference can be traced in **personnel**, which was used in French in distinction from *matériel*, often in descriptions of an army; it was adopted as a foreign word in English from eC19 and had lost its italics by lC19. In *personnel management* it retains its sense of managing human property, who are nominally but not emphatically **persons**; see MANAGEMENT).

What matters, in **personality**, is the development from a general to a specific or unique quality. If we read, from 1655, 'for a time he loses the sense of his own personality and becomes a mere passive instrument of the deity', we take, almost inevitably, the developed modern meaning, for which we could substitute *individuality*. But this, though suggestive – it is the period of the transition – is far from certain, since we could also, within that form of thought, substitute HUMANITY (q.v.). It was in C18 that the individualizing reference became quite clear. Johnson defined **personality** as 'the existence or individuality of any one', and there were several uses for distinct personal identity. What is perhaps even more interesting is the emergence of the sense of lively personal identity, which is essential if we are to understand an example from 1795: 'even a French girl of sixteen, if she has but a little personality, is a Machiavel.' This, while apparently consonant with the developing use for qualified identity (e.g. 'overpowering personality' (Emerson, 1847); 'strong personality', 'dominant personality', 'weak personality', etc.,), engages a dimension in which we can speak of someone, in absolute distinction from the earliest sense, as having 'no personality'. This whole range is still active, but there has been a specialized C20 development – significantly, as so often, in both politics and entertainment – of a new noun from the most limited sense. There are 'leading personalities' (**personages** or, in an early specialized use, **persons**; **Very Important Persons** as the phrase now goes) but there are also, emphatically, 'Personalities'. These are perhaps now more often well-known than lively people, though the sense of liveliness is intended to be close. In this use, presumably, most people are not 'personalities'.

We still, however, 'have' personality, of some kind. The formation can be compared with the development of 'character'. *Character* came into English from fw *caractère*, F, *character*, L from the Greek word for an engraving or impressing instrument: the rw is of sharpening, furrowing, engraving. This sense has persisted in the context of the letters of the alphabet or other graphic symbol; in the period C14-C16 it was widely used of any impressed sign. The application to people developed, metaphorically, from this, with special reference to the face: 'by characters graven on thy brows' (Marlowe, *Tamburlaine* I, 1, ii); 'a minde that suites with this thy faire and outward character' (*Twelfth Night*, 1, ii). A more general application, to describe the NATURE (q.v.) of something, supported a further application to persons which was fully developed, though with many intermediate uses, by eC18. Butler in 1729 wrote that 'there is greater variety of parts in what we call a character, than there are features in a face', and the transfer was then evidently complete. There were also other eC18 uses to indicate reputation (including the formal giving of a character, a *character reference* as we would now say) and, interlocking with the development of **personality**, to indicate a strong or striking quality: 'most Women have no Characters at all' (Pope, 1735); 'men of character' (1737). The writing of *characters*, formal descriptions and estimates of persons, was a popular literary exercise in C17 and C18. It became possible to describe a man as *a character* before his description as **a personality**; the dating is difficult but is probably mC19. Meanwhile, in an interesting echo of *persona*, the FICTIONAL (q.v.) persons of novels and plays were described from mC18 as *characters*. The recurrence of the metaphor, from both mask and graphic sign, and with overlap between dramatic or fictional presentation and the possession of a private as well as an evident nature, is very striking. The related *disposition*, from astrology and early physiology, is still, though it has lost these specific references, more DETERMINED (q.v.). But a **personality** or a *character*, once an outward sign, has been decisively internalized, yet internalized as a possession, and therefore as something which can be either displayed or interpreted. This is, in one sense, an extreme of possessive individualism, but it is even more a record of the increasing awareness of 'freestanding' and therefore 'estimable' existence which, with all its difficulties, gave us *individual* itself.

Personality and *character*, in some of their senses, can of course be distinguished. We know what we mean, or think we know what we mean, when we say, distinguishing liveliness from reliability, that someone 'has plenty of personality but no character'. The *private characters* of **personalities** who have created *characters* are also regularly looked into.

See DRAMATIC, HUMANITY, INDIVIDUAL, MAN, PRIVATE

PHILOSOPHY

Philosophy has retained its earliest and most general meaning, from fw *philosophia*, L, *philosophia*, Gk – the love of wisdom, understood as the study and knowledge of things and their causes. At different times it has taken on subsidiary senses, as in the widespread post-classical sense of practical wisdom, which could lead to a distinction such as that made by Penn in 1679: 'famous for her Virtue and Philosophy, when that word was understood not of vain Disputing but of Pious living.' The common use of **philosophical**, in phrases like **taking a philosophical attitude**, is of this kind, and usually in practice equates **philosophy** with *resignation*. In formal use, and especially in universities, **philosophy** was divided into the three categories of *metaphysical*, *moral* and *natural*; the last category has been replaced by SCIENCE (q.v.). At times **philosophy**, as human knowledge and reasoning, has been sharply distinguished from religion: 'that no man disseyve you bi filosofie and veyn fallace, aftir the tradicioun of men, aftir the elements of the world and not aftir Crist' (Wyclif, 1388); and notably during the Enlightenment, in a

scepticism noted in Hannah More's comment (1790): 'Philosophy. . . (as Unbelief . . . has lately been pleased to call itself)'.
Philosophy has also been a common name for any particular
system of ideas, defined by a specific description.

Two contemporary English uses need to be noticed. Academic
philosophy in England has for some time been largely limited to
logic and theory of knowledge, and there is a tendency to confine
philosophy to this sense and to regard its traditional association
with general moral and intellectual systems as an error. This is a
powerful but very local habit. Likewise is the increasing use of
philosophy in managerial and bureaucratic talk, where **philosophy**
can mean general policy but as often simply the internal assumptions or even the internal procedures of a business or institution:
from the **philosophy of selling** through the **philosophy of motor-
ways** to the **philosophy of supermarkets**. This can be traced back
to Ure's *Philosophy of Manufactures* (1835) but in mC20 it
became very much more widespread, as a dignified name for a
local line.

See SCIENCE

POPULAR

Popular was originally a legal and political term, from *popularis*,
L – belonging to the people. An **action popular**, from C15, was a
legal suit which it was open to anyone to begin. **Popular estate**
and **popular government**, from C16, referred to a political system
constituted or carried on by the whole people, but there was also
the sense (cf. COMMON) of 'low' or 'base'. The transition to the
predominant modern meaning of 'widely-favoured' or 'well-
liked' is interesting in that it contains a strong element of setting
out to gain favour, with a sense of calculation that has not quite
disappeared but that is evident in a reinforced phrase like
deliberately popular. Most of the men who have left records of
the use of the word saw the matter from this point of view,
downwards. There were neutral uses, such as North's 'more
popular, and desirous of the common peoples good will and
favour' (1580) (where **popular** was still a term of policy rather
than of condition), and evidently derogatory uses, such as
Bacon's 'a Noble-man of an ancient Family, but unquiet and

popular' (1622). **Popularity** was defined in 1697, by Collier, as 'a courting the favour of the people by undue practices'. This use was probably reinforced by unfavourable applications: a neutral reference to 'popular . . . theams' (1573) is less characteristic than 'popular error' (1616) and 'popular sickenesse' (1603) or 'popular disease' (C17–C19), in which an unwelcome thing was merely widespread. A primary sense of 'widely favoured' was clear by lC18; the sense of 'well liked' is probably C19. A lC19 American magazine observed: 'they have come . . . to take popular quite gravely and sincerely as a synonym for good'. The shift in perspective is then evident. **Popular** was being seen from the point of view of the people rather than from those seeking favour or power from them. Yet the earlier sense has not died. **Popular culture** was not identified by *the people* but by others, and it still carries two older senses: inferior kinds of work (cf. **popular literature**, **popular press** as distinguished from *quality press*); and work deliberately setting out to win favour (**popular journalism** as distinguished from *democratic journalism*, or **popular entertainment**); as well as the more modern sense of well-liked by many people, with which of course, in many cases, the earlier senses overlap. The recent sense of **popular culture** as the culture actually made by people for themselves is different from all these; it is often displaced to the past as *folk culture* but it is also an important modern emphasis. The range of senses can be seen again in **popularize**, which until C19 was a political term, in the old sense, and then took on its special meaning of presenting knowledge in generally accessible ways. Its C19 uses were mainly favourable, and in C20 the favourable sense is still available, but there is also a strong sense of 'simplification', which in some circles is predominant.

In mC20 **popular song** and **popular art** were characteristically shortened to **pop**, and the familiar range of senses, from unfavourable to favourable, gathered again around this. The shortening gave the word a lively informality but opened it, more easily, to a sense of the trivial. It is hard to say whether older senses of **pop** have become fused with this use: the common sense of a sudden lively movement, in many familiar and generally pleasing contexts, is certainly appropriate.

See COMMON, CULTURE, DEMOCRACY, MASSES

POSITIVIST

It is now virtually impossible to disentangle a popular sense of **positivist** from general arguments about EMPIRICISM (q.v.) and SCIENTIFIC (q.v.) method, though the actual history of the word should make us wary of some of its vaguer uses. The word was effectively introduced into French by Comte from 1830, and was often used in English in mC19. Its root was **positive** in one of its developing C17 senses, denoting real or actual existence; (a shift from the earliest use to denote 'formally laid down' – fw *positivus*, L, rw *ponere*, L, laid down; the sense of 'definite' or 'certain', in this formal context, obviously contributed to the sense of 'real'). Comte argued that the human mind passed from a primary stage of theological interpretation through a stage of metaphysical and abstract interpretation to a mature stage of **positive** or *scientific* understanding, based only on observable facts and the relations between them and the laws discoverable from observing them, all other kinds of inquiry into origin, cause or purpose being pre-scientific. In this sense, **positivist** was widely adopted and was often interchangeable with *scientific*. But in Comte **positivism** was not only a theory of knowledge; it was also a scheme of history and a programme of social reform. In this broader sense, **Positivism** became in England a free-thinking and radical as well as a scientific movement. Indeed, because it was so concerned with understanding and changing society, it was met by the charge that it was not *scientific* enough, or not *objective* enough (cf. *sociology*, the other main word that Comte invented). Moreover, one branch of **Positivism** broke away, in an attempt to found a **Positivist Church**: the new *Religion of Humanity*. These particular developments, however, belong firmly to the past. The general meaning that came through was at first *anti-dogmatic* – 'Positivism, i.e. the representation of facts without any admixture of theory or mythology' (1892) – and later, as part of a general and difficult argument about *empiricism* and *scientific* method, its largely negative and now popular sense of naive objectivity. It is significant that it is not now used, as are both *scientific* and *empirical*, to describe and justify a criterion of reliable knowledge. Rather, it is mainly used by opponents of this criterion as absolute. What they urge against it is not what

positivists themselves argued against, whether faith or *a priori* ideas. Instead, the critique of **positivism** is based on what is felt to be the ambiguity of the concept of 'observable facts', in its common limitation to facts subject to physical measurement, or repeatable and verifiable measurement. It is argued not only that this neglects the position of the observer, who is also a fact and not merely an instrument, but that it neglects experiences and questions which are not 'measurable' in this way; this would then limit THEORY (q.v.) and SCIENTIFIC (q.v.) method to certain areas, exposing other areas to mere convention or indifference.

This is an important argument, but the effect of using **positivist** as one of its central terms, when it has been practically dropped by those who actually defend the position being attacked, is often to distance the real conflict, or even to prevent its clarification. It becomes a swear-word, by which nobody is swearing. Yet the real argument is still there. It is simply that it would be more uncomfortable to centre it on *scientific*, where the issues would be at once harder and clearer.

See EMPIRICAL, SCIENCE, SUBJECTIVE, THEORY

PRAGMATIC

Pragmatic is now most often used, especially of politicians and politics, in contrast either with *dogmatic* or with *principled*, according to point of view. Its connections with **pragmatism** are uncertain, ranging from a generalization of *practical* as opposed to *theoretical* considerations, to more or less conscious reference to the particular philosophical theory known since lC19 as **Pragmatism**. It is thus an interesting instance of the very complex linguistic cluster around the notions of THEORY (q.v.) and *practice*.

Pragmatic came into English in C16 (at first with **pragmatic** as a noun and **pragmatical** as the adjective) with the particular senses of (i) a state decree and (ii) an agent or man of business, from rw *pragmaticus*, L – skilled in business, later related to matters of state, *pragmatikos*, Gk – (a man) skilled in business, from rw *pragma*, Gk – an act, a matter of business. (*Business*, from *bisig* (busy), oE, had a very wide range of meanings, from anxiety to eagerness to serious occupation, only a few of which survive, often in particular phrases, since the predominant specialization of the word to trade and commerce was evident from C17 and normal by C19.) The early uses of **pragmatic** persisted, though (i) became rare and confined to specific historical reference. In C17 the adjective was extended to (iii) practical and useful – 'not a curious and idle knowledge . . . but a pragmaticall knowledge, full of labour and business' (1597) – and (iv) interfering, intrusive, assertive – 'pragmatic medling people' (1674). A curious by-product of (iv) was a sense, (v), of opinionated, dogmatic, often used from C17 to C19: 'a pragmatical peremptory way of delivering their Opinions' (1704); 'a strong contrast to the pragmatic Cobbett was the amiable, indolent, speculative . . . Mackintosh' (1872); 'irrelevant and pragmatic dogmatism' (1872). There was then another C19 sense, (vi), from *pragmatisch* and *Pragmatismus*, G., to describe the systematic study of history, with special reference to its causes and results.

These later senses are now very surprising, and it is not easy to trace the C20 development. Sense (iii) was still available, and the implication not only of practical skill but of shrewdness and practicability was there in some C19 uses: 'political and pragmatical wisdom' (1822). Meanwhile, from the 1870s, the American philosopher Peirce used **pragmatism** for a method in logic: 'a method of ascertaining the meaning of hard words and abstract conceptions' (*Collected Papers of Charles Sanders Peirce*; 1931–5; V, 464). The method was 'to consider what effects, that might conceivably have practical bearings, we conceive the object of our conception to have . . . Our conception of the effects is the whole of our conception of the object' (*ibid.*, V, 2). This was a method of understanding, not (as later in William James's advocacy of **Pragmatism**) of justification. In the very complicated development of the theory of **Pragmatism**, the predominant stress was on 'keeping close to the facts' and on 'seeing what sequence of experiences follows from' an action or an idea. It is ironic that Peirce, who introduced the term in this context, put much more stress on the problems of ascertaining facts, and thus on knowledge and language as problematic. It is certain that the questions Peirce asked would stop any ordinary **pragmatist** dead in his tracks. But there is a sense in which the popularized version of 'the philosophy of attending to facts and practical results' connected with flattering descriptions in sense (iii), though the connection became false when it reached the reduced sense of 'the art of the possible', meaning only shrewd, manipulative political calculation. The latter is still justified by distinction from *dogmatic*, the popular reductive word for *theory, principle* or even consistency. At this level, all associations with the philosophical position are effectively false. Yet it is interesting that the word has been so widely used, and that senses (iv) and (v) have been dropped. From 'the pragmatic Cobbett' to today's 'pragmatic politician' is all the distance a word can travel. Yet the word has been useful as a dignified alternative to *unprincipled* or *timeserving*, especially in political movements which profess a set of beliefs and which decide, under pressure, to neglect, discard or betray them, but with a show of skill and intelligence.

See DOCTRINAIRE, THEORY

PRIVATE

Private is still a complex word but its extraordinary historical revaluation is for the most part long completed. It came into English from fw *privatus*, L – withdrawn from public life, from rw *privare*, L – to bereave or deprive (English *deprive* has kept the strongest early sense). It was applied to withdrawn religious orders, where the action was voluntary (C14) and from C15 to persons not holding public or official position or rank, as still in **private soldier** and **private member** (in Parliament). It acquired the sense of secret and concealed, both in politics and in the sexual sense of **private parts**. It acquired also (and this was one of the crucial moments of transition) a conventional opposition to *public*, as in **private house**, **private education**, **private theatre**, **private view**, **private hotel**, **private club**, **private property**. In virtually all these uses the primary sense was one of *privilege*; the limited access or participation was seen not as deprivation but as advantage (cf. *exclusive*). This favourable sense developed mainly from C16 and was still being rapidly extended in C19, even while **privation** retained its old sense of being deprived and **privateer** its sense (from the original **private man of war**) of seizing the property of others. *Privilege* meanwhile went with **private**; originally, in *privilegium*, L – a law or ruling in favour of or against an individual, it became a special advantage or benefit.

Private

But this general movement in **private** (the association with **privilege**) has to be set alongside an even more important movement, in which 'withdrawal' and 'seclusion' came to be replaced, as senses, by 'independence' and 'intimacy'. It is very difficult to date this. There is a positive use in Ridley (1549): 'the privits of my hart and consciance'. There was a common sense of privileged intimacy with some powerful or important person, and this allowed overlap with a developed uncalculating sense, as in **private friends**. In C17 and especially C18, seclusion in the sense of a quiet life was valued as **privacy**, and this developed beyond the sense of solitude to the senses of decent and dignified withdrawal and of the **privacy of my family and friends**, and beyond these to the generalized values of **private life**. This development was deeply connected with corresponding changes in the senses of INDIVIDUAL and FAMILY (qq.v.).

Private life still has its old sense, in special distinction from *public life* ('what he is in private life') but it is the steady association of **private** with *personal*, as strongly favourable terms, that now seems predominant. In certain contexts the word can still be unfavourable – **private profit**, **private advantage** – but the association with personal independence is strong enough to permit the extraordinary description of large joint-stock corporations as **private enterprise** (where the chosen distinction is not from *public* but from *State*). **Private**, that is, in its positive senses, is a record of the legitimation of a bourgeois view of life: the ultimate generalized privilege, however abstract in practice, of seclusion and protection from others (*the public*); of lack of accountability to 'them'; and of related gains in closeness and comfort of these general kinds. As such, and especially in the senses of the rights of the *individual* (to his **private life** or, from a quite different tradition, to his *civil liberties*) and of the valued intimacy of *family* and friends, it has been widely adopted outside the strict bourgeois viewpoint. This is the real reason for its current complexity.

See FAMILY, INDIVIDUAL, PERSONALITY, SOCIETY

PROGRESSIVE

Progressive as a term of political description is comparatively recent. It appeared in theological controversy in mC19 but had been preceded in politics by the formation **progressist**: 'socialists and progressists' (1848); 'two natural and inevitable parties . . . conservatives and progressists' (1856). The opposed term, *conservative*, was then itself recent in a political sense, though it had been used since C14 in the general sense of preservative or preserving, and *conservatory* had a rather earlier political application. The currency of *conservative* as a political term is usually dated from Croker (1830): 'what is called the Tory, and which might with more propriety be called the Conservative, party'. It was then widely used, formally and informally, in political argument, and extended during mC19 to describe more general attitudes. **Progressist** and **progressive** were natural counters within this argument. Disraeli (1844) wrote: 'Conservatism discards Prescription, shrinks from Principle, disavows Progress.' From the 1880s the **Progressives** were a generally Liberal group within municipal politics: 'there were Progressives who are not Liberals but . . . no Liberals who are not Progressives' (Rosebery, 1898). In C20 **progressive** has been widely extended, not only to indicate general positions and parties, but to describe particular policies and attitudes. Thus **progressive conservatism** has been heard of.

Quite apart from the complications of specific controversies, **progressive** is a complex word because it depends on the significantly complicated history of the word **progress**. This has been in English since C15, from fw *progressus*, L – a going forward, from rw *pro* – forward and the past participle of *gradi* – to step. Its early uses were of a physical march, journey or procession, then of a developing series of events. There is no necessary ideological implication in this sense of a forward movement or developing series, as we can still see in uses like the **progress of a disease**. All that is certainly meant is a discoverable sequence. On the other hand the very association of these senses – moving forward and discoverable sequence – made choice of the word natural when the new senses of CIVILIZATION and of HISTORY (qq.v.) were being established, especially in C18. Bunyan, in

The Pilgrim's Progress (1678), caught the primary C17 sense of a journey but in the way he completed his title, 'from this world to that which is to come' included the sense of a manifest destiny and *future* (which especially in *the future* gathered the same ambience), and this was soon to be secularized and given a wholly new content. The key specialization of sense, outside certain limited contexts, depended on understanding movement as from worse to better. It was the abstraction of this movement, as a discoverable historical pattern, that produced **Progress** as a general idea, in close association with the ideas of CIVI-LIZATION and of IMPROVEMENT (qq.v.). The further idea that this was an evident or discoverable general movement of history completed the abstraction, notably in the Universal Histories of the Enlightenment. The sense was further supported by the developing idea of EVOLUTION (q.v.), where an inherent principle of development to higher forms became the primary sense. Young, in 1742, used **progress** in the general sense of improvement:

> Nature delights in progress; in advance
> From worse to better; but when minds ascend,
> Progress, in part, depends upon themselves.

Yet even this is different from the eventual abstraction of an inherent process of social and historical improvement. Though based in C18, the full development of the idea of **Progress**, as a law of history ('you can't stop progress') belongs to the political and industrial revolutions of lC18 and C19. It is interesting that because of the mixed character of these changes **Progress** came to be questioned or opposed not only from conservative or metaphysical positions but also by those who saw different or contradictory movements in history, which made the abstraction of **Progress** as a universal social or historical law merely IDEALIST (q.v.). In C20 **progress** has retained its primary sense of improvement but has an important (as well as an ironic) sense which takes it simply as change: the working out of some tendency, in evident stages, as in the older sense. Any particular **progress** may then be approved or disapproved, on quite different criteria.

Progressive is a difficult term in politics because it has this history behind it. It can still be used simply as the term opposite to *conservative*; that is, for one who welcomes or advocates change. In its most general and improving sense it is an adjective applied, by themselves, to virtually all proposals of all parties. There is an important complexity in that, on the one hand, the phrase is used generally of the Left (by parts of the Left) as in **progressive-minded people**, but, on the other hand, is used to distinguish supporters of '*moderate* and orderly' change (as is EVOLUTION, opposed to REVOLUTION, (qq.v.)), where the sense of a steady step-by-step journey in some general direction is called upon, as in 'a **progressive** but not a socialist party', or 'Conservatism is orderly **progress**; we are the genuinely **progressive** party'. It is certainly significant that nearly all political tendencies now wish to be described as **progressive**, but for the reasons given it is more frequently now a persuasive than a descriptive term.

See CIVILIZATION, EVOLUTION, HISTORY, IMPROVE, RE-ACTIONARY, REFORM, REVOLUTION

PSYCHOLOGICAL

Psychologia was coined as a Latin word in Germany in C16. The Greek *psyche* – breath, soul – had developed in Latin as spirit, soul, mind (cf. *anima*, L – air, breath, life, soul). The original German use was *psychologia anthropologica, sive animae humanae doctrina*, and this in the general sense of science of the human soul or mind came through French to English as **psychology** in lC17. Its earliest sense was of a doctrine of souls; (there had been a sense in French of the science of apparitions). An **empiric psychology**, in a more modern sense, was defined in German by Wolff in 1732, and this use was taken into English by Hartley in 1748. Yet the word was not much used before C19.

Psychological is recorded from 1794: the 'psychological unity which we call the mind'. It was also used by D'Israeli, with a German reference, in 1812. Yet in 1818, distinguishing between Shakespeare's 'two methods . . . the Psychological . . . the Poetical', Coleridge begged 'pardon for the use of this *insolens verbum*: but it is one of which our language stands in great need. We have no single term to express the Philosophy of the Human Mind.' All these uses are at some distance from what was to be eventually the most common sense of the word. **Psychological** is still a specific adjective from **psychology**: 'psychological research', etc. But perhaps under influences from particular schools of psychology, and also in relation to the more general movement which gave us the modern senses of PERSONALITY, PRIVATE and SUBJECTIVE (qq.v.), **psychological** acquired two different senses: (i) of 'inner' feelings; (ii) of character and behaviour seen from this point of view. A third sense, as in **psychological moment**, was common in terms of the effect of some action on the feelings and especially the morale of others, from c. 1870.

Clearly, except in its scientific uses, **psychological** does not normally express the range indicated by Coleridge, of the human mind as a whole. It indicates what is felt to be an area of the mind (cf. UNCONSCIOUS), which is primarily that of 'feeling' rather than of 'reason' or 'intellect' or 'knowledge'. **Psychological reasons** are given, not usually because they are derived from **psychology** (except in its comparably extended sense of the understanding of the feelings or characters of others), but as a reference to this assumed area. (There is an interesting comparison with the use of *sociological*, which from mC20 has been widely used not so much to indicate facts or theories derived from *sociology*, but as a form of *social*: 'the sociological factors in this strike'. Often *sociological factors* are *social*, and **psychological factors** are *personal*, in the conventional division between SOCIETY and INDIVIDUAL (qq.v.). Yet while *social* is there as a simple alternative to this popular use of *sociological*, there is no such simple alternative to **psychological**; *psychic* and *psychical* have quite other meanings, persisting from the earlier uses of *psyche* and **psychology**. A comparable formation is *technological*, which is often used where it seems that *technical* is meant: matters pertaining to a *technique* (*tekhne*, Gk – art or craft; *technical*, C17; *technique*, C19 – method in art, later method generally) rather than to *technology*, C17 – study of arts and crafts, technical terminology, later – mainly C20 – the body of applied scientific and industrial knowledge and methods).

Whatever reservations are made about **psychology** and **psychological**, from scientific or academic standpoints, the general reference to matters of 'feeling' and 'character' is now predominant. It belongs, in this sense, with a cluster of other words: *personality, subjective, individual, sensibility* and some of the developed senses of *art, interest, creative*. The tension between the senses of this important cultural formation and the stricter senses of **psychology** is repeated, at a different level, within

psychology itself, with its intensely controversial range from experimental physical studies through experimental studies of *interpersonal* relations (with specialized applications in **social** and **industrial psychology**) to doctrines and practices of both a curative and philosophical kind, many of which themselves rest on the developed senses of the key words in the formation. Characteristically the strict sense of **psychology** is often mutually denied between these varying tendencies.

An important effect of the most general sense can be observed in certain uses of **psychological**: notably **psychological realism** and **the psychological novel**. These terms could not have been invented, and can still not be reasonably used, except on the assumption of a separable or at least radically distinguishable *inner world*, within which processes of feeling and relationship and activity can be described 'in their own terms', such processes often being taken as primary, with the *outside world – nature* or *society* – seen as secondary or contingent. The now conventional separation between **the psychological** and *the social* is one of the most significant marks of this formation as a whole.

See BEHAVIOUR, PERSONALITY, PRIVATE, SENSIBILITY, SUBJECTIVE, UNCONSCIOUS

R

RADICAL

Radical has been used as an adjective in English from C14, and as a noun from C17, from fw *radicalis*, lL, rw *radix*, L – root. Its early uses were mostly physical, to express an inherent and fundamental quality, and this was extended to more general descriptions from C16. The important extension to political matters, always latent in this general use, belongs specifically to lC18, especially in the phrase **Radical Reform**. **Radical** as a noun to describe a proponent of **radical reform** was common from eC19: 'Radical is a word in very bad odour here, being used to denote a set of blackguards . . .' (Scott, 1819); 'Love is a great leveller; a perfect Radical' (Cobbett, 1822); 'the term Radical once employed as a name of low reproach, has found its way into high places, and is gone forth as the title of a class, who glory in their designation' (1830); 'the radical mob' (Emerson, 1856). **Radicalism** was formed from this use, in eC19, and was followed by **radicalize**. The words then have a curious subsequent history. **Radical**, especially with a capital letter, was by the second half of C19 almost as respectable as *liberal*, and **Radicalism** generally followed. But **radical** was still available, in some uses, in the sharper eC19 sense. Where in 1852 we find 'incipient radicalism, chartist tendencies, or socialist symptoms' there was by lC19 a clear distinction between Radicals and Socialists, and in the course of time most Radical parties, in other countries, were found considerably to the right of the political spectrum.

C20 use has been complicated. **Radical**, with or without the capital, has continued to be used of the more vigorous elements of LIBERALISM (q.v.) and more generally to indicate relatively vigorous and far-reaching reforms. As such it has often been contrasted with 'dogmatic' *socialism* or *revolutionary* pro-grammes. It has also been widely used in its older general sense, as in 'radical re-examination'. Two further uses have complicated it. There is the now common use in the phrase **Radical Right**, either to indicate extreme right-wing politics or more strictly to indicate active policies of change of a right-wing kind, as distinct from a more conventional CONSERVATISM (q.v.). On the other hand, **radical** was re-adopted, especially in the United States from the late 1950s, in a sense very close to the eC19 use; as such it is often virtually equivalent to *socialist* or *revolutionary*, and has gathered the same range of responses as in that earlier period. The choice of **radical**, especially in the United States though it has been imitated in Europe and elsewhere, can probably be related to mC20 difficulties in the definitions of SOCIALIST and COMMUNIST (qq.v. and cf. *Marxist*). **Radical** seemed to offer a way of avoiding dogmatic and factional associations while reasserting the need for vigorous and funda-mental change. At the same time it avoided some of the difficulties in REVOLUTIONARY (q.v.), making a necessary distinction between an armed rising and militant opposition to the political system. **Radical** then went far beyond its received mC20 meanings, but the problems of definition (including matters of 'dogma' and 'faction', or of principle and organization) were in the end not evaded by revival of the word. Its use by its supporters is probably fading, though use by its opponents, very much in eC19 terms, is still common. It is interesting that as part of this development the old phrase **radical reform** (q.v.) has been split into the contrasted **radical** and *reformist*, within the radical movement, while elsewhere **radical** (with *militant*) does service as a contrast with *moderate* (which in practice is often a euphemistic term for everyone, however insistent and committed, who is not a **radical**).

See COMMUNISM, LIBERAL, PROGRESSIVE, REFORM, REVOLUTION, SOCIALIST

RATIONAL

The group of words which are derived from and include **rational** and *reason* is extremely complex. We have only to think of the contemporary distance between *reasonableness* and **rationalization**. The social and intellectual history involved in the development of these words is immense, but some main points can be picked out.

Reason (from fw *reisun* or *raison*, oF, *rationem*, L, from a root in the past participle of *reri*, L – to think) had from its earliest uses in C13 English two kinds of meaning. It was at once specific – a statement, account or understanding, as still in 'believed with reason' as well as in '*a* reason for believing' – and general – a (usually specifically human) faculty of connected thought and understanding. There is no absolute need to oppose these two senses, but distinction and even radical opposition between them have been features of a long and continuing argument. There have been times when *Reason*, often in this use capitalized, has been sharply distinguished from the giving of any specific reason or reasons. The two most notable instances are the lC16 and C17 theological use of *Reason*, often emphasized as *Right Reason*, against new kinds of *reasoning* and **rationality**, and the lC18 and eC19 Idealist use of *Reason* as the transcendent power of grasping first principles, as distinct from the processes of EMPIRICAL (q.v.) verification or **rational** calculation. Given this complexity, it is not surprising that in the most bitter disputes

211

most parties have claimed to have *reason* on their side. *Reason* in the specific sense, of a reason for something, has been relatively uncontroversial and has remained common. *Reason* in the most general sense, as a human faculty, has always been there but has been so variously applied, over a range from *reason* understood as 'informed by grace' as opposed to mere 'carnal reason', to *reason* understood as a set of universal principles as distinguished from *reason* as the faculty of connected and demonstrated argument, that it is, obviously, a word that cannot be taken far on its own. Some of the effects of this argument can be seen in the changing and varying senses of *reasonable*, but the most important effects are in the senses of **rational** and its derivatives.

Rational and *reasonable* have the same primary sense, of being endowed with *reason*, as a creature, or being characterized by *reason*, as an act or argument. But *reasonable* developed a very early specialized sense of moderation or limitation, which says much about the understanding of the human condition within a medieval theological perspective: a *resonable* prayer (Chaucer, 1366), a *resonable* request (1399), *ressonable desyris* (1561). It is interesting that this developed, from C17, not only into more general uses to indicate moderation (as now in '*reasonable* wage demands', where there is already significant tension between *reasonable* and *demand*, and where the underlying principles, though as strong, are hardly as explicit) but also into a persistent use to indicate cheapness: 'when paper is more *reasonable*' (1667); 'at a very reasonable cost'. **Rational** never really followed this development, though the sense of moderation is not far away in polemical uses of 'any **rational** person' or 'all **rational** men', where the results of specific **rationality** or *reasoning* are usually confidently assumed in advance.

Rational, in its predominant sense, has remained relatively constant. It still means having or evidently exercising the faculty of *reason*, and its negative, **irrational**, quite strictly corresponds to this. But it is another matter with **rationalist, rationalism** and even **rationality**. The **rational** or **rationalist** physicians (cf. EMPIRICAL) were a special case. The term really came through in theology and in the closely associated C17 social, political and intellectual arguments, where a *Reason* associated with faith, precedent and established law was challenged both by new *reasoning* and new concepts of the *reasonable*, and, in the complexity of the argument, by an appeal beyond (mere human) *reason.* (Cf. C. Hill: *Change and Continuity*, 1974; Ch. 4.) Thus from 1670: 'a mere Rationalist (that is to say in plain English, an Atheist of the late Edition)'. This use has continued, though with variations of detail: cf. 'the Rationalist . . . makes the whole subject of Religion and Revelation . . . a matter of sensible evidence or intellectual demonstration' (Myers, 1841). **Rationalism** was formed in C19, mainly in this sense. Constant attacks on it provoked the counter-term **Irrationalism**.

A **rationale**, however (from C17), was still a reasoned argument or an underlying reason. It is interesting to trace the development of another qualification of **rationality**, which now occasionally affects even **rationale** and certainly affects **rational** and **rationalist**, but is most evident in **rationalize**. The theological use was once fairly simple: men were trying to *reason* about matters which 'unaided reason' could not resolve; they needed the help either of revelation or of authoritative guidance; those who refused either were mere **rationalists**, whether professed believers or not. The argument about revelation has gone its own way; the argument about authoritative guidance has extended much more widely. Meanwhile Boswell's 'pretty dry rationality' (1791) expressed a new reaction; its context is religious but it is symptomatic of a distinction of **rationality** from *emotion* or *feeling*. These could be either established emotions (a feeling of loyalty or duty which **rationalist** thinkers were criticizing) or any emotions (which **rationalists** were held to undervalue or despise, humans being now *emotional* as well as **rational** creatures, and the **rational** merely one 'side' of human nature). There was a C17 use of 'only Mental or Rational' (Gale, 1677) as opposed to *Real*, but **rationalize**, much more specifically, passed in eC19 through a sense of explaining on a rational basis to explaining *away*: 'to rationalize away all the wonders' (Kingsley, 1855). This has remained an important sense, and supports the deprecatory meanings of **rationalist** and **rationalism**. But the distinction between *reason* and *emotion*, the 'two sides' of human nature which became conventional in lC18 and C19, was given a surprising new twist in C20. In Freudian and related psychology 'feelings' – *instinctual drives* – were given primacy; a reversal of the long definition of *reason* and the **rational** as central and constitutive human faculties. **Rationalization** was not now explaining away the divine or the wonderful; it was finding a false or covering 'reason' for an act or feeling which had quite other ('instinctual') origins. As this extended into common use, **rationalization** came to mean any false or substitute *reason*, even for the 'real' *reason*. Where this leaves *reasoning* and **rationality** has not been clear. **Rationalization** can be distinguished as false reasoning, but **irrational** is still avoided, since the distinction is not (or at least not consistently) made on that ground. Moreover, though more comfortable words are usually found, the associated conviction is usually that human beings are 'at root' or 'fundamentally' **irrational**; the **rational** is then mere reason-making and reason-finding, of a secondary kind. As in other matters, this position recalls certain earlier structures, of a theological or idealist kind, and *reason* where it is retained is defined by such a structure. **Rational**, in this structure, can be limited to sensible and coherent; *reasonable*, significantly, is 'moderate', a matter of accepting 'necessary' limitations.

The other significant tension, in this group of words in their contemporary use, is around **irrational** in quite another sense. Several new kinds of action, which have **rationales** and are often supported by extensive *reasoning*, are dismissed as **irrational** ('the new **irrationalism**'; another variant is *mindless*) because they are not *reasonable* (*moderate*) in the conventional sense. To be *reasonable* or **rational** is to have certain assumptions of purpose, system or method which are then so deeply held that for others to challenge them is not only *unreasonable* but **irrational** (and probably a **rationalization** of some quite other emotion or motive). It would help, against such confusion, if we could with any confidence call in *reason*, but we have seen how shifting that is. *Reasoning*, however, may still hold.

See EMPIRICAL, SUBJECTIVE, THEORY, UNCONSCIOUS

REACTIONARY

Reactionary is now widely used as a description of right-wing attitudes and positions (*right* and *left* having been conventional, from eC19, though much more common in C20, for broadly *conservative* and *progressive* positions, from a particular occasion in French parliamentary seating). But **reactionary** is a complicated word, if only because of the complications of *progress* and PROGRESSIVE (q.v.). **Reaction** came into English, in mC17, in a primarily physical sense: an action opposing or resisting another action – so that *action* and **reaction** became physical laws – and then, more widely, as an action influenced by or in response to a preceding action, especially in chemistry and physiology but more generally in the sense of a declared or observable response ('my reaction to that', 'public reaction to that'). The political use came first in French, in eC19, in a relatively precise political context: it was used of attitudes and actions opposing or resisting the Revolution, with a strong sense of wishing to *re-establish* a pre-revolutionary state of affairs. It was from this special context that the word was borrowed into the specialized English sense, but with an early and wide range: 'perpetuating of factious quarrels' (Scott, 1816) as well as the eventually predominant sense of 'opposing reform'. **Reaction** was then capitalized in a way comparable to the capitalization of *Progress*.

Reactionary has become difficult because it can mean (i) opposed to reforms, (ii) wishing to go back to some previous condition, (iii) by application, supporting a particular (right-wing) version of society. There are few difficulties when all impulses to change (*actions*) are from the Left, and all resistance (**reactions**) from the Right. But if, for example, a capitalist party is in an innovating phase, or if a fascist party is proposing a new social order, each side can call the other **reactionary**: (i) because capitalism and fascism are right-wing, **reactionary**, as such; (ii) because resistance to particular kinds of change, and especially changes and innovations in capitalism and capitalist society, is seen as **reactionary** (wishing to preserve or restore some other condition). Thus we can be invited to identify the **reactionary Right** (usually with a sense of the extreme Right, as distinguished from *progressive* or *reforming* conservatives, as well as from Liberals and the Left) but often, also, the **reactionary Left** (opposing types of change which they see as for the worse, or relying on particular senses of the democratic or socialist tradition which they oppose to current changes of a different kind).

The word will probably keep its predominant sense of extreme conservatism, but it would only be simple, outside this specific sense, if all political actions were good and all reactions therefore bad. It is interesting that **reaction** has kept its neutral sense, and its neutral adjective **reactive**, through all the specialization of **Reaction** and **reactionary**.

See PROGRESSIVE, REFORM

REALISM

Realism is a difficult word, not only because of the intricacy of the disputes in art and philosophy to which its predominant uses refer, but also because the two words on which it seems to depend, **real** and **reality**, have a very complicated linguistic history. The earliest **Realists**, in English, were at a great distance from anything now indicated by the term, for the philosophical school known as **Realist** was primarily opposed by the *Nominalists*, who themselves might in post-mC19 terms be classed as **realists** of an extreme kind. The old doctrine of **Realism** was an assertion of the absolute and objective existence of universals, in the Platonic sense. These universal Forms or Ideas were held either to exist independently of the objects in which they were perceived, or to exist in such objects as their constituting properties. Redness, for the nominalists, was merely a (confusing) name for a number of red things; for the conceptualists it became a generalizing mental idea; for the Realists it was an absolute and objective Form independent of red objects or essentially constituting such objects. It is very striking, and very confusing, that this **Realist** doctrine is what we would now call extreme IDEALISM (q.v.).

That use may be said to have faded. From eC19 quite different senses of **realist**, and the new word **realism** in a more modern sense, can be said to have overlain and suppressed it. But this is not wholly true. Our common distinction between *appearance* and **reality** goes back, fundamentally, to the early use – 'the reality underlying appearances' – and this has significantly affected many arguments about **realism**. **Real**, from the beginning, has had this shifting double sense. It is from fw *real*, oF, *realis*, lL, from rw *res*, L – thing. Its earliest English uses, from C15, were in matters of law and property, to denote something actually existing. There was a connected and persisting later use for immovable property, as still in **real estate**. The sense of something actually existing was transferred to general use, from lC16, in an implicit or explicit contrast with something *imaginary*: 'Is't reall that I see?' (*All's Well That Ends Well*, V, iii); 'not Imaginary, but Reall' (Hobbes, *Leviathan*, III, xxxiv). But at the same time there was an important sense of **real** as contrasted not with *imaginary* but with *apparent*: not only in theological arguments about the 'reall presence' of Christ in the materials of communion, but also in wider arguments about the true or fundamental quality of some thing or situation – the **real** thing, the **reality** of something. This use is still very common, if often not noticed as such, in phrases like 'refusing to face the real facts of his situation' or 'refusing to face reality'. Since the use to indicate something tangible, palpable or factual was also strongly continued, it can be seen that there is almost endless play in the word. A **Realist** in the pre-C18 sense of the word took **real** in the general sense of an underlying truth or quality; in the post-eC19 sense in the (often opposed) sense of *concrete* (as from C14 opposed to *abstract*) existence.

Realism was a new word in C19. It developed four distinguishable meanings: (i) as a term to describe, historically, the doctrines of Realists as opposed to those of Nominalists; (ii) as a term to describe new doctrines of the physical world as independent of mind or spirit, in this sense sometimes interchangeable with NATURALISM or MATERIALISM (qq.v.); (iii) as a description of facing up to things as they **really** are, and not as we imagine or would like them to be – 'let us replace sentimentalism by realism, and dare to uncover those simple and terrible laws which, be they seen or unseen, pervade and govern' (Emerson, 1860); (iv) as a term to describe a method or an attitude in art and literature – at first an exceptional accuracy of representation, later a commitment to describing **real** events and showing things as they actually exist.

It is not surprising that there should have been so fierce and often so confused a controversy, especially over sense (iv). Senses (i) and (ii) can now normally be disregarded: (i) because it is now an isolated and specific historical reference, (ii) because for all practical purposes this sense has been taken over by *materialism*. Sense (iii) is still very important in everyday use. In the Emerson example the familiar play of **real** is evident: the laws may be seen or unseen. But the use has come through as 'facing facts', as in the characteristic new mC19 adjective **realistic**: 'could not be reconciled to life by any plain view of things, by any realistic calculations' (Seeley, 1869). What matters is that in this sense most people hold that their own views of any matter are **realistic**. But there is an evident range of application, from the older sense of being based on a true understanding of a situation, to a now common sense which shares the implicit impatience of one sense of *practical*. 'Let's be realistic' probably more often means 'let us accept the limits of this situation' (*limits* meaning *hard facts*, often of power or money in their existing and established forms) than 'let us look at the whole truth of this situation' (which can allow that an existing **reality** is changeable or is changing). Thus though **realistic** (cf. *reasonable*) is an immensely popular word among businessmen and politicians, it has acquired some consequent tone of limited calculation, and is then often contrasted, from both points of view, with *idealistic*.

Sense (iv) remains the most difficult. It does not end but only begins a controversy in art and literature when it is said that the purpose is 'to show things as they really are'. There is a surviving sense of the old *idealism*, as in Shelley's lines on the Poet in *Prometheus Unbound*:

> He will watch from dawn to gloom
> The lake-reflected sun illume
> The yellow bees in the ivy bloom,
> Nor heed nor see, what things they be;
> But from these create he can
> Forms more real than living man,
> Nurslings of immortality.

Here the stress must fall not only on **real** but on *forms*: a poetic creation which is indifferent and certainly not tied to the objects of observation, but which **realizes** immortal essences or entities. (This use of **realize** began in C17, and was common from mC18: 'an Act of the Imagination, that realizes the Event however fictitious, or approximates it however remote' (Johnson, *Rambler 60*; 1750). The term is popular in modern criticism, to refer to the *means* and *effect* of bringing something vividly to life.) But this is the kind of use which was eventually distinguished from **realism** and which indeed allowed a contrast between **realism** and other words in this complex, as in Swinburne's contrast of 'prosaic realism' and 'poetic reality' (1880). Again and again, from positions of this kind, **realism** has been accused of evading the **real**.

The difficulty is most acute when we see that **realism** in art and literature is both a method and a general attitude. As the latter it is distinguished from ROMANTICISM (q.v.) or from *Imaginary* or **Mythical** (q.v.) subjects; things not of **the real world**. The use to describe a method is often a term of praise – the characters, objects, actions, situations are **realistically** described; that is, they are lifelike in description or appearance; they show **realism**. It is often also a term of blame or limitation, in these senses: (a) that what is described or represented is seen only super-ficially, in terms of its outward *appearance* rather than its inner **reality**; (b) in a more modern form of the same objection, that there are many **real** forces – from inner feelings to underlying social and historical movements – which are either not accessible to ordinary observation or which are imperfectly or not at all represented in how things appear, so that a **realism** 'of the surface' can quite miss important **realities**; (c) in a quite different objection, that the medium in which this REPRESENTATION (q.v.) occurs, whether language or stone or paint or film, is radically different from the objects *represented* in it, so that the effect of 'lifelike representation', 'the reproduction of reality', is at best a particular artistic convention, at worst a falsification making us take the forms of REPRESENTATION as *real*.

Objections (a) and (b) have been countered by a specialized sense of **realism**, which has used NATURALISM (q.v.) as the form to which these objections can properly be made, but then pre-serves **realism** – sometimes in even more specialized forms such as **psychological realism** or **socialist realism** – to include or to emphasize hidden or underlying forces or movements, which simple 'naturalistic' observation could not pick up but which it is the whole purpose of **realism** to discover and express. This depends on the old play in the senses of **real**, but it has been important not so much in an idealist sense, which would now normally avoid **realism** as a term, as in senses deriving from dynamic psychology or from DIALECTICAL (q.v.) as opposed to MECHANICAL MATERIALISM (q.v.). **Reality** is here seen not as static *appearance* but as the movement of psychological or social or physical forces; **realism** is then a conscious commitment to understanding and describing these. It then may or may not include **realistic** description or *representation* of particular features.

Objection (c) is directed primarily at **realistic** in the sense of *lifelike*. **Realist** art or literature is seen as simply one CONVENTION (q.v.) among others, a set of formal REPRESENTATIONS, in a particular MEDIUM (qq.v.) to which we have become accustomed. The object is not **really** lifelike but by convention and repetition has been made to appear so. This can be seen as relatively harmless or as extremely harmful. To see it as harmful depends on a sense that (as in *mechanical materialism*) a pseudo-objective *version* of reality (a version that will be found to depend, finally, on a particular phase of history or on a particular set of relationships between men and between men and things) is passed off as **reality**, although in this instance at least (and perhaps more generally) what is there is what has been made, by the specific practices of writing and painting and film-making. To see it as **reality** or as the **faithful copying of reality** is to exclude this active element and in extreme cases to pass off a FICTION (q.v.) or a CONVENTION (q.v.) as **the real world**.

This is a powerful argument against many of the claims of **realism** as accurate *representation*, but it is an accident of the way that the argument has gone, in relation to this one sense of **realism**, that it can be taken either way in relation to **realism** as a whole movement. Thus it could be made compatible with the sense of **realism** that was distinguished from *naturalism*, and especially with that sense of a conscious commitment to understanding and describing real forces (a commitment that at its best includes understanding the processes of consciousness and composition that are involved in any such attempt). More often, however, the argument has been linked, in particular intellectual formations, with the idealist modes of FORMALISM and of STRUCTURALISM (qq.v.), where the strength of attention to the detailed practice of composition, and especially to the basic forms and structures within which composition occurs, goes along with or can be used to justify an indifference to the forces other than literary and artistic and intellectual practice which it was the purpose of the broader **realism** (even at times naively) to take into radical account. The historical significance of **Realism** was to make social and physical **reality** (in a generally materialist sense) the basis of literature, art and thought. Many marginal points can be made against the methods historically associated with this purpose, and from a frankly idealist position many radical points can be made against the purpose itself. But what has most often happened, recently, is that the marginal points have been extended, loosely, as if they were radical points, or that making the marginal points has been so absorbing that the radical points at issue, from a materialist or an idealist standpoint, have been in effect ignored.

It is hardly necessary to add that the critical attention which is necessary in most cases of the use of **real**, **realistic** and **reality** is at least equally necessary in the case of this extraordinary current variation in uses of **realism**.

See CONVENTION, CREATIVE, FICTION, MATERIALISM, MYTH, NATURALISM, PRACTICAL, RATIONAL, SUBJECTIVE

REFORM

Reform as a verb came into English in C14, from fw *reformer*, oF, *reformare*, L – to form again. In most of its early uses it is very difficult to distinguish between two latent senses: (i) to restore to its original form; (ii) to make into a new form. There are clear early examples of each use, but in many contexts the idea of changing something for the better was deeply bound up with the idea of restoring an earlier and less corrupted condition (cf. *amend*, from fw *emendare*, L – to free from fault, which was often interchangeable with **reform** but which came through with a slighter or more limited reference; cf. also *reaction*). The first noun from the verb was **reformation**, from C15, and this shows the same ambiguity. The great religious **Reformation** of C16 had a strong sense of purification and restoration, even when it needed new forms and institutions to achieve this. The continuing play in **reform** is clear in the exchange in *Hamlet* (III, ii):

I hope we have reformed that indifferently with us, sir.
O, reform it altogether.

From lC17 an alternative spelling, **re-form** ('Re-form and New-Mold', 1695) made some of the stronger uses clearer. Nevertheless **reform** in its most general sense has continued to carry implications of amending an existing state of affairs in the light of known or existing principles, and this use can move towards *restoration* as often as towards *innovation*. The usual noun became **reform**, from mC17, but it was still mainly a noun of process, like **reformation**, until lC18. A C18 gloss (Bailey) gave '**Reform** . . . a re-establishment or revival of a former neglected discipline; also a correction of reigning abuses.' **Reform** as a definite noun, for a specific measure, was common from lC18. In the same period it was capitalized and abstracted as a political tendency, mainly in relation to Parliament and the suffrage, where quite new forms were being proposed but often with a sense of the *restoration* of liberty.

In the struggle over Parliamentary representation, **Reform** became a radical term (cf. **Radical Reform** from lC18) and **parliamentary reformists** who had been *subtle* (not a kind term) as early as 1641 were in correspondence with Jacobins (Windham, 1792) and were seen as **violent reformists** (meaning 'ardent') by Lady Granville in 1830. The play in the word is evident. Cf. 'these Unions were to be for the promotion of the cause of reform, for the protection of life and property against the detailed but irregular outrages of the mob . . .' (*The Times*, 1 December 1830); 'that reform which had thus been obtained appeared to him to have been the ultimate means of strengthening the hands of corruption and oppression' (Rider, *Leeds Times*, 12 April 1834; this and the preceding example are quoted in E. P. Thompson: *The Making of the English Working Class*; 1963; pp. 810–26).

It was from this kind of controversy, assisted by the play in the word, that the C20 sense of **reformism** and **reformist** emerged. **Reformism** was a new word coined in the controversy within the socialist movement, especially between 1870 and 1910. The issue was whether capitalist society could be changed, or was indeed changing itself, in gradual, local and specific ways, or whether such **reforms** were trivial or illusory, either masking the need for the replacement of capitalism by socialism (REVOLUTION, q.v.) or actually intended to prevent this replacement. **Reformism** in C20 use has had both these latter senses, and **reformist**, which from C16 had been generally equivalent to **reformer** (with which it was contemporary) has now been specialized to the sense of **reformism**, leaving **reformer** in the older general sense.

See FORM, RADICAL, REVOLUTION

REPRESENTATIVE

The group of words in which **represent** is central is very complex, and has long been so. **Represent** appeared in English in C14, by which time **present** already existed as a verb 'to make present' (the sense of offering something came in C14). **Represent** quickly acquired a range of senses of making present: in the physical sense of presenting oneself or another, often to some person of authority; but also in the sense of making present in the mind

('Aulde storys that men redys, Representis to thaim the dedys, Of stalwart folk', Barbour, 1375) and of making present to the eye, in painting ('representid and purtraid', c. 1400) or in plays ('this play . . . representyd now in yower syght', c. 1460). But a crucial extension also occurred in C14, when **represent** was used in the sense of 'symbolize' or 'stand for' ('ymagis that representen pompe and glorie of tho worlde', Wyclif, c. 1380). It is clear that at this stage there was considerable overlap between the sense (a) of making present to the mind and the sense (b) of standing for something that is not present. What was eventually a divergence between these senses, in some uses, might not at first have been perceived as a divergence at all. The emergence of the separable sense of 'standing for others' is very difficult to trace. Many early political uses have the sense of 'symbolize' rather than 'stand for'. When Charles I described the Houses of Parliament as 'the Representative Body of the Kingdome' (1643) it seems certain, especially when we remember what was then in dispute, that the sense was that of the Kingdom being made present, symbolized, rather than the later sense of members of Parliament 'standing for' the opinions of those who elected them. That is to say, an assumed whole state or condition was **represented** by a particular institution; the **representative** quality came from the whole state outwards, rather than from scattered and diverse opinions brought together and, in a more modern sense, **represented**. This use is still evident in such phrases as 'representing your country abroad'. The political representative is the political image.

Yet it was mainly in C17 that the sense of standing *for* others, in a more diverse way, began to come through. There had already developed a sense of **represent** meaning standing for some other named person ('our Generall sent Cap. Jobson, repraesentinge his person with his authoritie', 1595). This use has of course continued, most notably in matters of law. The extended political sense can be seen from mC17: in 'the Burgesses (the representatives of the people)' (1658), where the older sense is still partly present; in Cromwell's 'I have been careful of your safety, and the safety of those that you represented' (1655); and in Coke's 'We will therefore enquire . . . whether a House of Commons, as it now stands, can be their Representative' (1660). None of these uses is quite clear as equivalent to modern **represent**, and in some ways the uncertainty has continued, within the very structure of the term. On the one hand we find Steele introducing a necessary qualification in 'the Elected became true Representatives of the Electors' (1713) and 'Junius' using a necessary distinction in 'the English nation declare they are grossly injured by their representatives' (1769). But on the other hand we find Burke making a notorious distinction between a **representative** and a *delegate*, which in part relied on the symbolic sense of **representative** (standing for others, but in his own terms) rather than on the political sense (making present, **representing**, the opinions of those who elected him). This distinction is still conventionally repeated by most politicians, and **representative** still evidently contains this complexity or ambiguity of reference. This is clear in current arguments about whether **representatives** should be *mandated* (that is to say, given instructions by those who elect them, and whose opinions they will thus **represent**) or subject to *recall* (that is to say, capable of being declared **not representative** of the opinions of their electors). It is clear from the character of the opposition to ideas of *mandate* and *recall* (which seem merely to spell out one meaning of **represent**) that another meaning of **representative**, as symbolizing or generally characteristic of the others who are not present, is being heavily drawn upon. This is made easier by a common general use of **representative**, since mC17, to mean a typical sample or specimen.

The point becomes very important in arguments about **representative democracy** (q.v.) which can evidently mean (i) the periodic election of typical persons, or (ii) the periodic election of persons who will, in general, speak *for* ('on behalf of' or 'in the name of') those who elected them, or (iii) the periodic election of persons who will continually **represent** (make present) the views of those who elected them. The fact of competitive election to each of these functions, which is usually emphasized as the substance of **representative democracy**, does not alter the equally important fact that the functions themselves are radically different. In practice arguments about *mandate* and *recall* use sense (iii), and are countered by arguments depending on senses (i) and (ii). The arguments have been fierce enough to generate the alternative definition, *participatory democracy*, which in its emphasis on people governing themselves rather than being governed by '**representatives**', would rule out senses (i) and (ii) though often, for practical reasons, retain sense (iii).

Meanwhile **represent** has gone through an equally complex development in art and literature. A **representation** was, as we have seen, a symbol or image, or the process of presenting to the eye or the mind. From C18 the sense of **representative** as typical began to be used in description of characters or situations. From mC19 this became common and was eventually widely used as an identifying element of REALISM or NATURALISM (qq.v.). Later, an old meaning of **representation** – the visual embodiment of something – became specialized to a sense of 'accurate reproduction' and in this sense, probably not earlier than C20, produced the distinctive category of **representational art**. Yet there is nothing in the general sense of **represent** or of **representation** to make this specialization inevitable. Indeed its emphasis on accurate *reproduction* runs counter to the main development of the political sense. But it is now very strongly established and is even (ironically in terms of its history) contrasted with *symbolic* or *symbolizing*. (*Symbol* has developed a comparable ambiguity, from the early senses of a mark, token or summary of some general state or condition or doctrine, through the intermediate sense of something which **represents** something else, to the late sense of something significant but autonomous – not a **representation** but an *image*, which indicates either something not otherwise defined or something deliberately not defined in its own terms.) There is evidence of some overlap between the separate senses of **representative** and **representational** as terms of art and literature. This is characteristic of arguments about REALISM (q.v.), but there is obviously no necessary identity between the sense of *typical* and the sense of accurately *reproduced*; this is, rather, a local historical association.

The degree of possible overlap between **representative** and **representation** in their political and artistic senses is very difficult to estimate. In the sense of the *typical*, which then stands *for* ('as' or 'in place of') others or other things, in either context, there is probably a deep common cultural assumption. At the same time, within this assumption, there is the contradiction expressed both in the arguments about **representative democracy** and in the arguments in art about relations between the **representational** and the **representative**.

See DEMOCRACY, IMAGE, REALISM

REVOLUTION

Revolution now has a predominant and specialized political meaning, but the historical development of this meaning is significant. The word came into English from C14, from fw *revolucion*, oF, *revolutionem*, L, from rw *revolvere*, L – to revolve. In all its early uses it indicated a **revolving** movement in space or time: 'in whiche the other Planetes, as well as the Sonne, do finyshe their revolution and course according to their true tyme' (1559); 'from the day of the date heereof, to the full terme and revolution of seven yeeres next ensuing' (1589); 'they recoyl again, and return in a Vortical motion, and so continue their revolution for ever' (1664). This primary use, of a recurrent physical movement, survives mainly in a technical sense of engines: **revolutions** per minute, usually shortened to **revs**.

The emergence of the political sense is very complicated. It is necessary to look first at what previous word served for an action against an established order. There was of course *treason* (with its root sense of *betraying* a lawful authority) but the most general word was *rebellion*. This was common in English from C14. The sense had developed in Latin from the literal 'renewal of war' to the general sense of armed rising or opposition and, by extension, to open resistance to authority. *Rebellion* and *rebel* (as adjective, verb and noun) were then the central words for what we would now normally (but significantly not always) call **revolution** and **revolutionary**. There was also, from C16, the significant development of *revolt*, from fw *révolter*, F, *revolutare*, L – to roll or revolve, which from the beginning, in English, was used in a political sense. The development of two words, *revolt* and **revolution**, from the sense of a circular movement to the sense of a political rising, can hardly be simple coincidence.

Revolution was probably affected, in its political development, by the closeness of *revolt*, but in English its sense of a circular movement lasted at least a century longer. There are probably two underlying causes for the transfer (in both *revolt* and **revolution**) from a circular movement to a rising. On the one hand there was the simple physical sense of the normal distribution of power as that of the *high* over the *low*. From the point of view of any established authority, a *revolt* is an attempt to turn over, to turn upside down, to make topsy-turvy, a normal political order: the *low* putting themselves against and in that sense above the *high*. This is still evident in Hobbes, *Leviathan*, II, 28: 'such as are they, that having been by their own act Subjects, deliberately revolting, deny the Soveraign Power' (1651). On the other hand, but eventually leading to the same emphasis, there was the important image of the Wheel of Fortune, through which so many of the movements of life and especially the most public movements were interpreted. In the simplest sense, men revolved, or more strictly were revolved, on Fortune's wheel, setting them now up, now down. In practice, in most uses, it was the downward movement, the *fall*, that was stressed. But in any case it was the *reversal* between up and down that was the main sense of the image: not so much the steady and continuous movement of a wheel as the particular isolation of a top and bottom point which were, as a matter of course, certain to change places. The crucial change in **revolution** was at least partly affected by this. As early as 1400 there was the eventually characteristic:

It is I, that am come down
Thurgh change and revolucioun. (*Romance of the Rose*, 4366)

A sense of **revolution** as alteration or change is certainly evident from C15: 'of Elementys the Revoluciouns, Chaung of tymes and Complexiouns' (Lydgate, c. 1450). The association with *fortune* was explicit as late as mC17: 'whereby one may see, how great the revolutions of time and fortune are' (1663).

The political sense, already well established in *revolt*, began to come through in **revolution** from eC17, but there was enough overlap with older ways of seeing change to make most early examples ambiguous. Cromwell made a revolution, but when he said that 'God's revolutions' were not to be attributed to mere human invention (Abbott, *Writings and Speeches of Cromwell*; III, 590–2) he was probably still using the word with an older sense (as in *Fortune*, but now *Providential*) of external and DETERMINING (q.v.) movements. Indeed the most fascinating aspect of this complex of words, in C17, is that Cromwell's revolution was called, by its enemies, the *Great Rebellion*, while the relatively minor events of 1688 were called by their supporters the **Great** and eventually the **Glorious Revolution**. It is evident from several uses that **revolution** was gaining a political sense through C17, though still, as has been noted, with overlap to general mutability or to the movements of Fortune or Providence. But it is very significant that in lC17 the lesser event attracted the description **Revolution** while the greater event was still *Rebellion*. **Revolution**, that is to say, was still the more generally favourable word, and from as late as 1796 we can find that distinction: 'Rebellion is the subversion of the laws, and Revolution is that of tyrants'. (*Subversion*, it will be noted, depends on the same physical image, of turning over from below; and cf. *overthrow*.)

From lC17 the sense of **revolution** in English was dominated by specific reference to the events of 1688. The ordinary reference (Steele, 1710; Burke, 1790) was to 'the Revolution', and **revolutioner**, the first noun for one engaged in or supporting **revolution**, was used primarily in that specific context. Yet the general sense was slowly making its way through, and there was renewed cause for distinction between *rebellion* and **revolution**, according to point of view, in the rising and declaration of independence of the American states. **Revolution** won through in that case, both locally and generally. In a new climate of political thought, in which the adequacy of a political system rather than loyalty to a particular sovereign was more and more taken as the real issue, **revolution** was obviously preferred to **rebellion**, by anyone who supported *independent* change. There is a surviving significance in this, in our own time. *Rebellion* is still ordinarily used by a dominant power and its friends, until (or even after) it has to admit that what has been taking place – with its own *independent* cause and loyalties – is a **revolution**. The same distinction began to be made between *revolt* and **revolution**, though also with an added sense of scale: 'Sire . . . it is not a revolt, it is a revolution' (Carlyle, *French Revolution*, V, vii; 1837). (It is worth noting that *revolt* and *revolting* had acquired, from mC18, an application to feeling as well as to action: a feeling of disgust, of turning away, of *revulsion*; this probably accentuated the distinction. It is curious that *revulsion* is etymologically associated with *revel*, which itself goes back to *rebellare*, L – to rebel. *Revel* became specialized, through a sense of riotous mirth, to any lively festivity; *rebel* took its separate unfavourable course; *revulsion*, from a physical sense of drawing away, took on from eC19 its sense of drawing away in disgust.)

It was in this state of interaction between the words that the specific effects of the French Revolution made decisive the modern sense of **revolution**. It was a matter of confirmation and emphasis, though, rather than innovation. Already in 1727 there had been 'Savage, restless, turbulent **Revolutionists**', and in 1774 a distinction between 'stationary' and '**revolutionary**' principles of government, the former being preferred. But the full sense of **revolutionary**, and the new word **revolutionize**, belong to the 1790s, and the words have resounded through C19 to our own day. The sense of making a new social order was always as important as that of overthrowing an old order. That, after all, was the crucial distinction from *rebellion* or from what was eventually distinguished as a **palace revolution** (changing the leaders but not the forms of society). Yet in political controversy arising from the actual history of armed risings and conflicts, **revolution** took on a specialized meaning of violent overthrow, and by lC19 was being contrasted with EVOLUTION (q.v.) in its sense of a new social order brought about by peaceful and constitutional means. The sense of **revolution** as bringing about a wholly new social order was greatly strengthened by the socialist movement, and this led to some complexity in the distinction between **revolutionary** and *evolutionary* socialism. From one point of view the distinction was between violent overthrow of the old order and peaceful and constitutional change. From another point of view, which is at least equally valid, the distinction was between working for a wholly new social order (SOCIALISM as opposed to CAPITALISM, (qq.v.)) and the more limited modification or REFORM (q.v.) of an existing order ('the pursuit of equality' within a 'mixed economy' or 'post-capitalist society'). The argument about means, which has often been used to specialize **revolution**, is also usually an argument about ends.

Revolution and **revolutionary** and **revolutionize** have of course also come to be used, outside political contexts, to indicate fundamental changes, or fundamentally new developments, in a very wide range of activities. It can seem curious to read of 'a **revolution** in shopping habits' or of the '**revolution** in transport', and of course there are cases when this is simply the language of publicity, to describe some 'dynamic' new product. But in some ways this is at least no more strange than the association of **revolution** with VIOLENCE (q.v.), since one of the crucial tendencies of the word was simply towards important or fundamental change. Once the factory system and the new technology of lC18 and eC19 had been called, by analogy with the French

Revolution, the INDUSTRIAL (q.v.) **Revolution**, one basis for description of new institutions and new technologies as **revolutionary** had been laid. Variations in interpretation of the **Industrial Revolution** – from a new social system to simply new inventions – had their effect on this use. The **transistor revolution** might seem a loose or trivial phrase to someone who has taken the full weight of the sense of **social revolution**, and a **technological** or **second industrial revolution** might seem merely polemical or distracting descriptions. Yet the history of the word supports each kind of use. What is more significant, in a century of major revolutions, is the evident discrimination of application and tone, so that the storm-clouds that have gathered around the political sense become fresh and invigorating winds when they blow in almost any other direction.

See EVOLUTION, REFORM, VIOLENCE

ROMANTIC

Romantic is a complex word because it takes its modern senses from two distinguishable contexts: the content and character of **romances**, and the content and character of the **Romantic Movement**. The latter is usually dated to lC18 and eC19; it is in itself exceptionally complex and diverse. But **romantic** was in use in English well before this, with most of its still predominant modern associations. The adjective was formed in C17 from **romance** as it was then generally understood. But **romance** was itself then changing. The word in varying forms, *romanz, romaunz, roman, romaunt*, etc., had come through oF and Provençal from *romanice*, mL – 'in the Romanic tongue': that is to say, in the neo-Latin vernacular languages. Medieval romances, broadly speaking, were verse-tales of adventure, chivalry or love, and as late as *Paradise Lost* Milton still used **Romance** in this sense: 'what resounds in Fable or Romance of Uther's son'. But the effective development which led to **romantic** was the popularity of new kinds of prose **romance**, based mainly on C16 Spanish forms. These were widely seen as sentimental and extravagant, but also as characterized by freedom of imagination. Both senses got into the new adjective: 'the romantic and visionary scheme of building a bridge over the river at Putney' (1671); 'upon the onely security of Mr Harrington's romantick Commonwealth' (1660); 'these things are almost romantique, and yet true' (Pepys, 1667); 'that Imagination which is most free, such as we use in Romantick Inventions' (1659). This range of uses continued through C18, and was joined by a popular use as a description of certain places: 'so Romantic a Scene' (Addison, 1705).

Romantic as a new kind of description of a literary, artistic and philosophical movement was essentially a development of eC19. Its English use was heavily influenced by German thought, where the particular distinction between **Romantic** and *Classical* originated (most influentially, but with opposite implications, in Goethe and Hegel). Except in specific contexts, with reference to particular periods and styles, **Romantic** in this sense was and has remained difficult to separate from the earlier general uses. The existing sense of a free or liberated imagination was undoubtedly greatly strengthened. An extended sense of liberation from rules and conventional forms was also powerfully developed, not only in art and literature and music but also in feeling and BEHAVIOUR (q.v.). A corresponding sense of strong feeling, but also of fresh and *authentic* feeling, was also important. The **romantic hero** developed from an extravagant to an ideal character. New valuations of the 'irrational', the 'unconscious' and the 'legendary' or MYTHICAL (q.v.) developed alongside new valuations of the *folk-cultures* within which some of these materials seemed to be found, and, in a different dimension, alongside new valuations of SUBJECTIVITY (q.v.), which connected with the emphasis on liberated imagination and on strong ORIGINAL (q.v.) feeling. The degree of overlap between some of these senses and some of the earlier senses is obvious; what was new but remains difficult to make precise was the general philosophical basis for what were previously regarded as specific and separable features.

In C20, **Romantic** as a historical description, and as a disputed but still necessary generalization for the philosophical and literary movement from lC18, has remained common. But the older uses are still active, with considerable ambivalence. A **romantic** place is still approved; a **romantic** scheme is not. The derived C19 words, **romanticism** and **romanticize** (outside the specific historical references) are heavily unfavourable. **Romantic feelings** and **romance** itself have meanwhile been commonly specialized (with support from the subjects of many **romances** and **romantic stories**, now specialized as **romantic fiction**) to love between men and women. There is a subsidiary distinction between **romantic** love and *sexual* love, but a sexual relationship is still, in popular use, a **romance**, and **romantic** places and **romantic** situations are much influenced by this. This has often affected understanding of the earlier **Romances** and **Romantic literature**, which in real terms remain very different.

See CREATIVE, FICTION, MYTH, NOVEL, ORIGINAL, SUBJECTIVE

S

SCIENCE

Science may now appear to be a very simple word, even if we remember that before C19 it had other meanings. Yet, precisely in its separation from these meanings, there is a significant and still active social history. **Science** came into English in C14, from fw *science*, F, *scientia*, L – knowledge. Its earliest uses were very general. It was a term for knowledge as such, as in 'for God of sciens is lord' (1340), and this use was still active in Shakespeare:

. . . hath not in natures mysterie more science
Then I have in this Ring. (*All's Well That Ends Well*, V, iii)

This sense was sometimes distinguished from *conscience*, to express the difference between knowing something, as we would say theoretically (**science**) and knowing it with conviction and commitment (*conscience*). But **science** became more generally used, often interchangeably with *art*, to describe a particular body of knowledge or skill: 'his science Of metre, of rime and of cadence' (Gower, 1390); 'thre Sciences . . . Divinite, Fisyk, and Lawe' (1421); 'Liberal Sciencis . . . fre scyencis, as gramer, arte, fisike, astronomye, and otheris' (1422).

The general use for knowledge and learning, and the particular uses for some branch or body of learning, continued until eC19. Cf: 'those seeds of science call'd his ABC' (Cowper, 1781); 'no science, except reading, writing and arithmetic' (Godwin, 1794). But from mC17 certain changes became evident. In particular there was the distinction from *art*: not at all the modern distinction (see ART) but in its own way significant. In 1678 'dyalling' (the making of dials) was described as 'originally a Science . . . yet . . . now . . . no more difficult than an Art', which seems to express a distinction between a skill requiring theoretical knowledge and a skill requiring only practice. Then in 1725: 'the word science is usually applied to a whole body of regular or methodical observations or propositions . . . concerning any subject of speculation.' This can be read, loosely, as a modern definition, but it concerns propositions as well as observations and relates to 'any subject'. This is in line with an earlier use of **scientific** (lC16, fw *scientificus*, L) to mean either theoretical or, commonly, a demonstrative proof in an argument. (**Scientific** had also been used earlier, in alternation with LIBERAL (q.v.), to distinguish the learned from the MECHANICAL (q.v.) arts.) The meaning that was thus coming through, from the whole body of learning, had elements both of method and of demonstration, at a theoretical level; science was a kind of knowledge or argument, rather than a kind of subject. This would seem to be so even in what reads at first sight like a modern example, from 1796: the statement that until recently 'mineralogy, though tolerably understood by many as an art, could scarce be deemed a Science', where the distinction is probably between practical and theoretical knowledge. Theory necessarily implied methodical demonstration, which might occur in any subject.

The key distinction was not at first in **science** but in the crucial C18 distinction between *experience* and *experiment* (see EMPIRICAL). This supported a distinction between *practical* and *theoretical* knowledge (see THEORY), which was then expressed as a distinction between *art* and **science** in their C17 and C18 general senses. The practice of what we would now call **experimental science**, and indeed of what is now called, retrospectively, the **scientific revolution**, had been growing remarkably since mC17. Yet **science**, in lC18, still meant primarily methodical and theoretical demonstration, and its specialization to particular studies had not yet decisively occurred. The distinction between *experience* and *experiment*, however, was a sign of a larger change. *Experience* could be specialized in two directions: towards practical or customary knowledge, and towards inner (SUBJECTIVE, (q.v.)) knowledge as distinct from external (*ob-*

jective) knowledge. Each of these senses was already present in *experience*, but the distinction of *experiment* – an arranged methodical observation of an event – allowed new specializing emphasis in *experience* also. Changes in ideas of NATURE (q.v.) encouraged the further specialization of ideas of method and demonstration towards the 'external world', and the conditions for the emergence of **science** as the theoretical and methodical study of *nature* were then complete. Theory and method applied to other kinds of *experience* (one area was metaphysical and religious; another was social and political; another was *feeling* and the *inner life*, now acquiring its new specialized association with ART, (q.v.)) could then be marked off as not **science** but something else.

The distinction hardened in eC19 and mC19. Though there were still many residual uses, we can find by 1867 the significantly confident, yet also significantly conscious, statement: 'we shall . . . use the word "science" in the sense which Englishmen so commonly give to it . . . as expressing physical and experimental science, to the exclusion of theological and metaphysical'. That particular exclusion was the climax of a decisive argument, but the specialization excluded, under that cover, many other areas of knowledge and learning. **Scientific**, **scientific method** and **scientific truth** became specialized to the successful methods of the **natural sciences**, primarily physics, chemistry and biology. Other studies might be theoretical and methodical, but this was not now the main point; it was the hard *objective* character of the material and the method, which in these areas went together, which was taken as defining.

In 1840 Whewell wrote: 'we need very much a name to describe a cultivator of science in general. I should incline to call him a scientist.' This is a significant mark of a general grouping within the new specializing emphasis. A further distinction, but at an earlier stage, can be seen, also from 1840, in 'Leonardo was mentally a seeker after truth – a scientist; Correggio was an assertor of truth – an artist'. Distinctions of this kind became conventional, though as late as 1836, and convincingly, Constable was saying: 'painting is a science, and should be pursued as an inquiry into the laws of nature. Why . . . may not landscape painting be considered as a branch of natural philosophy, of which pictures are but the experiments?' (*Fourth Lecture at the Royal Institution*). But the predominant tendency was in another direction. Method was specialized to one kind of method, just as *experience*, of a demonstrable kind, had been specialized to a certain kind of *experiment*. This was later to have its own internal consequences, especially in biology but also in physics. It was also to have profound consequences in other areas of human learning, where a particular and highly successful model of neutral methodical observer and external object of study became generalized, not only as **science**, but as *fact* and *truth* and *reason* or RATIONALITY (qq.v.). This was made worse by conventional criticism of the model in terms of an even older method, now reserved and specialized: the distinction of *subjective* facts and truths, and of 'areas' – religious, *artistic, psychological, moral* (the doubtful straddling one was *social*) – to which these, rather than **scientific** method, were appropriate.

The specialization of **science** is perhaps more complete in English than in most comparable languages. This causes considerable problems in contemporary translation, notably from French: cf. the alternation of **science** and *studies* in the **social** or **human sciences**, and the pressure around **scientific** when it is still used in an old sense, of 'a demonstrative proof in an argument', or in the developed sense of 'methodological rigour' – yet then where are the *experiments*, and is this not merely (*subjective, literary, speculative*) *experience*? As the simplifications of the conventional divisions, and especially those between **science** and *art* and *objective* and *subjective*, become more evident, the critical term **scientism** has been used to define the limited character of one side of the argument, but there is as yet no common term (though its formation may be seen in current re-examination of such concepts as *literature, aesthetic*, and *subjective*) to define the equally evident limitation of the 'other', in fact complementary, position.

See ART, EMPIRICAL, MATERIALISM, POSITIVIST, SUB-JECTIVE, THEORY

SENSIBILITY

Sensibility became a very important word in English between mC18 and mC20, but in recent years this importance has quite sharply declined. It is a very difficult word, both in its senses and variations within this historical period, and in its relations within the very complicated group of words centred on *sense*. We have only to remember that **sensibility** is not a general noun for the condition of being *sensible* to realize how difficult this group can be. Some of the interrelations of the group have been brilliantly analysed by William Empson in *The Structure of Complex Words*, 1951; 250–310.

The earliest uses of **sensibility**, fw *sensibilitas*, L, followed the earliest uses of **sensible**, fw *sensible*, F, *sensibilis*, lL – felt, perceived, through the (physical) *senses*. This use of **sensible**, from C14, underlay **sensibility** as physical feeling or sense perception from C15. But it was not a word often used. The significant development in *sense* was the extension from a process to a particular kind of product: *sense* as good sense, good judgment, from which the predominant modern meaning of **sensible** was to be derived. (*Common sense* has followed this track, ending in a blunt assertion of the obvious – what everybody knows, or knows to be practical – after its earlier and more active reference to a *sense* achieved by common process; the variations of COMMON (q.v.) are crucial here.) But before **sensible** was specialized to this limited use, it had moved, temporarily, in another direction, towards 'tender' or 'fine' feeling, from C16. This just survives in **sensible of** (cf. the special use of *touched*); *sense of* has a wider actual range, including neutrality. It was from **sensible** in this particular use that the important C18 use of **sensibility** was derived. It was more than *sensitivity*, which can describe a physical or an emotional condition. It was, essentially, a social generalization of certain personal qualities, or, to put it another way, a personal appropriation of certain social qualities. It thus belongs in an important formation which includes TASTE (q.v.), *cultivation* and *discrimination*, and, at a different level, CRITICISM (q.v.), and CULTURE (q.v.) in one of its uses, derived from **cultivated** and **cultivation**. All describe very general human processes, but in such a way as to specialize them; the negative effects of the actual exclusions that are so often implied can best be picked up in *discrimination*, which has survived both as the process of fine or informed judgment and as the process of treating certain groups unfairly. *Taste* and *cultivation* make little sense unless we are able to contrast their presence with their absence, in ways that depend on generalization and indeed on CONSENSUS (q.v.). **Sensibility** in its C18 uses ranged from a use much like that of modern *awareness* (not only *consciousness* but *conscience*) to a strong form of what the word appears literally to mean, the ability to feel: 'dear Sensibility! source . . . un-exhausted of all that's precious in our joys, or costly in our sorrows' (Sterne, 1768).

It was at this point that its relation to *sentimental* became important. *Sentiment*, from fw *sentimentum*, mL, rw *sentire*, L – to feel, had ranged from C14 uses for physical feeling, and feeling of one's own, to C17 uses for both opinion and emotion. In mC18 *sentimental* was widely used: '*sentimental*, so much in vogue among the polite . . . Everything clever and agreeable is comprehended in that word . . . a *sentimental* man . . . a *sentimental* party . . . a *sentimental* walk' (Lady Bradshaugh, 1749). The association with **sensibility** was then close: a conscious openness to feelings, and also a conscious consumption of feelings. The latter use made *sentimental* vulnerable, and in C19 this was, often crudely, pushed home: 'that rosepink vapour of Sentimentalism, Philanthropy and Feasts of Morals' (Carlyle, 1837); 'Sentimental Radicalism' (Bagehot on Dickens, 1858). Much that was moral or radical, in intention and in effect, was washed with the same brush that was used to depict self-conscious or self-indulgent displays of *sentiment*. Southey, in his conservative phase, brought the words together: 'the sentimental classes, persons of ardent or morbid sensibility' (1823). This complaint is against people who feel 'too much' as well as against those who 'indulge their emotions'. This confusion has permanently damaged *sentimental* (though limited positive uses survive, typically in *sentimental value*) and wholly determined *sentimentality*.

Sensibility escaped this. It maintained its C18 range, and became important in one special area, in relation to AESTHETIC (q.v.) feeling. (Jane Austen, of course, in *Sense and Sensibility*, had explored the variable qualities which the specialized terms appeared to define. In *Emma* she may have picked up one tendency in 'more acute sensibility to fine sounds than to my feelings' (II, vi; 1815).) Ruskin wrote of 'sensibility to colour' (1843). The word seems to have been increasingly used to distinguish a particular area of interest and response which could be distinguished not only from RATIONALITY (q.v.) or *intellectuality* but also (by contrast with one of its C18 associations) from *morality*. By eC20 **sensibility** was a key word to describe the human area in which artists worked and to which they appealed. In the subsequent development of a CRITICISM (q.v.) based on distinctions between *reason* and *emotion*, *sensibility* was a preferred general word for an area of human response and judgment which could not be reduced to the *emotional* or *emotive*. What T. S. Eliot, in the 1920s, called the **dissociation of sensibility** was a supposed disjunction between 'thought' and 'feeling'. **Sensibility** became the apparently unifying word, and on the whole was transferred from kinds of response to a use equivalent to the formation of a particular mind: a whole activity, a whole way of perceiving and responding, not to be reduced to either 'thought' or 'feeling'. *Experience*, in its available senses of something active and something formed, took on the same generality. For an important period, **sensibility** was that from which art proceeded and through which it was received. In the latter use, *taste* and *cultivation*, which had been important associates in the original formation, were generally replaced by *discrimination* and *criticism*. But for all the interest of this phase, which was dominant to c. 1960, the key terms were still pre-dominantly social generalizations of personal qualities or, as became increasingly apparent, personal appropriations of social qualities. **Sensibility** as an apparently neutral term in discussion of the sources of art, without the difficult overtones of *mind* or the specializations of *thought* and *feeling*, proved more durable than as a term of appeal or ratification for any particular response. But, as in the C18 emergence, the abstraction and generalization of an active personal quality, as if it were an evident social fact or process, depended on a consensus of particular valuations, and as these broke down or were rejected **sensibility** came to seem too deeply coloured by them to be available for general use. The word faded from active discussion, but it is significant that in its actual range (which is what is fundamentally at issue) no adequate replacement has been found.

See AESTHETIC, ART, CRITICISM, CULTURE, RATIONAL, SUBJECTIVE, TASTE

SOCIALIST

Socialist emerged as a philosophical and political description in eC19. Its linguistic root was the developed sense of SOCIAL (q.v.). But this could be understood in two ways, which have had profound effects on the use of the term by radically different political tendencies. *Social* in sense (i) was the merely descriptive term for *society* in its now predominant sense of the system of common life; a *social reformer* wished to reform this system. *Social* in sense (ii) was an emphatic and distinguishing term, explicitly contrasted with *individual* and especially *individualist* theories of society. There has of course been much interaction and overlap between these two senses, but their varying effect can be seen from the beginning in the formation of the term. One popular form of sense (i) was in effect a continuation of LIBERAL-ISM (q.v.): reform, including radical reform, of the social order, to develop, extend and assure the main *liberal* values: political freedom, the ending of privileges and formal inequalities, social justice (conceived as equity between different individuals and groups). A popular form of sense (ii) went in a quite different direction: a competitive, *individualist* form of society – specifically, industrial capitalism and the system of wage-labour – was seen as the enemy of truly *social* forms, which depended on practical co-operation and mutuality, which in turn could not be achieved while there was still *private* (*individual*) ownership of the means of production. Real freedom could not be achieved, basic inequalities could not be ended, social justice (conceived now as a just social order rather than equity between the different individuals and groups produced by the existing social order) could not be established, unless a society based on PRIVATE (q.v.) property was replaced by one based on *social* ownership and control.

The resulting controversy, between many groups and tendencies all calling themselves **socialist**, has been long, intricate and bitter. Each main tendency has found alternative, often derogatory terms for the other. But until c. 1850 the word was too new and too general to have any predominant use. It seems to have been first used in the English Owenite *Cooperative Magazine* of November, 1827; its first recorded appearance in French is in 1833. On the other hand, *socialisme* seems to have been first used in French in 1831, and in English in 1837 (Owen, *New Moral World*, III, 364). (A use of *socialismo* in Italian, in 1803, seems to have no connection with the later development; its meaning was quite different.) Given the intense political climate, in France and in England in the 1820s and 1830s, the exact dates are less important than the sense of a period. Moreover, it could not then have been known which word would come through as decisive. It was a period of very intense and rapid political argument and formation, and until well into the 1840s other terms stood level with **socialist**, or were indeed more common: *co-operative, mutualist, associationist, societarian, phalansterian, agrarianist, radical*. As late as 1848 Webster's *Dictionary* (USA) defined **socialism** as 'a new term for agrarianism', although in France and Germany, and to a lesser extent in England, **socialist** and **socialism** were by then common terms. The active verbs, **socialize** and *socialiser*, had been current in English and French from around 1830.

One alternative term, COMMUNIST (q.v.), had begun to be used in France and England from 1840. The sense of any of these words could vary in particular national contexts. In England in the 1840s *communist* had strong religious attachments, and this was important since **socialist**, as used by Robert Owen, was associated with opposition to religion and was sometimes avoided for that reason. Developments in France and Germany were different: so much so that Engels, in his *Preface* of 1888 looking back to the *Communist Manifesto* which he and Marx had written in 1848, observed:

> We could not have called it a *Socialist* manifesto. In 1847, Socialism was a middle-class movement, Communism a working-class movement. Socialism was, on the continent at least, respectable; Communism was the very opposite.

Communist had French and German senses of a militant movement, at the same time that in England it was being preferred to **socialist** because it did not involve atheism.

Modern usage began to settle from the 1860s, and in spite of the earlier variations and distinctions it was **socialist** and **socialism** which came through as the predominant words. What also came through in this period was a predominance of sense (ii), as the range of associated words – *co-operative, mutualist, associationist* and the new (from the 1850s) COLLECTIVIST (q.v.) – made natural. Though there was still extensive and intricate internal dispute, **socialist** and **socialism** were, from this period, accepted general terms. *Communist*, in spite of the distinction that had been made in the 1840s, was very much less used, and parties in the Marxist tradition took some variant of *social* and **socialist** as titles: usually *Social Democratic*, which meant adherence to **socialism**. Even in the renewed and bitter internal disputes of the period 1880–1914, these titles held. COMMUNISM (q.v.) was in this period most often used either as a description of an early form of society – *primitive communism* – or as a description of an ultimate form, which would be achieved after passing through **socialism**. Yet, also in this period, movements describing themselves as **socialist**, for example the English Fabians, powerfully revived what was really a variant of sense (i), in which **socialism** was seen as necessary to complete *liberalism*, rather than as an alternative and opposed theory of society. To Shaw and others, **socialism** was 'the economic side of the democratic ideal' (*Fabian Essays*, 33) and its achievement was an inevitable prolongation of the earlier tendencies which *Liberalism* had represented. It is interesting that opposing this view, and emphasizing the resistance of the capitalist economic system to such an 'inevitable' development, William Morris used the word *communism*. The relative militancy of *communist* had also been affected by the example of the Paris Commune, though there was a significant argument whether the correct term to be derived from that was *communist* or *communard*.

The decisive distinction between **socialist** and *communist*, as in one sense these terms are now ordinarily used, came with the renaming, in 1918, of the *Russian Social-Democratic Labour Party* (*Bolsheviks*) as the *Communist Party of the Soviet Union* (*Bolsheviks*). From that time on, a distinction of **socialist** from *communist*, often with supporting definitions such as *social democrat* or **democratic socialist**, became widely current, although it is significant that all *communist* parties, in line with earlier usage, continued to describe themselves as **socialist** and dedicated to **socialism**. Each tendency continues to deny the title to its opponents and competitors, but what has really happened is a re-surfacing, in new terms, of the originally variant senses of *social* and thence **socialist**. Those relying on sense (ii) are right to see other kinds of **socialist** as a new stage of *liberalism* (and thus to call them, often contemptuously, *liberals*), while those relying on sense (i), seeing a natural association between *liberal* values and **socialism**, have grounds for opposing **socialists** who in their view are enemies of the *liberal* tradition (where the difficulty, always, is in the alternative interpretations: (a) political freedom understood as an *individual* right and expressed socially in competitive political parties; (b) *individualism* understood as the competitive and antagonistic ethos and practice of capitalism, which *individual* rights and political competition merely qualify).

Some other associated political terms provide further complications. There is the significant development, in mC19, of *anarchy* and its derivatives in new political senses. *Anarchy* had been used in English from C16 in a broad sense: 'this unleful lyberty or lycence of the multytude is called an Anarchie' (1539). But this specific political sense, often interpreted as opposition to a single ruler – '*Anarchism* . . . the being itself of the people without a Prince or Ruler', (1656) (where the sense is close to that of early *democracy*) – was on the whole less common than the more general sense of disorder and chaos. Yet in 1791 Bentham defined the *anarchist* as one who 'denies the validity of the law . . . and calls upon all mankind to rise up in a mass, and resist the execution of it', a sense again near that of early *democrat*. What was really new from mC19 was the positive adoption of the term by certain groups, as a statement of their political position; most of the earlier descriptions were by opponents. *Anarchism* and *anarchist*, by lC19, represented a specific continuation of earlier senses of *democracy* and *democrat*, but at a time when both *democracy* and, though less widely, **socialism** had acquired new general and positive senses. Anarchists opposed the *statist* tendencies of much of the socialist movement, but stressed *mutuality* and *co-operation* as the principles of the self-organization of society. Particular *anarchist* groups opposed particular tyrannies and governments by *militant* and VIOLENT (q.v.) means, but this was not a necessary or universal result of *anarchist* principles, and there was in any case a complicated overlap between such policies and **socialist** definitions of REVOLUTION (q.v.). Yet the persistent general senses of disorder and chaos were relatively easily transferred (often with obvious injustice) to *anarchists*: the variant senses of *lawlessness* – from active criminality to resistance to laws made by others – were in this context critical. *Militant*, meanwhile, had been going through a related development: its early senses in English were stronger in the context of dedicated activity than in the root *military* sense, and the predominant use, to lC19, was in religion: *church militant* (from eC15); 'our condition, whilst we are in this world, is militant' (Wilkins, *Natural Religion*, 251; 1672); 'the Church is ever militant' (Newman, 1873). The word was effectively transferred from religious to social activity during C19: 'militant in the endeavour to reason aright', (Coleridge, *Friend*, 57; 1809); 'a normal condition of militancy against social injustice' (Froude, 1856). The further development from political to industrial *militancy* came in C20, and much of the earlier history of the word has been forgotten, except in residual uses. There has also been a marked association

– as in *anarchism* – with senses of disorder and of VIOLENCE (q.v.). *Solidarity*, in its sense of unity in industrial or political action, came into English in mC19, from fw *solidarité*, F, lC18. *Exploitation* appeared in English from eC19, originally in the sense of profitable working of an area or a material, and from mC19 in the sense of using other persons for (selfish) profit; it depended in both senses on fw *exploitation*, F, lC18.

Nihilist was invented by Turgeniev in *Fathers and Sons* (1862). Its confusion with *anarchist* has been widespread. *Populist* began in the United States, from the People's Party, in the early 1890s; it spread quickly, and is now often used in distinction from **socialist**, to express reliance on popular interests and sentiments rather than on particular (*principled*) theories and movements. *Syndicalist* appeared in French in 1904 and in English in 1907; it has gone through varying combinations with *anarchism* (in its stress on *mutuality*) and with **socialism**.

The widest term of all, the *Left*, is known from C19 from an accident of parliamentary seating, but it was not common as a general description before C20, and *leftism* and *leftist* do not seem to have been used in English before the 1920s. The derisive *lefty*, though it has some currency from the 1930s, belongs mainly to the 1950s and after.

See CAPITALISM, COMMUNISM, DEMOCRACY, INDIVIDUAL, LIBERAL, SOCIETY

SOCIETY

Society is now clear in two main senses: as our most general term for the body of institutions and relationships within which a relatively large group of people live; and as our most abstract term for the condition in which such institutions and relationships are formed. The interest of the word is partly in the often difficult relationship between the generalization and the abstraction. It is mainly in the historical development which allows us to say 'institutions and relationships', and we can best realize this when we remember that the primary meaning of **society** was companionship or fellowship.

Society came into English in C14 from fw *société*, oF, *societas*, L, rw *socius*, L – companion. Its uses to mC16 ranged from active unity in fellowship, as in the Peasants' Revolt of 1381, through a sense of general relationship – 'they have neede one of anothers helpe, and thereby love and societie . . . growe among all men the more' (1581) to a simpler sense of companionship or company – 'your society' (lC16). An example from 1563, 'society between Christ and us', shows how readily these distinguishable senses might in practice overlap. The tendency towards the general and abstract sense thus seems inherent, but until lC18 the other more active and immediate senses were common. The same range can be seen in two examples from Shakespeare. In 'my Riots past, my wilde Societies' (*Merry Wives of Windsor*, III, iv) **society** was virtually equivalent to relationship or to one of our senses of *associations*, whereas in 'our Selfe will mingle with Society' (*Macbeth*, III, iv) the sense is simply that of an assembled company of guests. The sense of a deliberate association for some purpose (here of social distinction) can be illustrated by the 'societe of saynct George' (the Order of the Garter, C15), and over a very wide range this particular use has persisted.

The general sense can be seen as strengthening from mC16. It was intermediate in 'the yearth untilled, societie neglected' (1553) but clear though still not separate in 'a common wealth is called a society or common doing of a multitude of free men' (1577). It was clear and separate in 'societie is an assemblie and consent of many in one' (1599), and in C17 such uses began to multiply, and with a firmer reference: 'a due reverence . . . towards Society wherein we live' (1650). Yet the earlier history was still evident in 'the Laws of Society and Civil Conversation' (Charles I, 1642; *conversation*, here, had its earliest sense of mode of living, before additional (C16) familiar discourse; the same experience was working in this word, but with an eventually opposite specialization). The abstract sense also strengthened: 'the good of Humane Society' (Cudworth, 1678; see HUMAN) and 'to the benefit of society' (1749). In one way the abstraction was made more complete by the development of the notion of 'a society', in the broadest sense. This depended on a new sense of relativism (cf. CULTURE) but, in its transition from the notion of the general laws of fellowship or association to a notion of specific laws forming a specific society, it prepared the way for the modern notion, in which the laws of society are not so much laws for getting on with other people but more abstract and more impersonal laws which determine social institutions.

The transition was very complex, but can now be best seen by considering **society** with *state*. *State* had developed, from its most general and continuing sense of condition (*state of nature*, *state of siege*, from C13), a specialized sense which was virtually interchangeable with *estate* (both *state* and *estate* were from fw *estat*, oF, *status*, L – condition) and in effect with rank: 'noble stat' (1290). The word was particularly associated with monarchy and nobility, that is to say with a hierarchical ordering of society: cf: 'state of prestis, and state of knyghtis, and the thridd is staat of comunys' (1300). The *States* or *Estates* were an institutional definition of power from C14, while *state* as the dignity of the king was common in C16 and eC17: 'state and honour' (1544); 'goes with great state' (1616); 'to the King . . . your Crowne and State' (Bacon, 1605). From these combined uses *state* developed a conscious political sense: 'ruler of the state' (1538); 'the State of Venice' (1680). But *state* still often meant the association of a particular kind of sovereignty with a particular kind of rank. *Statist* was a common term for politician in C17, but through the political conflicts of that century a fundamental conflict came to be expressed in what was eventually a distinction between **society** and *state*: the former an association of free men, drawing on all the early active senses; the latter an organization of power, drawing on the senses of hierarchy and majesty. The crucial notion of **civil society** (see CIVILIZATION) was an alternative definition of social order, and it was in thinking through the general questions of this new order that **society** was confirmed in its most general and eventually abstract senses. Through many subsequent political changes this kind of distinction has persisted: **society** is that to which we all belong, even if it is also very general and impersonal; the *state* is the apparatus of power.

The decisive transition of **society** towards its most general and abstract sense (still, by definition, a different thing from *state*) was an C18 development. I have been through Hume's *Enquiry Concerning the Principles of Morals* (1751) for uses of the word, and taking 'company of his fellows' as sense (i) and 'system of common life' as sense (ii) found: sense (i), 25; sense (ii), 110; but also, at some critical points in the argument, where the sense of **society** can be decisive, sixteen essentially intermediate uses. Hume also, as it happens, illustrates the necessary distinction as **society** was losing its most active and immediate sense; he used, as we still would, the alternative *company*:

As the mutual shocks in *society*, and the oppositions of interest and self-love, have constrained mankind to establish the laws of justice . . . in like manner, the eternal contrarieties, in *company*, of men's pride and self-conceit, have introduced the rules of *Good Manners* or *Politeness* . . . (*Enquiry*, VIII, 211)

At the same time, in the same book, he used **society** for *company* in just this immediate sense, where we now, wishing for some purposes to revive the old sense, would speak of 'face-to-face' relationships; usually, we would add, within a COMMUNITY (q.v.).

By lC18 **society** as a system of common life was predominant: 'every society has more to apprehend from its needy members than from the rich' (1770); 'two different schemes or systems of morality' are current at the same time in 'every society where the distinction of rank [see CLASS] has once been established' (Adam Smith, *Wealth of Nations*, II, 378–9; 1776). The subsequent development of both general and abstract senses was direct.

A related development can be seen in **social**, which in C17 could mean either associated or sociable, but by lC18 was mainly general and abstract: 'man is a Social creature; that is, a single man, or family, cannot subsist, or not well, alone out of all Society', . . . (though note that **Society** here, with the qualification *all*, is still active rather than abstract). By C19 **society** can be seen clearly enough as an object to allow such formations as **social reformer** (although **social** was also used, and is still used, to describe personal company; cf. **social life** and **social evening**). At the same time, in seeing **society** as an object (the objective sum of our relationships) it was possible, in new ways, to define the relationship of **man and society** or **the individual and society** as a problem. These formations measure the distance from the early sense of active fellowship. The problems they indicate, in the actual development of society, were significantly illustrated in the use of the word **social**, in eC19, to contrast an idea of **society** as mutual co-operation with an experience of **society** (the **social system**) as individual competition. These alternative definitions of society could not have occurred if the most general and abstract sense had not, by this period, been firm. It was from this emphasis of **social**, in a positive rather than a neutral sense, and in distinction from INDIVIDUAL (q.v.), that the political term SOCIALIST (q.v.) was to develop.

One small specialized use of **society** requires notice if not comment. An early sense of **good society** in the sense of good company was specialized, by the norms of such people, to **Society** as the most distinguished and fashionable part of **society**: the *upper* CLASS (q.v.). Byron (*Don Juan*, XIII, 95) provides a good example of this mainly C19 (and residual) sense:

Society is now one polish'd horde
Formed of two mighty tribes, the *Bores* and *Bored*.

It is ironic that this special term is the last clear use of **society** as the active companionship of one's (class) fellows. Elsewhere such feelings were moving, for good historical reasons, to COMMUNITY (q.v.), and to the still active senses of **social**.

See   CLASS,   COMMUNITY,   INDIVIDUAL,   SOCIALIST, SOCIOLOGY

SOCIOLOGY

Sociology was first used by Comte in 1830, and first appeared in English in 1843: Mill, *Logic*, VI and *Blackwood's Magazine* (in an article on Comte). Spencer wrote *Principles of Sociology* in three volumes between 1876 and 1896. From the work of Durkheim, in French, and Weber, in German, at the turn of the century, the subject was remarkably extended. The term depended on the developed senses of SOCIETY and SOCIAL (qq.v.). It has been defined within a number of intellectual systems as the SCIENCE (q.v.) of society. **Sociological** has two senses: a reference to the forms of this science, and a looser and more general reference (in which it often replaces *social*) to some social fact or tendency (cf. 'sociological factors'; cf. also *technological*, where a similar transfer from the abstract formation is common). **Sociologist**, used first in general ways for a student of society, has acquired a more limited professional sense since the subject became defined in university courses; it is still, however, also used generally, in the same area as the general use of **sociological**. One interesting result of this overlap of professional and general references is that **sociology** itself is often used to indicate any general interest in social processes, often by contrast with other kinds of interest which assume that they can separate or exclude the *social*. Meanwhile professional **sociology**, especially in

247

countries where it is weak, often insists on its distance from *social theory* or *social criticism*, and re-defines itself as the *science of society* in the special and limited senses of empirical investigation and quantification. Within a more general tradition of **sociology** other modes of investigation are still emphasized.

See SCIENCE, SOCIETY

STANDARDS

Standard, in the singular, is a complicated but not especially difficult word. The same is true of its ordinary plural. But **standards** is also a case of an exceptional kind of plural – what can be called a plural singular – in which the plural form covers a singular reference; other common examples are *morals* and *values*.

Standard is etymologically complicated. Its main development was by aphesis (loss of an initial letter) from fw *estaundart*, AN, *estendart*, oF, from rw *extendere*, L – stretch out (which more directly led to *extend* and *extension*). In its transitional forms – *standardum*, *standardus* – it applied this root sense to the flag (as still in **Royal Standard**) stretched out from its pole (from C12). But from C13 it acquired the different sense of an erect or upright object, perhaps from association with the display of flags, more probably from confusion with the noun from *stand*, *stander*, which underlies certain modern uses (**standard lamp**, **standard rose**), in a different physical sense. The most interesting modern sense, in the range from 'a source of authority' to 'a level of achievement', developed in C15, probably from association with the **Royal Standard** as marking a source of authority. It was widely used in the precise context of weights and measures: the **standard foot**. But it was also extended to other matters, with the general sense of an authoritative example of correctness. Thus in C15 there was reference to a **standard book**, in alchemy.

All these uses have continued, but in C19 there were some significant developments. In mC19 there was the curious case of **Standard English**: a selected (class-based) use taken as an authoritative example of correctness, which, widely backed by educational institutions, attempted to convict a majority of native speakers of English of speaking their own language 'incorrectly'. There was the prescription, also in education, of certain levels of competence – **standards** – in reading, writing and arithmetic; in one period these were factors in the calculation of teachers' pay. Classes aiming at these levels of competence were described, in elementary education, as **Standards** (Two to Six). The word was much emphasized as a term of assessment or grading, and was more generally associated with a concept of graded progress within a hierarchy (cf. the contemporary phrase *the educational ladder*, probably introduced by T. H. Huxley and applied in the *board* – controlled by an *Educational Board* – schools).

From this period, **standards** both as an ordinary plural and as a plural singular became common. In many contexts the **standards** thus grouped could be precisely stated, as still in the **British Standards Institution**. It was also natural that this use should be extended to matters in which less precise measurement was possible but in which, on demand, quite specific levels of attainment or competence could be exemplified or described. These are the ordinary plurals. The plural singular is the quite different use where the reference is essentially CONSENSUAL (q.v.) ('we all know what real standards are') or, with a certain deliberate vagueness, suasive ('anyone who is concerned with standards will agree'). It is often impossible, in these uses, to disagree with some assertion of **standards** without appearing to disagree with the very idea of quality; this is where the plural singular most powerfully operates. Some comparable cases can help us to understand this. 'A person of no *morals*' can mean a person with no moral sense or a person whose moral ideas or actions are at variance with current local norms. 'A concern for *values*' can mean a concern to distinguish relative values or to uphold certain (consensual) valuations. If we think about common phrases like *Western values* or *University standards* we can see the variation fairly clearly. Each phrase can be further defined, in some uses. But since *Western Civilization* is not only a TRADITION (q.v.) but a complex and historically varied social process, containing radical disagreements and conflicts as well as intellectual and practical agreements, and since *universities*, while at any given time they have certain precise standards, also change these and disagree about them and vary between different societies and periods, it is soon apparent, by the character of any further definition, or by the kind of response to a request for it, whether *values* and **standards** are true plurals, grouping a number of specific positions and judgments, or plural singulars, in which a generalizing version of the essence of a civilization or a university is being projected as if it were a specific grouping of certain defined *valuations* and **standardizations**. It is very significant that the popular use of **standards** – laudatory – is at odds with a popular use of **standardization** – derogatory. **Standardization** came into use in lC19, from science (standardizing the conditions of an experiment) and then industry (standardizing parts). It is not controversial in these uses, but in its application to matters of mind and experience it has been widely resisted – 'people can't be **standardized**', 'teaching mustn't be **standardized**' – by, among others, those who insist on the 'maintenance of **standards**'. This odd usage probably depends on exploiting the range of senses from **Royal Standard** (respectful) to **standard foot** (all right in its place but here inappropriate). The power of the plural singular always depends on its not being spotted as a singular. If it is not spotted, it can be used to override necessary arguments or to appropriate the very process of valuation and definition to its own particular conclusions.

A further note is necessary on the phrase **standard of living**. This is now common but sometimes difficult. Its earliest form, from mC19, was **standard of life**, and this is still often used interchangeably. Yet as we realize when we think about **standard**, the term seems to imply a defined level or a necessary level, rather than, as in its now common use, a general condition or an averaged condition. It was first used in the strict sense of **standard**: **standard of life** meant the necessary level of income and conditions to maintain life satisfactorily. (This was of course argued about, and could vary in different groups, times and places, but it had a precise sense when it was first used in the campaign for a minimum wage: a **standard** would be set, and a wage could be judged by reference back to it.) This was **standard of life** in a defining and retrospective (referential) sense. But the phrase developed (subsequent to its definition, for example, in OED) towards its now more common meaning: the income and conditions we actually have. As it lost the measurable reference of **standard** it retained, nevertheless, a sense of measurement. There has been controversy whether a standard of *life* or *living* can really be measured, while at the same time statistics of income, consumption, and so on have been used to define it. Standard Past, we might say, has been replaced by Standard Present. But there is also a use which draws on another sense of **standard**: not the agreed measure but, metaphorically, the flag: the **standard** we set ourselves; proper **standards** of health care; a proper **standard** of living. This is Standard Future: the old measures, or the existing grades, are inadequate, and we will aim at something better. It is a very interesting use. Instead of referring back to a source of authority, or taking a current measurable state, a **standard** is set, projected, from ideas about conditions which we have not yet realized but which we think should be realized. There is an active social history in this development of the phrase.

STATUS

Status has become a significant word in C20. It was taken directly into English from *status*, L – condition, which had earlier led to STATE and ESTATE (qq.v.). It is still often used in specific Latin formations such as *status quo*. It had legal uses from C18, to define 'rights, duties, capacities or incapacities' (1832) and has survived in this sense (cf. **marital status**). Its extension to a more general social sense came from this kind of use: '*status* as free or slave' (1865); 'legal status of negroes' (1888); 'civil status of actors' (1904). There was evident extension in Mill's 'status of a day-labourer' (1848) and perhaps in 'professional status' (1883), where general rather than legal condition was implied. Thus far the word is not difficult.

It became difficult from its use in a new general sense in some modern sociology, where it is frequently offered, as a more precise and measurable term, in preference to CLASS (q.v.). It is impossible to clarify this without reference to the three main social senses of *class*, as group, rank and formation. Clearly **status** has no clear use in the senses either of group or of formation, and its real significance is that it is a new and modernizing term for *rank* (losing the inherited and formal associations of that term). It can thus be substituted for *class* in only this one of its senses. But the substitution is significant, in that this sense is chosen. The use is often traced to Max Weber, and to his critique of Marx's notion of *class*. But this is a confusion. Weber's word *Stand*, often now translated as **status**, could more properly be translated as *Estate* (which has, however, lost the relevant early sense). It refers primarily to a social group who have motivations other than the strictly economic factors of *class* in Marx's main sense: motivations such as social beliefs and ideals proper to the group, or to a distinct social condition. In more recent sociology this important social observation has been transferred to the abstract sense of a generalized rank order: 'social status . . . the position occupied by a person, family, or kinship group in a social system relative to others . . . Social status has a hierarchical distribution in which a few persons occupy the highest positions . . .' (*A Dictionary of Sociology*; G. D. Mitchell, 1968). An extraordinary technical sophistication has been brought to the elaboration of this competitive and hierarchical model of society. **Status** is a 'continuous variable' but with observable 'clusters'; these are its advantages, as a term of measurement, over *class* as rank, with its overtones of definite group or formation. They are also its disadvantages, since the term inherits (from its associations with Weber) elements of respect and self-respect, which are bound to confuse the apparently objective process of **status-determination**. Where *rank* had titles and ribbons, **status** has *symbols*. But it is characteristic that these can be not only displayed but acquired: the objective or pseudo-objective signs are then confused with the subjective or merely pretentious emphases. It is especially significant that the language of **status**, in this specialized but now common sense, turns out to be the language of *class* in a deliberately reduced sense (*rank*). This has the double advantage, of appearing to cancel *class* in the sense of formation or even of broad group, and of providing a model of society which is not only hierarchical and individually competitive but is essentially defined in terms of consumption and display (see CONSUMER). Thus one 'continuous scale of social status' has been based on 'the style of life reflected in the main living room of the home', which is certainly a matter of interest but which has reduced *society* to this series of units interpreted in terms of private possessions. As the units are grouped into **status-groups** or even a **status system**, the 'life' style which is being measured is life as defined by market-research, whether as goods and services or as 'public opinion'. What was once a term of legal condition or general condition (and which in its earlier adoption, in *estate*, had indicated effective social formations) is then, in its conventional modern use, an operational term for the reduction of all social questions to the terms of a mobile consumer society.

See CLASS, CONSUMER, SOCIETY

STRUCTURAL

Structure, with its associated words, is a key term in modern thought, and in many of its recent developments it is especially complex. The word is from fw *structure*, F, *structura*, L, rw *struere*, L – build. In its earliest English uses, from C15, **structure** was primarily a noun of process: the action of building. The word was notably developed in C17, in two main directions: (i) towards the whole product of building, as still in 'a wooden structure'; (ii) towards the manner of construction, not only in buildings but in extended and figurative applications. Most modern developments follow from (ii), but there is a persistent ambiguity in the relations between these and what are really extended and figurative applications of (i).

The particular sense that became important as an aspect of (ii) is that of 'the mutual relation of constituent parts or elements of a whole as defining its particular nature'. This is clearly an extension of the sense of a method of building, but it is characteristic that it carries a strong sense of *internal* structure, even while **structure** is still important to describe the whole construction. The earliest specialized uses were in anatomy – 'structure of the Hand' (eC17) – and the word remained important in the general development of biology, often with a distinction from *function* (fw *functionem*, L, rw *fungi* – perform), where observation of the (proper) *functioning* of an organ could be distinguished from observation of the **structure** of the organism. Still, however, in C18 developments there was an understandable range from the sense of the whole construction to the sense of internal conformation. **Structure** was used, for example, to describe not only bodies but statues. It was used to describe the main features of a region. In the biological uses, sense (ii) is usually clear: 'structure and internal conformation' (1774). But when we find, for example, from 1757, 'every one's private structure of mind and sensations', it is far from clear whether this refers primarily to internal relations or to the whole result of a process of (building and) development. In applications to writing there was a similar uncertainty: 'the Structure of his Line' (1746) and 'structure of... periods' (1749) both carry a sense of the process of building, but the former probably referred primarily to the whole result and the latter primarily to internal relations. In geology, from 1813, there is an unambiguous example in the strengthening analytic sense: 'structure of the internal parts'.

Structural appeared in mC19. In its early uses it repeated the range of **structure** but there was an increasing emphasis on the internal construction as constitutive. It was used in quite general ways for matters of building and engineering (cf. a modern definition of engineering as 'to design or develop structures, machines, apparatus or manufacturing processes . . .') where the principles of construction were recognized to be **structural**, but where **structure**, as a matter of course, referred both to the method and process of construction and to the completed work. However the sense of **structure** as constitutive was drawn upon to express not only a sense of basic construction but, emphatically, of internal construction: in geology, for example: 'structural, as affecting the intimate character of the mass, and not merely its external form'. This was repeated in, for example, 'structural differences which separate Man from the Gorilla' (1863). This was the completion of the earlier sense of 'mutual relations of constituent parts of a whole', with particular stress on the identification of the arrangement and mutual relations of elements of a complex unity. **Structural evidences** and **structural relations**, from the 1870s, expressed this sense. In building, by lC19, there was a conventional distinction between **structural** and *decorative*, which reinforced the sense of an internal framework or process. Sciences using this emphasis were named as **structural**: **structural botany** (1835); **structural geology** (1882); **structural chemistry** (1907); **structural engineering** (1908).

We need to know this history if we are to understand the important and difficult development of **structural** and later **structuralist** as defining terms in the human sciences, notably linguistics and anthropology. The stress in linguistics, though at first not given this name, represents a shift from historical and comparative to analytic studies, made necessary especially by the problems of understanding languages which were outside the traditional groups in which earlier methods had been developed. Especially in the case of the languages of the American Indians, it was found necessary to discard presuppositions and assimilations drawn from historical and comparative studies of Indo-European languages, and to study each language 'from the inside' or, as it was later put, **structurally**. At the same time, more rigorous and objective methods were applied to the study of language as a whole, and its basic procedures began to be described by the word which was already available, from the physical sciences, for this emphasis: **structures**. Thus far there was no particular difficulty, but the problem of naming turned out to be crucial and has led to some obvious problems. **Structure** was preferred to *process* because it emphasized a particular and complex organization of relations, often at very deep levels. But what were being studied were nevertheless living processes, while **structure**, characteristically, from its uses in building and engineering, and in anatomy, physiology and botany, expressed something relatively fixed and permanent, even hard. The intensive development of notions of **structure** in physics, though in themselves demonstrating the difference between *static* and *dynamic* structures, added to the sense of deep internal relations, discoverable only by special kinds of observation and analysis. The initial move, to discard some received modes of study because they included presuppositions drawn from quite different material, did not necessarily lead to all the subsequent senses of **structural** or, as now, **structuralist**. Indeed the early phase of **structuralist** linguistics used the adjective to mean little more than taking each language in its own terms, so as to discover *its* structure. Similarly, **structural** linguistics was a form of analysis of the general phenomenon of language, in terms of the fundamental organization of its basic procedures. It is an irony that the *functionalist* and **structuralist** schools of anthropology are now often contrasted, with support from a traditional distinction in biology between *function* (performance) and **structure** (organization) itself emphasized in sociology by Spencer, but that early **structuralist** linguistics and *functionalist* anthropology shared an emphasis on studying a particular organization, a language or a culture, in its own terms, setting aside general or conventional presuppositions drawn from other languages and cultures, or from generalizations about languages and cultures as wholes. This overlap is now past, but it reminds us of the complexity of the distinctions. We can compare the similar complexities of *form* and FORMALIST (q.v.), where *formal* can mean either the external (often superficial) appearance or those qualities and details of *formation* which explain a particular shaping. The difficulties of *systematic* are also relevant. *System*, from fw *systema*, Gk – organized whole, was used from C17 to describe particular organizations: either a *set* or such organizations as the *solar system* or the *nervous system*. What was involved in describing these was discovering the organization and mutual relations of a particular complex whole: a sense which overlaps with one sense of **structural** and is still close to it, down to details of procedure, in matters like *systems analysis*. But *system* also continued in its sense of a whole organization: a set of principles; an organized treatise; a THEORY (q.v.) (there was a mC18 distinction between *system* and *practice*); or a whole social organization ('the social system', 'the system'). *Systematic* can then mean either orderly and complete inquiry and exposition, or that **structural** quality which pertains to the essential 'constitutive' character of an organization. The shades of meaning are obviously very difficult to distinguish. It is not as easy as it is often made to seem to distinguish one kind of procedure or one kind of definition of interest from another, by the use of terms as complex and variable as these.

This is especially the case in the popularization of **structuralist**. In America, linguistics and anthropology, for historical reasons, have always been closely linked, and the effective popularization of **structuralist** can only be understood when this is taken into account. There have been many variations and many areas of uncertainty, but the primary emphasis is on deep permanent structures of which the observed variations of languages and cultures are forms. There has been a radical rejection of 'historical' (*historicist*) and EVOLUTIONARY (q.v.) assumptions, and comparative methods are applied only to **structures**, which in this use has quite lost (and indeed rejected) the alternative sense of finished constructions and intends only the sense of internal *formal* relations. In what can be called orthodox structuralism, these **structures**, over a range from kinship to myth and grammar, are permanent constitutive human formations: the defining features of human consciousness and perhaps of the physical human brain. Observed or observable variations are interpreted in terms of these structures. (There is an evident association, in this, with the psychoanalytic generalizations of human nature, and with earlier rationalist generalizations of the *properties* of the mind, to say nothing of the practical overlap, in some cases, with forms of IDEALISM (q.v.). There is an alternative tendency, named GENETIC (q.v.) **structuralism**, which still emphasizes deep constitutive formations, of a **structural** kind, but which sees these as being built up and broken down at different stages in history, as distinct from being permanent and humanly constitutive. (The claim that Hegel and Marx were

genetic structuralists, in this sense, bears some examination.) The dispute between these tendencies is important, but it is necessary to analyse the uses of **structure** if any full argument is to be developed. Often 'orthodox' and 'genetic' structuralists share the conviction that the **structures** DETERMINE (q.v.) human life, whether absolutely or historically. One influential tendency sees not human beings living in and through **structures**, but **structures** living in and through human beings. (This is the ground for a recent derogatory sense of *humanism*: the reduction of **structural** matters to *human* – *individual* or *moral* – tendencies and motivations.) It is clear that in many cases the hypothesis of a **structure**, followed by its detailed analysis, has been very fruitful in investigation. It can encourage clarification of fundamental relationships, often of a kind screened by assumption or habit. This has given great strength to **structuralism** as an emphasis, but the transition represented by one aspect of the transfer from **structural** to **structuralism** – the sense not of a procedure or set of procedures but of an explanatory *system* – has had quite different effects. There has been an evident tendency to take the categories of thought and analysis as if they were prime substances. It is here, especially, that *structuralism* joins with particular tendencies in psychology (when Id, Ego, Superego, Libido or Death-Wish function as primary characters, which actual human beings perform in already **structured** ways) and in Marxism (where CLASSES (q.v.) – or *modes of production* are primary, and human beings live out their inherent properties). It is a very fine point, in description of any *system* or **structure**, whether emphasis is put on the *relations* between people and between people and things, or on the *relationships*, which include the relations and the people and things related. It is clear from the history of **structure** and **structural** that the words can be used with either emphasis: to include the actual construction with special reference to its mode of construction; or to isolate the mode of construction in such a way as to exclude both ends of the process – the producers (who have intentions related to the mode chosen, as well as experience derived from the material being worked) and the product, in its substantive sense, which is more than the sum of its formal constructive relations, and distinctly more than an abstraction of them. In orthodox structuralism the effective exclusion of both producers and substantial products – their analytic reduction to the determining general relations – has been especially acceptable to people accustomed to similar procedures in industrial technology and in MANAGERIAL (q.v.) versions of society. Actual people and actual products are made theoretically subordinate to the decisive abstracted relations. GENETIC (q.v.) structuralism, with its emphasis on the building (**structuration**) and dismantling of structures, is better able to include both producers and products (who in this emphasis are more than the bearers of permanent structures) but is not really able to include them in substantial ways while the **structural** emphasis is still on deep internal relations rather than on what can be dismissively described as *content*. The problems of *formalism*, and of the complex bearings of *form* and *formation*, are very close at this point. Much **structuralist** analysis is *formalist* in the sense of separating *form* and *content* and giving *form* priority, as well as *formalist* in the wider and more acceptable sense of detailed analysis of specific formation. This need not separate content but can be concerned precisely with the *forms of content* and the *content of forms*, as integral processes. This can also be a concern with **structures**, in the wide sense which includes the activity of building and the thing built as well as (in and through) the modes of construction. But this is very different from a concern with **structures** in the sense of abstracted and constitutive internal relations.

The issues involved in this difficult group of words are very important. Indeed structural analysis of the group itself is particularly necessary, since one effect of the abstracted emphasis of **structure** is an assumption of the **structuralist** as an independent 'objective' observer, freed from both the habits and the substances of more superficial or EMPIRICAL (q.v.) kinds of observation. Some associated words may help. There has been an interesting use of *code*, to describe *sign-systems* in language and other forms of BEHAVIOUR (q.v.). *Code* (fw *codex*, L) was a systematic collection of laws and statutes (from C14) and, later, after extension to any systematic collection of laws in a less formal sense, a system of signals, in military (eC19) and telegraphic (mC19) use; thence, and now predominantly, an opaque system through which, but not in which, meanings are communicated. It is very significant, as a form of metaphorical support for the assumption of hidden internal relations of a decisive kind, that *code* is now used as if it were equivalent to any system of signals, thus making every element of communication (and especially its communicators) intrinsically abstract. *Code* may retain the sense of a system of constitutive laws, but the element of arbitrariness which its modern development indicates has been repeated in significant uses of words like *model* and *paradigm*. *Model* was indeed, from C16, a representation of a structure that it was proposed to build. It was then extended and used figuratively to express a pattern or type. It is still so used, but it is significantly often used to express not merely an abstract configuration of a process, but the sense that the particular abstract configuration chosen is at once decisive and, in a key sense, arbitrary: another *model* might have been chosen, giving substantially different results. Similarly *paradigm*, a pattern or example, used generally from C15 and in grammar from lC16, has been recently popularized in the sense of a characteristic (often arbitrary) mental hypothesis. Clearly all these words, like **structure** in its critical development, are important ways of thinking beyond habit and presupposition. Their recognition of variable forms is very important. But, as with **structure**, a necessary category of hypothesis or analysis can be converted, sometimes unconsciously, into a definition of substance. In one form of contemporary thought there are only **structures**, *codes*, *models* and *paradigms*: relations as distinct from relationships. The analytic importance of the categories is qualified by the implicit or explicit reduction of all processes to category relations. This (as in *games theory*) can, at times even against the intentions of their users, reduce substantial relations to formal and abstract relations (**structural** relations in the narrow sense), not only in analysis but in effective practice. If the analysis is to be carried through, this structural characteristic of the terms will have to be made conscious, and all its effects – within and beyond the analysis – assessed.

See FORMALIST, THEORY

SUBJECTIVE

Subjective is a profoundly difficult word, especially in its conventional contrast with *objective*. Historically this contrast is especially difficult, since it was also made in medieval thought but in a very different and virtually opposite way. This lasted until C17, when each term began to be used in new ways. The modern contrast, though it has precedents in C17 and C18, was not fully developed in English until eC19, and is still, under analysis, highly variable. The philosophical assumptions revealed by its conscious use, or concealed by its conventional use, are in each stage fundamental. Moreover, even if we decide to ignore the earlier and very different contrast, as now of merely historical interest, we are still left with senses of **subject**, deriving from that earlier period, which make the relationships between **subject** and **subjective** especially difficult.

Subject – in mE *soget*, *suget* or *sugiet* – is from fw *suget*, *soget*, *subjet*, oF, *subjectus* and *subjectum*, L, from rw *sub* – under, *jacere* – throw, cast. The Latin root sense was evident in its earliest English meanings: (i) a person under the dominion of a lord or sovereign; (ii) substance; (iii) matter worked upon. Senses (i) and (iii) are still current in English: (i) residually, in one kind of political thinking, as in **British subject** or **liberties of the subject**, where later senses of **subject** may suggest a more favourable gloss but where the continuing meaning is of someone under dominion or sovereignty, LIBERTIES (q.v.) being not the positive modern sense but the older sense of certain permitted rights, within an otherwise absolute sovereignty; (iii) commonly, in the sense of an area or topic or theme which is studied, or written or spoken about, or modelled or painted: a **subject** being worked on. Sense (i) is continuous from C14 and is still especially common in **subjection**. Sense (iii) has been common from eC16.

Object is from fw *objectum*, L, from rw *ob* – towards, against, in the way of, *jacere* – throw, cast. Its earliest English senses were of an 'opposing point in argument' – as still in the verb *object* and in *objection*, and of an 'obstacle'. A separate and crucial sense was taken from *objectum*, mL – a thing 'thrown before' the mind: hence something seen or observed, and thence, in a general sense from C16, a thing. From the sense of 'thrown before' the mind, a further sense developed, of a purpose, as still in *the object of this operation* and in the noun *objective*.

The complexities and difficulties of these developing senses are already evident. We can imagine a nightmare sentence: 'the object of this subject is to subject certain objects to particular study'. If we then add, in their modern senses, either *objective* or **subjective** to define the kind of study, we might feel we shall never wake up.

Yet each development is comprehensible. The normal scholastic distinction between **subjective** and *objective* was: **subjective** – as things are in themselves (from the sense of **subject** as substance); *objective* – as things are presented to consciousness ('thrown before' the mind). These perfectly reasonable uses, however, were parts of a radically different world-view from that which, developing from lC17 and especially from Descartes, proposed the thinking self as the first substantial area of knowledge – the **subject** – from the operations of which the independent existence of all other things must be deduced – as *objects* thrown before this consciousness. It is not that the terms were at all quickly clarified in this way; any such distinction is a much later summary. And there are many intermediate complications, as in the term **subject-matter.** But two tendencies of meaning assisted the transition: in *object* quite clearly, given the already developed sense of 'thing'; in **subject** more indirectly, and probably not primarily through the sense of substance but through the particular use, known from Aristotle, of the *predicate*, for which, in grammar, **subject** was used from C17. The use of *object* in grammar was later, from C18.

In the two centuries of essential transition there were many inconsistencies and overlaps. In the Authorized Version of the Bible, **subject** was always used in the sense of domination; the one use of *object* was of the verb – to speak against. A particular form of the medieval distinction can be found in Jeremy Taylor (1647); where the 'confession of Peter' was seen as 'the objective foundation of Faith, Christ and his apostles the subjective, Christ principally, and St Peter instrumentally'. Another example, 'a Light within them and a Light without them, Subjective and Objective Light', can, interestingly, be read in either way: in the modern sense, which it happens to fit, or in the old sense, where the distinction, as in Taylor, would be between funda-mental and essential, on the one hand, and instrumental and operative on the other. The deep changes going on in these uses are now very difficult to grasp. There occurs an interesting tran-sitional use, in 1725, when an 'objective certainty . . . when the proposition is certainly true in itself' was distinguished from a 'subjective certainty . . . when we are certain of the truth of it'.

The next crucial development of the terms was in German classical philosophy, in which, though with many difficulties, most uses of the modern distinction originated. Both the dis-tinction of **subject** and *object*, and the many attempts to prove their ultimate unity or identity, took place within the main senses: **subject** – the active mind or the thinking agent (in ironic contrast with the passive subject of political dominion); *object* – that which is other than the active mind or the thinking agent (in the development of the argument this was classified into several categories of *object*). This specific tradition, with its extraordinary intricacies, is still very active, and in many translations and transfers, especially from German and French, **subject**, *object*, **subjective** and *objective* can be understood only by specific reference to its terms. As the specific consequence of the dominant modern form of idealist thought, and of an influential form of critique of its position from an alternative standpoint but often using the same terms, the senses and distinctions belong – like the contrast of IDEALISM and MATERIALISM (qq.v.) to which, in its most current form, they are closely related – to a very particular and in its way enclosed tradition. This is important to realize, even if we value that tradition highly, since the development of senses in English, though of course affected, and in some contexts even determined, by it has also another dimension.

This is critically important for the most current modern English senses of **subjective** and *objective*. Coleridge wrote in 1817: 'the very words *objective* and *subjective* of such constant recurrence in the schools of yore, I have ventured to reintroduce'. His reference was scholastic but his usage was from German idealist thought. De Quincey later observed of *objective*: 'this word, so nearly unintelligible in 1821, so intensely scholastic, and . . . so apparently pedantic, yet . . . so indispensable to accurate thinking, and to wide thinking, has since 1821 become too common to need any apology.' We must take his and Coleridge's word for it; the C17 and C18 examples are probably rare. But there was a very significant use in 1801: 'objective, i.e., taken from an external object . . . or . . . subjective, i.e., they exist only in the mind of him who judges'. There is something in the tone of this definition of **subjective** which casts its shadows ahead. In philosophical uses the German distinction was mainly followed: 'subjective . . . the thinking subject . . . objective . . . what belongs to the object of thought' (Hamilton, 1853). But in mC19, in relation to the changes that can be observed in ART (q.v.) and *artistic*, there was talk of a **subjective** style in painting and literature, and the outline of an explicit dualism can be seen to be forming. It is wholly within the spirit of German idealist philosophy and its critical descendants to speak of the **subjective** – actively shaping – character of art. But the distinction between **subjective** and *objective* kinds of art, or kinds of thinking, is in the end a very different matter, if only because it supposes that there can be a kind of art or kind of thinking in which the active **subject** is not present. And it is this use that came through into common currency. It is difficult to date precisely. It was clearly not established for Bryce, when he wrote, in 1888: 'to complete the survey of the actualities of party politics by stating in a purely positive, or as the Germans say "objective" way, what the Americans think about . . . their system', where **subjective** might now be as readily used. The presence there of POSITIVE (q.v.) is also puzzling. What has really to be looked for is the strengthening sense of *objective* as factual, fair-minded (neutral) and hence reliable, as distinct from the sense of **subjective** as based on impressions rather than facts, and hence as influenced by personal feelings and relatively unreliable. There can be no doubt where these senses come from. They are from the procedures of POSITIVIST SCIENCE (qq.v.) and from the associated social, political and administrative senses of 'impartial' and 'neutral' judgment. Their roots thus lie very deep, but it is perhaps only from lC19, and with increasing confidence in C20, that the conventional contrast has settled. The coexistence of these positivist terms with the terms of the idealist tradition and its critique is then exceptionally confusing. In judgments and reports we are positively required to be *objective*: looking only at the facts, setting aside personal preference or interest. In this context a sense of something shameful, or at least weak, attaches to **subjective**, although everyone will admit that there are **subjective factors**, which have usually to be put in their place. The necessary philosophical framework for assessing this kind of definition already exists, meanwhile, in the alternative uses of **subject** and *object* already defined, and hence in a sophisticated epistemology. But at the ordinary current level, **subjective**, and a newly derived **subjectivism** and especially **subjectivity**, have to be reintroduced in a different critique of *objectivism*, seeing it as a wrong kind of concern with the 'external' world to the neglect of the 'inner' or 'personal' world.

This is the range we now have. It is easy enough to say that it is both a subject and an object of concern. But the real problem lies in the historical layering within each word and in the surpassing confidence of the very different surviving traditions which now shape the alternative senses. What must be seen, in the end, as deeply controversial uses of what are nevertheless, at least in **subject** and *object*, inevitable words, are commonly presented with a certainty and at times a glibness that simply spread confusion. **Subjective** and *objective*, we might say, need to be thought through – in the language rather than within any particular school – every time we wish seriously to use them.

See EMPIRICAL, IDEALISM, INDIVIDUAL, MATERIALISM, POSITIVISM, SCIENCE

T

TASTE

Taste in a physical sense has been in English since C13, though its earliest meaning was wider than **tasting** with the mouth and was nearer to the modern *touch* or *feel*. It came from fw *taster*, oF, *tastare*, It – feel, handle, touch. A predominant association with the mouth was evident from C14, but the more general meaning survived, for a time as itself but mainly by metaphorical extension. 'Good taast' in the sense of good understanding is recorded from 1425 and 'no spiritual tast' from 1502. A more extended use is evident in Milton's 'Sion's songs, to all true tasts excelling' (*Paradise Regained*, IV). The word became significant and difficult from lC17 and especially in C18, when it was capitalized as a general quality: 'Rules . . . how we may acquire that fine Taste of Writing, which is so much talked of among the Polite World' (Addison, 1712). **Taste** became equivalent to *discrimination*: 'the word Taste . . . means that quick discerning faculty or power of the mind by which we accurately distinguish the good, bad or indifferent' (Barry, 1784). **Tasteful** and **tasteless** developed with the same reference in the same period.

It is then important to look at the terms of Wordsworth's attack on **Taste** (in the 1800 *Preface* to *Lyrical Ballads*). He was against those

who will converse with us gravely about a *taste* for poetry, as they express it, as if it were a thing as indifferent as a taste for rope-dancing, or Frontiniac or Sherry.

Taste was

> a metaphor, taken from a *passive* sense of the human body, and transferred to things which are in their essence *not* passive – to intellectual *acts* and *operations*. The profound and the exquisite in feeling, the lofty and universal in thought and imagination . . . are neither of them, accurately speaking, objects of a faculty which could ever without a sinking in the spirit of Nations have been designated by the metaphor *Taste* . . . Without the exertion of a co-operating *power* in the mind of the Reader, there can be no adequate sympathy with either of these emotions: without this auxiliary impulse, elevated or profound passion cannot exist.

The question whether physical tasting is indeed a 'passive' sense may be left on one side. What Wordsworth did was to reanimate **taste** as a metaphor, in order to dismiss it; (his examples, incidentally, are not only of wines but also of rope-dancing, for which the metaphor would already have been conventional). He seems not to have known the long duration of the metaphorical transfer – some four centuries before he was writing – or the reference to the 'sinking in the spirit of Nations' would not have its point. Yet what he said is still extremely important, because he was attacking not so much **taste** as **Taste**. It was the abstraction of a human faculty to a generalized polite attribute, emphasized by the capital letter and significantly associated, as in the Addison example, with the notion of *Rules*, and elsewhere with *Manners* (which was itself narrowing from a description of general conduct to a more local association with *etiquette*), which he correctly identified. The strong and active sense of **taste** had been replaced by the weak because habitual attributes of **Taste**. We have only to think of related sense words, such as *touch* or *feel* in their extended and metaphorical uses, which have not been abstracted, capitalized and in such ways regulated, to realize the essential distinction. **Taste** and **Good Taste** have become so separated from active human senses, and have become so much a matter of acquiring certain habits and rules, that Wordsworth's attack is still relevant, in spite of its ironic relation to the actual history of the word. It is interesting that **tasteful** has become compromised, in a related way, with just this sense of (often trivial) conformity to an external habit, but that **tasteless** has on the whole been separated from **Taste** and carries, though in a relatively weak way, the older and wider sense of *feel* and *touch* and understanding, often in a moral rather than an aesthetic context.

It is worth noting, finally, that the idea of **taste** cannot now be separated from the idea of THE CONSUMER (q.v.). The two ideas, in their modern form, have developed together, and responses to ART and LITERATURE (qq.v.) have been profoundly affected (even at the level of highly developed theory, cf. CRITICISM) by the assumption that the viewer, spectator or reader is a *consumer*, exercising and subsequently showing his **taste**. (A popular sub-critical vocabulary directly associated with food – *feast*, *on the menu*, *goodies*, etc., – continually supports this assumption.)

See AESTHETIC, CONSUMER, CRITICISM, SENSIBILITY

THEORY

Theory has an interesting development and range of meanings, and a significant distinction from (later an opposition to) *practice*. The earliest English form was *theorique* (C14), followed by *theory* (C16), from fw *theoria*, lL, *theoria*, Gk – contemplation, spectacle, mental conception (from *theoros*, Gk – spectator, rw *thea*, Gk – sight; cf. *theatre*). In C17 it had a wide range: (i) spectacle: 'a Theory or Sight' (1605); (ii) a contemplated sight: 'the true Theory of death when I contemplate a skull' (Browne, 1643); 'all their theory and contemplation (which they count Science) represents nothing but waking men's dreams, and sick men's phantasies' (Harvey, 1653); (iii) scheme (of ideas): 'to execute their owne Theorie in this Church' (Hooker, 1597); (iv) explanatory scheme: 'leave such theories to those that study Meteors' (1638). A distinction between **theory** and *practice* was widely made in C17, as in Bacon (1626); 'Philosophy . . . divided into two parts, namely, speculative and practical' (1657); 'only pleasing in the Theory, but not in the Practice' (1664); 'Theorie without Practice will serve but for little' (1692).

It is interesting that **theory** and *speculation*, **theoretic(al)** and *speculative*, were ready alternatives, with the same root senses. In our own time, one use of **theory** is sharply distinguished from *speculation*, and, even more strongly, one use of **theoretical** from the relevant sense of *speculative* (the commercial sense of *speculative* is from C18). This depends on an important development of the sense of **theory**, basically from sense (iv), which is in effect 'a scheme of ideas which explains practice'. There is still a qualification in 'scheme'; cf. 'were a theory open to no objection it would cease to be theory and would become a law' (1850). But **theory** in this important sense is always in active relation to *practice*: an interaction between things done, things observed and (systematic) explanation of these. This allows a necessary distinction between **theory** and *practice*, but does not require their opposition. At the same time it is clear that forms of senses (ii) and (iii) survive actively, and the **theory**/*practice* relation, which is neutral or positive in sense (iv), is radically affected by them, at times confusingly. In sense (ii) the clearer word is now *speculation*: a projected idea, with no necessary reference to practice. In sense (iii) the relevant words are *doctrine* or IDEOLOGY (q.v.), a largely programmatic idea of how things should be. Of course these senses interact: (ii) may lead to (iii) and especially (iv); in certain areas of the human sciences, as distinct from the physical sciences, (iii) and (iv) are often inseparable, because *practice* itself is complex. There is *practice* in the sense of a particular thing done (and observed) which can be immediately related to **theory** (iv). There is also *practice* in the sense of a repeated or customary action (cf. *practise* as a verb), in which the **theory**/*practice* relation is often a contrast between one way of doing a thing and another, the **theoretical** being that which is proposed and the *practical* that which is now usually done. It is especially important to distinguish this relation not only from the relation in sense (iv), which it often confuses, but from the weaker forms of the relation in sense (ii), where 'waking men's dreams, and sick men's phantasies' can be powerfully contrasted with *practice* in the sense of doing anything (though to ignore the stronger forms of sense (ii), overlapping with sense (iii), would be damaging; cf. IDEALISM). It also needs to be noted that the very strength of **theory** (iv), its (systematic) explanation of *practice*, with which it is in regular and active relation, can be made prejudicial. *Practice* which has become CONVENTIONAL (q.v.) or habitual can be traced to (or made conscious as) a base in **theory** ((iii) or (iv)), and **theory** is then used derogatively just because it explains and (implicitly or explicitly) challenges some customary action.

The word *praxis* is now increasingly used, in specialized contexts, to express a sense related to **theory** (iv) but in a new relation to *practice*. **Theory** (iv) is simple in relation to the physical sciences: an active interrelation between explanation and things happening or made to happen in controlled conditions. *Praxis* (fw *praxis*, mL, *praxis*, Gk – practice, action) has been used in English since lC16 to express the practice or exercise of an art or an idea, a set of examples for practice, and accepted practice. In none of these is it quite separate from *practice*, though the notion of a 'scheme for practice' obviously distinguishes it from **theory**/*practice* oppositions: the *praxis* is systematic exercise in an understood and organized skill. But this was not predominant in the English development. As late as 1800 Coleridge used the wider sense: 'in theory false, and pernicious in praxis'. The specialized modern sense comes from a development in German, c. 1840, in origin late Hegelian but now especially Marxist, where *praxis* is *practice* informed by **theory** and also, though less emphatically, **theory** informed by *practice*, as distinct both from *practice* uninformed by or unconcerned with **theory** and from **theory** which remains **theory** and is not put to the test of *practice*. In effect it is a word intended to unite **theory** (iii) and (iv) with the strongest sense of *practical* (but not conventional or customary) activity: *practice* as action. *Praxis* is then also used, derivatively, to describe a whole mode of activity in which, by analysis but only by analysis, **theoretical** and *practical* elements can be distinguished, but which is always a whole activity, to be judged as such. The opposition between *theory* and *practice* is then, it is said, broken down, by the interactive redefinition of each term.

See DOCTRINAIRE, EMPIRICAL, IDEOLOGY, RATIONAL, STRUCTURAL

TRADITION

Tradition in its most general modern sense is a particularly difficult word. It came into English in C14 from fw *tradicion*, oF, *traditionem*, L, from rw *tradere*, L – to hand over or deliver. The Latin noun had the senses of (i) delivery, (ii) handing down knowledge, (iii) passing on a doctrine, (iv) surrender or betrayal. The general sense (i) was in English in mC16, and sense (iv), especially of betrayal, from lC15 to mC17. But the main development was in senses (ii) and (iii). Wyclif wrote in c. 1380: 'a positive lawe or a tradycion that thai han hem silfe made', which is an active sense, but there was a more passive sense in the characteristic mC15 'the trewe tradicion'. It is this range that remains important. It is one thing to say 'old songs delivered to them, by tradition, from their fathers' (1591): an active, and oral, handing down, or again: 'the expressing or transferring our knowledge to others . . . I will tearme by the general name of Tradition or Deliverie' (Bacon, 1605). But another sense was coming strongly through: 'Will you mocke at an ancient Tradition began uppon an honourable respect' (*Henry V*, V, i) or:

'Throw away Respect, Tradition, Forme
And Ceremonious Dutie . . .' (*Richard II*, III, ii)

It is easy to see how a general word for matters handed down from father to son could become specialized, within one form of thought, to the idea of necessary respect and duty. **Tradition** survives in English as a description of a general process of handing down, but there is a very strong and often predominant sense of this entailing respect and duty. When we look at the detailed processes of any of these **traditions**, indeed when we realize that there are **traditions** (real plural, as distinct from the 'plural singular' present also in *values* and STANDARDS (q.v.)), and that only some of them or parts of them have been selected for our respect and duty, we can see how difficult **Tradition** really is, in an abstract or exhortatory or, as so often, ratifying use.

It is sometimes observed, by those who have looked into particular **traditions**, that it only takes two generations to make anything **traditional**: naturally enough, since that is the sense of **tradition** as active process. But the word moves again and again towards *age-old* and towards ceremony, duty and respect. Considering only how much has been handed down to us, and how various it actually is, this, in its own way, is both a betrayal and a surrender.

See LITERATURE, STANDARDS

U

UNCONSCIOUS

Conscious came into English in eC17, from fw *conscius*, L, rw *con*, L – together, *scire*, L – to know. Its two earliest English senses are now unfamiliar: (i) a sense difficult to define, related to a kind of animism, in which inanimate things are described as aware of human actions: 'Thence to the coverts, and the conscious groves' (Denham, 1643); 'to these conscious stones we two pilgrims were alike known and near' (Emerson on Stonehenge, 1856); (ii), as in the root words, knowing something *with* another or others (cf. CONSCIENCE): 'where two, or more men, know of one and the same fact, they are said to be Conscious of it one to another' (Hobbes, 1651). But the word took on a general sense of 'awareness', with four common specializations: (iii) self-aware: 'being so conscious unto my selfe of my great weakenesse' (Ussher, 1620); (iv) actively aware and reflecting: 'to be happy or miserable without being conscious of it, seems to me utterly inconsistent and impossible' (Locke, 1690); (v) 'self-conscious', with implications of vanity or calculation: 'too conscious of their face' (Pope, 1714); 'the conscious simper' (Pope, 1728); (vi) active and waking: 'when at last he was conscious' (Lytton, 1841). A further general sense, (vii), distinguished a class of beings, as in *thinking* or *rational*: 'thinking or conscious beings' (Watts, 1725). **Consciousness** was used from mC17 in senses applied from (ii), (iii), (iv), and from mC19 from (vi). A new sense, with indirect relation to (ii), also developed from mC19: **consciousness** as a term for the mutual self-awareness of a group: 'national consciousness', 'class consciousness'.

It is necessary to understand this range of **conscious** before we can understand the now common **unconscious**. The word is recorded from eC18. In Blackmore's 'unconscious we these motions never heard', the sense was clearly a negative of (iv), and this is probably also true, though with some broadening of meaning, in Johnson's 'a kind of respect perhaps unconsciously paid' (1779). Blackmore's couplet of 1712 –

Unconscious causes only still impart
Their utmost skill, their utmost power exert

– is much more difficult; it seems to imply 'not known', almost in the later sense of 'not knowable', rather than simply 'not aware'. Two uses in Coleridge present some difficulty. 'With forced unconscious sympathy' (*Christabel*) presumably has the general sense of 'unaware', the negative of (iv), but the association with *forced* seems to introduce a dimension which, in including involuntary unawareness, has elements of a later meaning. Then 'the conscious is so impressed on the unconscious as to appear in it' (1817) – probably the first use of the phrase **the unconscious** – seems to imply two normal categories, **conscious** and **unconscious**, though with a significant priority to the former, which in this instance is the source. The physical senses of both **conscious** and **unconscious** were C19 developments. In limited uses – 'he was knocked unconscious' – they are not difficult, but in the development of C19 psychology there was increasing attention to several ambiguous conditions, where the line between *physical* and PSYCHOLOGICAL (q.v.) conditions of **consciousness** was difficult to draw. Cf. 'sleep, fainting, coma, epilepsy and other "unconscious" conditions' (William James, 1890). Another crucial state was the condition under hypnosis. Very different and controversial interpretations of these states have been made, and **conscious** and **unconscious** have become variable keywords within them. Moreover, many physical actions, within ordinary **consciousness**, were defined as **unconscious** in a new sense – as not requiring conscious initiation or control, or indeed as not capable of either, as in certain fundamental physical processes. It was not difficult to attach this specialized sense to sense (iv) and its negative.

The more difficult but now most extended use came in the work of Freud. Here **unconscious** has three elements: of processes (a) dynamically repressed from (**conscious**) awareness; (b) capable of being made **conscious** (brought to awareness and reflection) only by special techniques – hypnosis, psychoanalysis; (c) not under voluntary control, as in the new physical sense noted above but without a limitation to physical causes. The controversy that has followed these definitions is enormous and very difficult, but as it affects the words it can be noted that the original definitions imply that what has become **unconscious** was once (but too painfully) **conscious**, and that the sense of

unconscious as 'unknowable' is specialized to the individual concerned; the **unconscious** can be made **conscious** by the application of particular skills. These relatively precise senses become difficult, obviously, when they move from their generalization as processes to a generalized condition: **the unconscious** and especially **the unconscious mind**. The dynamic sense of something being made **unconscious** is often replaced, in these general terms, by the assumption of a primary and autonomous **unconscious** mind or being. This is especially true in Jung's hypothesis of **the collective unconscious**, which as a common human property precedes (both in time and in importance) the ordinary development of consciousness. But it is also true of more general uses, in which **the unconscious** (not in the physical sense of fundamental and 'involuntary' bodily processes, but in the sense of the generation of basic feelings and ideas) is taken not only as stronger than **conscious** mental and emotional activity, but as its true (if ordinarily hidden) source. This has been a powerful modern form of IDEALISM (q.v.).

The overlap and confusion between different senses, affected by different theories, are now formidable. The most general sense is strongly sustained by an increasing awareness (**consciousness**) of motives and preferences of which someone had not previously been **conscious** (iv) or is still **unconscious** (simple negative of (iv)). It is not clear that this implies the hypothesis of **the unconscious**, or of **the unconscious mind**, but it is in practice very difficult, within the linguistic formation, to distinguish between: (1) generalization of such experiences, which are ordinarily of transition from **unconscious** to **conscious**, and which imply some failures of transition; (2) abstraction of such transitions, so that the two states – **conscious** and **unconscious** – are categorized; (3) reification of such categories, so that **the conscious** (*mind*) and **the unconscious** (*mind*) are taken to exist as physical entities or as distinct forms of neural or even social organization. Steps (1) and (2) sometimes become a sliding staircase to (3), though they are evidently separable.

There has also been uncertainty about the relation between **unconscious** and **subconscious**, which came into English (probably first in De Quincey) in mC19. *Sub*, as a prefix, includes the senses 'under' or 'below' – which would make the word coincide with many late uses of **unconscious**. But it also has the sense of 'imperfectly', 'not completely', which would make it coincide with many uses of **unconscious** which allow for normal transition between unawareness and awareness. In the popularization of Freud in the 1920s, and subsequently in common use, **unconscious** and **subconscious** have often been interchangeable. But this has been resisted by one school, which, taking the sense of 'imperfectly', 'not completely', resists the implication of 'normal' transition and insists on a fully **unconscious** area, from which transition is not possible except by special methods; **subconscious** is then treated as a popular misunderstanding. Yet it remains in common use both because of the other sense, of what is 'below' consciousness, and, it would seem, because many people who accept, from experience, sense (1) of **unconscious**, find that **subconscious** (even or especially with the implication of some or many 'normal' transitions) adequately expresses this. ('I was not aware (**conscious**, (iv)) of my motive for doing that, but I have since become aware (**conscious**, (iv)) of my real motive.' But it is not then clear whether to add 'it was probably **subconscious**' means only, self-evidently, 'I was not then aware of it'; or whether it implies an area which was not then knowable (which, across many theories, seems to need the stronger word, **unconscious**) as distinct from not then known or realized, for some specific discoverable cause (as opposed to the hypothesis of **the unconscious**, where such causes naturally reside).) It would seem that the uncertainty between **unconscious** and **subconscious** largely replays the disputes about **unconscious** itself.

The specialized C20 uses of **unconscious** have led to a preference for the alternative negative, **not conscious**, for the persistent senses (iii), in general usage, (v) and, in some contexts, (vi).

See PSYCHOLOGICAL

UNEMPLOYMENT

There has been some controversy about the history of the word **unemployment**, since G. M. Young said that 'unemployment was beyond the scope of any idea which early Victorian reformers had at their command, largely because they had no word for it ... I have not observed it earlier than the sixties'. (*Victorian England*, 27; 1936). This was challenged by E. P. Thompson: '*unemployed*, *the unemployed*, and (less frequently) *unemployment* are all to be found in trade union and Radical or Owenite writings of the 1820s and 1830s: the inhibitions of "Early Victorian reformers" must be explained in some other way.' (*The Making of the English Working Class*, 776n; 1963).

Certainly Thompson is right, but the history is complicated. **Unemployed** is much older. It was first used of something not being put to use, from C16, but was applied to people from C17, as in Milton's 'rove idle unimploid' (1667), where the sense is of not doing something rather than being out of work, and is clear in a modern sense from an example of 1677: 'in England and Wales a hundred thousand poor people unimployed'. The developing sense is important, because it represents the specialization of productive effort to paid employment by another, which (cf. WORK, *job*, LABOUR) has been an important part of the history of capitalist production and wage-labour. In several related words this development can be traced. On the one hand INDUSTRY (q.v.) developed from the sense of a general quality of diligent human effort to its modern sense of productive institution. On the other hand **unemployed** and *idle*, which were general terms for being unoccupied with anything at that time (though *idle* had the much wider original meaning, from oE, of empty and useless), developed their modern senses of being 'out of paid employment', or of being 'in employment but not working'. **Employ** itself developed from a general sense – 'emploied in affaires' (1584) – to the sense of regular paid work: 'publick employ' (1709); 'in their employ' (1832). There were 'Secretaries and Employd Men' in Bacon (1625), and from C18 **employer** (originally usually *imployer*) had its modern sense; *employé* and the American *employee* followed in C19. **Employ** as a noun of condition is recorded from C17, and **employ** as an abstract social term can be found from C18. Both **employ** and **unemploy**, as nouns of condition acquiring a general and abstract social sense, can be found from lC18 and eC19; they pre-date their modern equivalents **employment** and **unemployment**. Thus all the necessary words were available by at latest lC18, and became common, in the new scale of the problem but also in the way that the problem was seen, as a social condition, from eC19.

Employ was from fw *employer*, F, from the passive form, *implicari*, L – involved in or attached to, rw *implicare*, L – enfold, involve (which also gave us *imply*). Its early sense was to apply something (C15) or someone (C16) to some purpose; both senses are still active. In the history of wage-labour this became, as we have seen, taking into paid work. The interaction with *idle* is particularly interesting. The wide sense, in application to people, can be illustrated from c. 1450:

> To devocionne evre and Contemplacionne
> Was sho gyven and nevre ydel.

But in an Act of 1530–1 we find the characteristic 'to arest the sayde vacaboundes and ydell persones'. This has lasted long enough, but already in 1764 Burn observed: 'they are idle for want of such work as they are able to do' – a perception of **unemployment** in the modern sense. Clearly the modern (from lC18) sense of **unemployment** depends upon its separation from the associations of *idle*; it describes a social situation rather than a personal condition (*idleness*). There has been a steady ideological resistance to this necessary distinction; that is the point of Thompson's criticism not only of Young's history but of Young. The resistance is still active, and in relation to the words is especially evident in the use of *idle*, in news reporting, to describe workers laid off, locked out or on strike. With its strong moral implications, *idle* in this context must have ideological intentions or effects. 'Many thousands idle' sticks in the mind.

The significant **unemployable** – not fit for **employment** in the modern sense – dates from lC19.

We can add a note on *dole*, the common name for **unemployment benefit** or compensation. *Dole* was from C10 a division or portion (from *dal*, oE), and from C14 a gift of food or money as charity. It is not how unemployment benefit was intended but it seems to have been how it was perceived.

See CAPITALISM, LABOUR, WORK

UTILITARIAN

Utilitarian has one complication: that it is a description of a particular philosophical system, which in practice has been widely adopted, though usually without reference to the formal name. It is also a description of a limited class of qualities or interests, *practical* or *material*. Many would say that this double sense has a single root; that this is the inevitable consequence of a particular kind of MATERIALIST (q.v.) philosophy. But **utilitarian** is very like *materialist* in that it has been loaded with the aspersions of its enemies just as much as with the consequences of its own assumptions. The word was taken from **utility** (fw *utilitas*, L, rw *uti*, L – use) which in the general sense of usefulness has been in English since C14. The isolation of **Utility**, as the primary test of the value of anything, belongs principally to C18 French and English thought. It was a sharp tool against definitions of social purpose which excluded the interests of a majority of people, or in one sense of all people, such as definitions of value in terms of an existing social order, or in terms of a god. The test of value was to be whether something was useful to people, and specifically, as the idea developed, to the majority, 'the greatest number'. **Utilitarian**, as a conscious description, was first used in English by Jeremy Bentham: to express an emphasis, in 1781, and to name, with a capital letter, the 'professors of a new religion' (1802). An action was 'conformable to the principle of utility . . . when the tendency it has to augment the happiness of the community is greater than any it has to diminish it.' *Happiness*, in fact, was a key word of the system, as again in John Stuart Mill (*Utilitarianism*, 1861): 'happiness . . . the only thing describable as an end'. But it often alternated with *pleasure*, which not only attracted familiar objections to *pleasure*, especially the pleasure of others, but was also so variable, and even by serious people could be made to seem so light, as to be a difficult term for the most difficult discussions of value. Moreover, within the specific **utilitarian** system, characteristically limited definitions of *usefulness* – both its characteristic specialization to the individual and the brisk but limited practicality which Mill described as adequate only for 'regulating the merely *business* part of the social arrangements' – came to predominate, and to limit the concepts of both *pleasure* and *happiness*. It became, ironically, the working philosophy of a bureaucratic and industrial capitalist society.

The other sense is not directly connected, though it was eventually affected by the philosophical development. 'Turning from the picturesque or romantic to the utilitarian view of this tree', wrote Coleman in 1859, and the terms on one side of the distinction are as significant as the term on the other. He was writing, very reasonably, about the uses of a particular tree, but *use*, by this period, had been predominantly specialized to the production of things or commodities, so that other uses of the tree needed the specialized *romantic* or *picturesque* (both significantly terms of art). It might be said that people use trees for shade or shelter or for looking at as well as for timber, but *use* – with its available and strengthening sense of consume – is not easy in such a range. What **utilitarian** in this spelled-out sense emphasizes is a split of some kinds of activity from others. ART (q.v.), that eminently practical word, was specialized as part of the same movement to a different kind of activity and a different kind of happiness or pleasure: contemplative or AESTHETIC (q.v.). So the longstanding practice of using things to make other things was specialized by purpose, into one kind, *art*, and another kind, **utility**.

This is the division at the root of capitalist production, where things are specialized to commodities. It is the transfer that occurred, for example, in 'this money-getting utilitarian age' (1839), and in one sense it is a real transfer. But, as with *materialist*, different kinds of objection were gathered and confused. Many of the opponents of **utilitarianism** and *materialism* have used the difficulties of these ways of seeing the world, which in practice have been so widely accepted, to urge residual values which, in terms of a traditional social order or a god, take priority over the 'greatest happiness of the greatest number'. But they have been wonderfully assisted in this by the theoretical and practical specialization of **utility** to the terms of capitalist production, and especially by the translation of 'the greatest happiness of the greatest number' into the terms of the organized *market* (in its increasingly abstract C19 sense), which was taken to be the mechanism for regulating this ultimate purpose. **Utility**, once a critical concept, became, in this context, at once ratifying and demeaning, and other terms had to be found to assert the principle of most people's happiness.

See CONSUMER, WELFARE

V

VIOLENCE

Violence is often now a difficult word, because its primary sense is of physical assault, as in 'robbery with violence', yet it is also used more widely in ways that are not easy to define. If we take physical assault as sense (i) we can take a clear general sense (ii) as the use of physical force, including the distant use of weapons or bombs, but we have then to add that this seems to be specialized to 'unauthorized' uses: the **violence** of a terrorist but not, except by its opponents, of an army, where 'force' is preferred and most operations of war and preparation for war are described as 'defence'; or the similar partisan range between 'putting under restraint' or 'restoring order', and 'police violence'. We can note also a relatively simple sense (iii), which is not always clearly distinguished from (i) and (ii), as in 'violence on television,' which can include the reporting of violent physical events but indicates mainly the dramatic portrayal of such events.

The difficulty begins when we try to distinguish sense (iv), **violence** as threat, and sense (v), **violence** as unruly behaviour. Sense (iv) is clear when the threat is of physical violence, but it is often used when the real threat, or the real practice, is unruly behaviour. The phenomenon known as 'student violence' included cases in senses (i) and (ii), but it clearly also included cases of sense (iv) and sense (v). The emotional power of the word can then be very confusing.

It is a longstanding complexity. **Violence** is from fw *violence*, oF, *violentia*, L – vehemence, impetuosity – ultimately from rw *vis*, L – force. **Violence** had the sense of physical force in English from lC13, and was used of hitting a priest in 1303. From the same period we hear, in what seems a familiar tone, that the world is in a state

> Of filthe and of corrupcion
> Of violence and oppression.

But this use is interesting, because it reminds us that **violence** can be exercised both ways, as Milton insisted of Charles I: 'a tedious warr on his subjects, wherein he hath so farr exceeded his arbitrary violences in time of peace' (1649). There has been obvious interaction between **violence** and *violation*, the breaking of some custom or some dignity. This is part of the complexity. But **violent** has also been used in English, as in the Latin, for intensity or vehemence: 'marke me with what violence she first lov'd the Moore' (*Othello*, II, i); 'violence of party spirit' (Coleridge, 1818). There was an interesting note in 1696: 'violence . . . figuratively spoken of Human Passions and Designs, when unruly, and not to be govern'd'. It is the interaction of this sense with the sense of physical force that underlies the real difficulties of senses (iv) and (v); a sense (vi), as in 'violently in love', is never in practice misunderstood. But if it is said that the State uses force, not only in senses (i) and (ii) but more critically in sense (iv) – the threat implied as the consequence of any breach of 'Law and order' as at any one time or in any one place defined – it is objected that **violence** is the wrong word for this, not only because of the sense of 'authorized' force but because it is not 'unruly'. At the same time, questions of what it is to be 'unruly' or 'not to be govern'd' can be side-stepped. It is within the assumption of 'unruly', and not, despite the transfer in the word, of physical force, that loud or vehement (or even very strong and persistent) verbal criticism has been commonly described as **violent**, and the two steps beyond that – threat to some existing arrangement, threat of actual force – sometimes become a moving staircase to the strong meanings of **violence** in senses (i) and (ii).

It is then clearly a word that needs early specific definition, if it is not (as in yet another sense, (vii)), to be done **violence** to – to be wrenched from its meaning or significance (from lC16).

W

WEALTH

Wealth was formed, perhaps by analogy with *health*, from the associated words *well*, adverb, fw *wel* or *well*, oE and *weal*, noun, fw *wela*, oE. It indicated happiness and prosperity but, if the question arose, it could clearly be specialized to either. The modern sense is clear enough in:

> For here es welth inogh to win
> To make us riche for evermore (1352).

But the wider meaning is evident in the need to distinguish 'worldly welthe' (1340), and 'nullus est felicior' (no man is more happy) was translated in 1398 as 'no man hath more welth'. In c. 1450 there was 'with-oute you have I neither joye ne welthe' and in Wyatt (1542) there was the clear sense of happiness: 'syns every wo is joynid to some welth'. **Commonwealth**, from *common weal*, *commonweal* and **common wealth**, had the general sense of the well-being of the community before it developed into a special but related sense of a kind of social order. It was still also possible to write 'for the welth of my soul' (1463).

Wealthy was more often used in the general sense (from C14) until perhaps mC15, and specialization to the wealth of a country seems earlier than that to the wealth of a man. From lC16 **wealth** was used in a surviving sense to indicate abundance of something: 'wealth of saumon'; wealth of examples. In C17 and C18 the word acquired not only a more definite association with money and possessions, but a strong subsidiary deprecative sense. The political economists from Adam Smith (who in his best-known work used as a title the already well-known C17 phrase **wealth of nations**) sought to distinguish between **wealth** in a man and the **wealth** of a society. The former had sufficient and often derogatory association with possessions to require a distinction of the latter as production: cf. 'a man of wealth . . . implies quantity . . . a source of wealth . . . quantity is not implied . . . products' (1821). But on the whole **wealth** and

wealthy have come through in individualist and possessive senses, with a predominant reference to money. Other words such as *resources* have been found for the other economic meaning. The general reference to happiness and well-being had been so far lost and forgotten that Ruskin (*Unto this Last*, iv. 26) was forced to coin a word to express a sense of the unhappiness and waste which followed from some kinds of production. These led, in the specialized sense, to **wealth**, but there was need for the opposite term, *illth*. This recalls the original formation, however oddly it may now read, and there was some precedent in *illfare* (see WELFARE) which was used occasionally between C14 and C17 and briefly revived in C19 and C20.

See COMMON, WELFARE

WELFARE

Welfare was originally the phrase *wel fare*, mE, from *well* in its still familiar sense and *fare*, primarily a journey or arrival but later also a supply of food. **Welfare** was commonly used from C14 to indicate happiness or prosperity (cf. WEALTH): 'thy negheburs welfare' (1303); 'welfare or ilfare of the whole realm' (1559). A subsidiary meaning, usually derogatory in the recorded instances, was of merrymaking: 'such ryot and welfare and ydlenesse' (1470); 'wine and such welfare' (1577). The extended sense of **welfare**, as an object of organized care or provision, came in eC20; most of the older words in this sense (see especially CHARITY) had acquired unacceptable associations. Thus **welfare-manager** (1904); **welfare policy** (1905); **welfare work** (1916); **welfare centres** (1917). The **Welfare State**, in distinction from the *Warfare State*, was first named in 1939.

See CHARITY, UTILITARIAN, WEALTH

WORK

Work is the modern English form of the noun *weorc*, oE and the verb *wyrcán*, oE. As our most general word for doing something, and for something done, its range of applications has of course been enormous. What is now most interesting is its predominant specialization to paid employment. This is not exclusive; we speak naturally of **working** in the garden. But, to take one significant example, an active woman, running a house and bringing up children, is distinguished from a woman who **works**: that is to say, takes paid employment. The basic sense of the word, to indicate activity and effort or achievement, has thus been modified, though unevenly and incompletely, by a definition of its imposed conditions, such as working for a wage or salary: being hired.

There is an interesting relation between **work** and LABOUR (q.v.). *Labour* had a strong medieval sense of pain and toil; **work**, earlier, in one of its senses, had also the strong sense of *toil*. *Toil* itself was derived from a Latin rw for stirring and crushing, and came through first as a synonym for trouble and turmoil before it acquired its sense of arduous labour in C14. *Labour* and *toil* are still harder words than work, but manual workers were generalized as *labourers* from C13, and the supply of such work was generalized as *labour* from C17. **Work** was then still available for a more general sense of activity: 'Fie upon this quiet life, I want worke' (1 *Henry IV*, II, iv). But a *labourer* was also a **worker** from C14. **Workman** had come through from oE and was joined by **workingman** from C17. An effective class of **workfolk** was spoken about from at latest C15, and of **workpeople** from C18: often, in the kind of records we have, in a familiar tone: 'You cannot imagine what a parcel of cheating brutes the work people here are' (1708). The specialization of one sense of **working** to the **working class**, in eC19 (see CLASS) drew on these earlier effective class definitions.

The specialization of **work** to paid employment (see UNEMPLOYMENT) is the result of the development of capitalist productive relations. To be **in work** or **out of work** was to be in a definite relationship with some other who had control of the means of productive effort. **Work** then partly shifted from the productive effort itself to the predominant social relationship. It is only in this sense that a woman running a house and bringing up children can be said to be **not working**. At the same time, because the general word is necessary, a person may be said to do his real work on his own, sometimes quite separately from his *job*. Time other than that spent in paid employment is significantly described as 'your own time', 'free time', or as 'holiday' (the old word for a day of religious festival), or as 'leisure-time'. (*Leisure* came from a Latin word for permit (*licere*), and from C14 meant opportunity or free time; it is significant of the narrowing specialization of work that we now have 'leisure-time activities', often requiring considerable effort but not described as **work**, which belongs to our 'paid time'.)

The development of *job* is perhaps even more significant. Its origins are obscure; it has always been predominantly a colloquial word. There are uses as 'lump' or 'piece' from C14, and as 'cartload' from C16. From 1557 we have 'certen Jobbes of woorke'. The sense of a limited piece of work came through strongly in C17, and *jobbing* and *jobber*, in senses we still have, came to mean doing occasional small 'jobs of work'. The range of application is then very interesting. It is recorded in thieves' slang from eC18, and is still active in this sense. It is recorded in the context of preferential treatment, moving towards sharp practice and corruption, from mC17; this is still just current in *jobbery*. Stocks were *jobbed*, from C17, by brokers and dealers who did not own them but made their money from them. Yet in spite of all these senses *job* has also come through as the now primary and virtually universal term for normal employment. By mC20 it had effectively completed a process of substitution for older terms, not only in manual work or in dealing, but in work previously described as *situation, position, post, appointment* and so on. These may still be formally used, but in practice nearly everyone describes them all as *jobs* (from a *job* in the Government or the Foreign Office – where people also have CAREERS (q.v.) – to a job on the buses or in a university or on a building site). What has then happened is that a word formerly specifically reserved to limited and occasional employment (and surviving in this sense, as in a *price for the job*; in view of the word's history the description of individual subcontracting in building as *the lump* might be significant) has become the common word for regular and normal employment. Certainly we say *a regular job*, but we also distinguish *a proper job* from going around doing this and that – *jobbing*. The *jobs problem* is a problem of regular paid employment.

It is extraordinarily difficult to trace this history. There is evidence that it first developed this modern sense in the United States. But the word has always been a description of a certain amount of work from the point of view of the person doing it. Even the criminal and corrupt senses have this essential element, before the word was picked up and used, often derogatorily, by others. **Work** is still centrally important, and in much everyday use means only *labour* or *a job*. But experience of every kind of work has qualified some of its more positive senses. **Works**, plural, is still neutral, but **a work** is relatively dignified. *Labour*, from its general sense of hard, difficult or painful work, became a term for a commodity and a class. As the latter it was adopted as a conscious term for a political movement which, among other things, asserted the *dignity of labour*. All these developments have interacted; many are still important. But running along at their base has been this short, colloquial and popular word *job*, with its significant practical range: the piece of work, the activity you get paid for, the thing you have to shift or to do, the ordinary working experience.